COLLECTED WHEEL PUBLICATIONS

VOLUME 17

NUMBERS 248 – 264

BPE

BPS Pariyatti Editions

BPS Pariyatti Editions
An imprint of Pariyatti Publishing
www.pariyatti.org

Copies of this book for sale in the Americas only. Although this is an American edition, we have left any British spelling of words unchanged.

First BPS Pariyatti Edition, 2025
ISBN: 978-1-68172-188-0 (Print)
ISBN: 978-1-68172-189-7 (PDF)
ISBN: 978-1-68172-190-3 (ePub)
ISBN: 978-1-68172-191-0 (Mobi)
LCCN: 2018940050

Contents

WH 248 & 249 The Buddha's Words on Kamma
Ñāṇamoli Thera 1

WH 250 Concept and Meaning
C.F. Knight and *Carlo Gragnani* 37

WH 251 & 253 The Roots of Good and Evil
Nyanaponika Thera 57

WH 254 & 256 Life's Highest Blessings
Dr. R. L. Soni 133

WH 258 The Contemporary Relevance of Buddhist Philosophy
K. N. Jayatilleke 203

WH 259 & 260 Nourishing the Roots
Bhikkhu Bodhi 229

WH 261 Buddhism and Death
M. O'C. Walshe 263

WH 262 Faith in the Buddha's Teaching and Refuge in the Triple Gem; Saddhā: Buddhist Devotion
Soma Thera; *Sister Dhammadinnā* 285

WH 263 & 264 Mahā-Moggallāna
Hellmuth Hecker 305

Key to Abbreviations

A	Aṅguttara Nikāya	Paṭis	Paṭisambhidamagga
Ap	Apadāna	Peṭ	Peṭakopadesa
Bv	Buddhavaṃsa	S	Saṃyutta Nikāya
Cp	Cariyāpiṭaka	Sn	Suttanipāta
D	Dīgha Nikāya	Th	Theragātha
Dhp	Dhammapada	Thī	Therigātha
Dhs	Dhammasaṅgaṇī	Ud	Udāna
It	Itivuttaka	Vibh	Vibhaṅga
Ja	Jātaka verses and commentary	Vin	Vinaya-piṭaka
Khp	Khuddakapāṭha	Vism	Visuddhimagga
M	Majjhima Nikāya	Vism-mhṭ	Visuddhimagga Sub-commentary
Mil	Milindapañha	Vv	Vimānavatthu
Nett	Nettipakaraṇa	Nidd	Niddesa

The above is the abbreviation scheme of the Pali Text Society (PTS) as given in the *Dictionary of Pali* by Margaret Cone.

The commentaries, *aṭṭhakathā*, are abbreviated by using a hyphen and an "a" ("-a") following the abbreviation of the text, e.g., *Dīgha Nikāya Aṭṭhakathā* = D-a. Likewise the sub-commentaries are abbreviated by a "ṭ" ("-ṭ") following the abbreviation of the text.

The sutta reference abbreviation system for the four Nikāyas, as is used in Bhikkhu Bodhi's translations is:

AN	Aṅguttara Nikāya	DN	Dīgha Nikāya
MN	Majjhima Nikāya	Sn	Saṃyutta Nikāya
J	Jātaka story	Mv	Mahāvagga (Vinaya Piṭaka)
Cv	Cullavagga (Vinaya Piṭaka)	SVibh	Suttavibhaṅga (Vinaya Piṭaka)

The Buddha's Words on Kamma

Four Discourses of the Buddha from the Majjhima Nikāya

by

Ñāṇamoli Thera

Edited with Preface and Introductions by

Khantipālo Bhikkhu

WHEEL PUBLICATION NO. 248/249

Preface

Kamma concerns everyone. We make it, a great deal of it, every day while we are awake. We decide whether or not to get up—kamma. (Good kamma if one gets up vigorously, bad kamma if slothfully or grudgingly.) Let's have a cup of tea, breakfast—maybe some greed is involved, so bad kamma. We sympathise with someone's sickness and give help—good kamma. We get flustered because the bus is late to take us to work—bad kamma. Once we're there perhaps we get impatient with someone, or angry with them, or threaten them—worse and worse kamma. But perhaps we are generous and kindly to someone there—excellent kamma. Work brings on dull mental states, then we shake ourselves out of that listlessness and resentment (bad kamma) and vigorously try to get back to mindfulness (good kamma).

In the crowded bus returning home someone stamps on one's foot, one curses—bad kamma—but after quick reflection one realises "Ah, no mindfulness" and this is good kamma. At home at last, one comforts the sick, then plays with the children and tells them some Jātaka stories—all good kamma. But then, tired and dull, one switches the radio (and/or television) on and, not listening to it, leaves it going as a sound to drown silence, then one eats too much and feels lethargic—bad kamma. But perhaps instead one pays respect to the Buddha-image, does some chanting and then meditates—all kinds of good kamma. When the body is tired one goes to sleep holding some meditation subject in mind—good kamma.

All these decisions, choices and desires are kammas made in the mind. More kamma is made when one talks after having decided. Still more kamma is added if after this one acts as well.

"Good" and "bad" kamma are distinguished by *the roots* of the actions. What is one's motivating force when one helps the sick? This is a case where there are various possibilities. Is it just because one wants rich Aunty's money when she dies, or out of genuine compassion? Obviously, in the latter case much better kamma is made. But there are examples where there is no doubt. One's toes are stamped on and one curses: this can never be good kamma simply because it is *rooted in hatred.* Or one gobbles down too much food—just *greed-rooted* kamma in this case. Again those dull or day-dream periods at work, not looking at things as they are at all, this is *rooted in delusion.* When any of the mentally defiled states of mind has arisen, when these three "roots of evil" are in control, then bad kamma is sure to be made.

Once it is made there is no way of erasing it or changing it and some day or other it will begin to fruit. The fruit of bad kamma is never happiness, as we can read in these discourses. It always comes up as pain, anguish, frustration or the limitation of opportunities. Who wants them? Then make no more bad kamma! Everyone has laid in a stock already quite capable of giving rise to sufferings for lifetimes to come. There is no need to increase it.

Everyone wants happiness! But it too arises conditionally. Now a great producer of happiness is the making of good kamma. What is good about it? It is *rooted in non-greed* (generosity, renunciation), or in *non-hate* (loving kindness, compassion) or finally in *non-delusion* (wisdom, understanding). The sure way to gain happiness, then, is to make good kamma, as much as possible every day.

It is only people who make a real effort to grow in Dhamma (that is, to make good kamma) who have any chance to succeed in meditation on the path to final liberation. Whatever one's goal in this life—happiness here and now, a good rebirth in the future or to end the whole birth and death process by attainment of Nibbāna one cannot go wrong by making good kamma.

And what about those who do not believe in kamma and its fruits? They still make it whether they believe or not! And they get the fruits of the kamma they make, too. But the doing, not the believing, is the important thing.

"Do good, get good,
do evil, get evil."

Majjhima Nikāya 57: The Dog-duty Ascetic (Kukkuravatika Sutta)

Introduction

There were some strange people around in the Buddha's days believing some strange things—but that is no different from our own days when people still believe the most odd off-balance ideas. In this sutta we meet some people who believed that by imitating animals they would be saved. Maybe they're still with us too!

Belief is often one thing, action another. While beliefs sometimes influence actions, for other people their beliefs are quite separate from what they do. But the Buddha says all intentional actions, whether thoughts, speech or bodily actions, however expressed, are *kamma* and lead the doer of them to experience a result sooner or later. In this sutta the Buddha classifies kamma into four groups:

(i) dark with a dark result,
(ii) bright with a bright result,
(iii) dark and bright with a dark and bright result,
(iv) neither dark nor bright with a neither dark nor bright result.

Dark (evil) kamma does not give a bright (happy) result, nor does bright (beneficial) kamma lead to dark (miserable) result. Kamma can be mixed, where an action is done with a variety of motives, some good, some evil. And that kind of kamma also exists which gives up attachment to and interest in the other three and so leads beyond the range of kamma.

The Sutta

1. Thus have I heard. On one occasion the Blessed One was living in the Koliyan country: there is a town of the Koliyans called Haliddavasana.

2. Then Puṇṇa, a son of the Koliyans and an ox-duty ascetic, and also Seniya, a naked dog-duty ascetic, went to the Blessed One, and Puṇṇa the ox-duty ascetic paid homage to the Blessed

One and sat down at one side, while Seniya the naked dog-duty ascetic exchanged greetings with the Blessed One, and when the courteous and amiable talk was finished, he too sat down at one side curled up like a dog. When Puṇṇa the ox-duty ascetic sat down, he asked the Blessed One: "Venerable sir, this naked dog-duty ascetic Seniya does what is hard to do: he eats his food when it is thrown on the ground. That dog duty has long been taken up and practised by him. What will be his destination? What will be his future course?"[1]

"Enough, Puṇṇa, let that be. Do not ask me that."

A second time... A third time Puṇṇa the ox-duty ascetic asked the Blessed One: "Venerable sir, this naked dog-duty ascetic Seniya does what is hard to do: he eats his food when it is thrown on the ground. That dog duty has long been taken up and practised by him. What will be his destination? What will be his future course?"

"Well, Puṇṇa, since I certainly cannot persuade you when I say 'Enough, Puṇṇa, let that be. Do not ask me that,' I shall therefore answer you.

3. "Here, Puṇṇa, someone develops the dog duty fully and unstintingly, he develops the dog habit fully and unstintingly, he develops the dog mind fully and unstintingly, he develops dog behaviour fully and unstintingly. Having done that, on the dissolution of the body, after death, he reappears in the company of dogs. But if his view is such as this: 'By this virtue or duty or asceticism or religious life I shall become a (great) god or some (lesser) god,' that is wrong view in his case. Now there are two destinations for one with wrong view, I say: hell or the animal womb. So, Puṇṇa, if his dog duty is perfected, it will lead him to the company of dogs; if it is not, it will lead him to hell."

4. When this was said, Seniya the naked dog-duty ascetic wept and shed tears. Then the Blessed One told Puṇṇa, son of the Koliyans and an ox-duty ascetic: "Puṇṇa, I could not persuade you when I said, 'Enough Puṇṇa, let that be. Do not ask me that.'"

"Venerable sir, I am not weeping that the Blessed One has spoken thus. Still, this dog duty has long been taken up and practised by me. Venerable sir, there is this Puṇṇa, a son of the

1. Of births in saṃsāra, the wandering-on in birth and death.

Koliyans and an ox-duty ascetic: that ox duty has long been taken up and practised by him. What will be his destination? What will be his future course?"

"Enough, Seniya, let that be. Do not ask me that." A second time... A third time Seniya the naked dog-duty ascetic asked the Blessed One: "Venerable sir, there is this Puṇṇa, a son of the Koliyans and an ox-duty ascetic; that ox duty has long been taken up and practised by him. What will be his destination? What will be his future course?"

"Well, Seniya, since I certainly cannot persuade you when I say 'Enough, Seniya, let that be. Do not ask me that,' I shall therefore answer you.

5. "Here, Seniya, someone develops the ox duty fully and unstintingly, he develops the ox habit fully and unstintingly, he develops the ox mind fully and unstintingly, he develops the ox behaviour fully and unstintingly. Having done that, on the dissolution of the body, after death, he reappears in the company of oxen. But if his view is such as this: 'By this virtue or duty or asceticism or religious life I shall become a (great) god or some (lesser) god,' that is wrong view in his case. Now there are two destinations for one with wrong view, I say: hell or the animal womb. So, Seniya, if his ox duty is perfected, it will lead him to the company of oxen; if it is not, it will lead him to hell."

6. When this was said, Puṇṇa, a son of the Koliyans and an ox-duty ascetic, wept and shed tears. Then the Blessed One told Seniya, the naked dog-duty ascetic: "Seniya, I could not persuade you when I said, 'Enough, Seniya, let that be. Do not ask me that.'"

"Venerable sir, I am not weeping that the Blessed One has spoken thus. Still, this ox duty has long been taken up and practised by me. Venerable sir, I have confidence in the Blessed One thus: 'The Blessed One is capable of teaching me the Dhamma in such a way that I may abandon this ox duty and that this naked dog-duty ascetic Seniya may abandon that dog duty.'"

7. "Then, Puṇṇa, listen and heed well what I shall say."

"Yes, venerable sir," he replied. The Blessed One said this:

8. "Puṇṇa, there are four kinds of kamma proclaimed by me after realisation myself with direct knowledge. What are the four? There is dark kamma with dark ripening, there is bright kamma

with bright ripening, there is dark-and-bright kamma with dark-and-bright ripening, and there is kamma that is not dark and not bright with neither-dark-nor-bright ripening that conduces to the exhaustion of kamma.

9. "What is dark kamma with dark ripening? Here someone produces a (kammic) bodily process (bound up) with affliction,[2] he produces a (kammic) verbal process (bound up) with affliction, he produces a (kammic) mental process (bound up) with affliction. By so doing, he reappears in a world with affliction. When that happens, afflicting contacts[3] touch him. Being touched by these, he feels afflicting feelings entirely painful as in the case of beings in hell. Thus a being's reappearance is due to a being: he reappears owing to the kammas he has performed. When he has reappeared, contacts touch him. Thus I say are beings heirs of their kammas. This is called dark kamma with dark ripening.

10. "And what is bright kamma with bright ripening? Here someone produces a (kammic) bodily process not (bound up) with affliction, he produces a (kammic) verbal process not (bound up) with affliction, he produces a (kammic) mental process not (bound up) with affliction. By doing so, he reappears in a world without affliction. When that happens, unafflicting contacts touch him. Being touched by these, he feels unafflicting feelings entirely pleasant as in the case of the Subhakiṇha, the gods of Refulgent Glory. Thus a being's reappearance is due to a being: he reappears owing to the kammas he has performed. When he has reappeared, contacts touch him. Thus I say are beings heirs of their kammas. This is called bright kamma with bright ripening.

11. "What is dark-and-bright kamma with dark-and-bright ripening? Here someone produces a (kammic) bodily process both (bound up) with affliction and not (bound up) with affliction... verbal process... mental process both (bound up) with affliction and not (bound up) with affliction. By doing so, he reappears in a world both with and without affliction. When that happens, both afflicting and unafflicting contacts touch him. Being touched by these, he feels afflicting and unafflicting feelings with mingled pleasure and pain as in the case of human beings and some gods

2. A defiled kamma expressed through the body (speech, mind).
3. Painful "touches" through eye, ear, nose, tongue, body, mind.

and some inhabitants of the states of deprivation. Thus a being's reappearance is due to a being: he reappears owing to the kammas he has performed. When he has reappeared, contacts touch him. Thus I say are beings heirs of their kammas. This is called dark-and-bright kamma with dark-and-bright ripening.

12. "What is neither-dark-nor-bright kamma with neither-dark-nor-bright ripening that leads to the exhaustion of kamma? As to these (three kinds of kamma), any volition in abandoning the kind of kamma that is dark with dark ripening, any volition in abandoning the kind of kamma that is bright with bright ripening and any volition in abandoning the kind of kamma that is dark-and-bright with dark-and-bright ripening: this is called neither-dark-nor-bright kamma with neither-dark-nor-bright ripening.

"These are the four kinds of kamma proclaimed by me after realisation myself with direct knowledge."

13. When this was said, Puṇṇa, a son of the Koliyans and an ox-duty ascetic, said to the Blessed One: "Magnificent, Master Gotama! Magnificent, Master Gotama! The Dhamma has been made clear in many ways by Master Gotama as though he were turning upright what had been overthrown, revealing the hidden, showing the way to one who is lost, holding up a lamp in the darkness for those with eyesight to see forms.

14. "I go to Master Gotama for refuge and to the Dhamma and to the Sangha of bhikkhus. From today let Master Gotama remember me as a lay follower who has gone to him for refuge for life."

15. But Seniya the naked dog-duty ascetic said: "Magnificent, Master Gotama!... The Dhamma has been made clear... for those with eyesight to see forms.

16. "I go to Master Gotama for refuge and to the Dhamma and to the Sangha of bhikkhus. I would receive the going forth under Master Gotama and the full admission."[4]

17. "Seniya, one who belonged formerly to another sect and wants the going forth and the full admission in this Dhamma and Discipline lives on probation for four months. At the end of the four months bhikkhus who are satisfied in their minds give him

4. That is, the novice ordination and the full ordination as a bhikkhu, or monk.

the going forth into homelessness and also the full admission to the bhikkhus' state. A difference in persons has become known to me in this (probation period)."

"Venerable sir, if those who belonged formerly to another sect and want the going forth and the full admission in this Dhamma and Discipline live on probation for four months and at the end of four months bhikkhus who are satisfied in their minds give them the going forth into homelessness and the full admission to the bhikkhus' state, I will live on probation for four years and at the end of the four years let bhikkhus who are satisfied in their minds give me the going forth into homelessness and the full admission to the bhikkhus' state."

18. Seniya the naked dog-duty ascetic received the going forth under the Blessed One, and he received the full admission. And not long after his full admission, dwelling alone, withdrawn, diligent, ardent, and self-controlled, the venerable Seniya by realisation himself with direct knowledge here and now entered upon and abode in that supreme goal of the holy life for the sake of which clansmen rightly go forth from the home life into homelessness. He had direct knowledge thus: "Birth is exhausted, the holy life has been lived, what had to be done has been done, there is no more of this to come."

And the venerable Seniya became one of the arahats.

Majjhima Nikāya 135: The Shorter Exposition of Kamma (Cūḷakammavibhaṅga Sutta)

Introduction

You want: long life, health, beauty, power, riches, high birth, wisdom? Or even some of these things? They do not appear by chance. It is not someone's luck that they are healthy, or another's lack of it that he is stupid. Though it may not be clear to us now, all such inequalities among human beings (and all sorts of beings) come about because of the kamma they have made individually. Each person reaps his own fruits. So if one is touched by short life, sickliness, ugliness, insignificance, poverty, low birth or stupidity and one does not like these things, no need to just accept that that is the way it is. The future need not be like that provided that one makes the right kind of kamma now. Knowing what kamma to make and what not to make is the mark of a wise man. It is also the mark of one who is no longer drifting aimlessly but has some direction in life and some control over the sort of events that will occur.

The Sutta

1. Thus have I heard. On one occasion the Blessed One was living at Sāvatthī in Jeta's Grove, Anāthapiṇḍika's Park.

Then Subha the student (brahman), Todeyya's son, went to the Blessed One and exchanged greetings with him, and when the courteous and amiable talk was finished, he sat down at one side. When he had done so, Subha the student said to the Blessed One:

2. "Master Gotama, what is the reason, what is the condition, why inferiority and superiority are met with among human beings, among mankind? For one meets with short-lived and long-lived people, sick and healthy people, ugly and beautiful people, insignificant and influential people, poor and rich people, low-born and high-born people, stupid and wise people. What is the

reason, what is the condition, why superiority and inferiority are met with among human beings, among mankind?"

3. "Student, beings are owners of kammas, heirs of kammas, they have kammas as their progenitor, kammas as their kin, kammas as their homing-place. It is kammas that differentiate beings according to inferiority and superiority."

4. "I do not understand the detailed meaning of Master Gotama's utterance spoken in brief without expounding the detailed meaning. It would be good if Master Gotama taught me the Dhamma so that I might understand the detailed meaning of Master Gotama's utterance spoken in brief without expounding the detailed meaning."

"Then listen, student, and heed well what I shall say."

"Even so, Master Gotama," Subha the student replied. The Blessed One said this:

5. "Here, student, some woman or man is a killer of living beings, murderous, bloody-handed, given to blows and violence, merciless to living beings. Due to having performed and completed such kammas, on the dissolution of the body, after death, he reappears in a state of deprivation, in an unhappy destination, in perdition, in hell. If, on the dissolution of the body, after death, instead of his reappearing in a state of deprivation, in an unhappy destination, in perdition, in hell, he comes to the human state, he is short-lived wherever he is reborn. This is the way that leads to short life, that is to say, to be a killer of living beings, murderous, bloody-handed, given to blows and violence, merciless to living beings.

6. "But here some woman or man, having abandoned the killing of living beings, abstains from killing living beings, lays aside the rod and lays aside the knife, is considerate and merciful and dwells compassionate for the welfare of all living beings. Due to having performed and completed such kammas, on the dissolution of the body, after death, he reappears in a happy destination, in the heavenly world. If, on the dissolution of the body, after death, instead of his reappearing in a happy destination, in the heavenly world, he comes to the human state, he is long-lived wherever he is reborn. This is the way that leads to long life, that is to say, to have abandoned the killing of living beings, to abstain from killing living beings, to lay aside the rod and lay aside the knife, to

be considerate and merciful, and to dwell compassionate for the welfare of all living beings.

7. "Here, student, some woman or man is one who harms beings with his hands or with clods or with sticks or with knives. Due to having performed and completed such kammas, on the dissolution of the body, after death, he reappears in a state of deprivation... If instead he comes to the human state, he is sickly wherever he is reborn. This is the way that leads to sickness, that is to say, to be one who harms beings with one's hands or with clods or with sticks or with knives.

8. "But here some woman or man is not one who harms beings with his hands, or with clods, or with sticks, or with knives. Due to having performed and completed such kammas, on the dissolution of the body, after death, he reappears in a happy destination... If instead he comes to the human state, he is healthy wherever he is reborn. This is the way that leads to health, that is to say, not to be one who harms beings with his hands or with clods or with sticks or with knives.

9. "Here, student, some woman or man is angry, much given to rage; even when little is said, he is furious, angry, ill-disposed, resentful, he shows ill-temper, hate and surliness. Due to having performed and completed such kammas, on the dissolution of the body, after death, he reappears in a state of deprivation... If instead he comes to the human state, he is ugly wherever he is reborn. This is the way that leads to ugliness, that is to say, to be furious, angry, ill-disposed, resentful and to show ill-temper, hate and surliness.

10. "But here some woman or man is not angry or much given to rage; even when much is said, he is not furious, angry, ill-disposed, resentful, nor does he show ill-temper, hate or surliness. Due to having performed and completed such kammas, on the dissolution of the body, after death, he reappears in a happy destination... If instead he comes to the human state, he is beautiful wherever he is reborn. This is the way that leads to beauty, that is to say, not to be angry or given to much rage; even when much is said, not to be furious, angry, ill-disposed or resentful, or to show ill-temper, hate or surliness.

11. "Here, student, some woman or man is envious; he envies, begrudges and harbours envy about others' gains, honour, veneration, respect, salutations and offerings. Due to having performed

and completed such kammas, on the dissolution of the body, after death, he reappears in a state of deprivation... If instead he comes to the human state, he is insignificant wherever he is reborn. This is the way that leads to insignificance, that is to say, to be envious, to envy, begrudge and harbour envy about others' gain, honour, veneration, respect, salutations and offerings.

12. "But here some woman or man is not envious, he does not envy, begrudge or harbour envy about others' gain, honour, veneration, respect, salutations and offerings. Due to having performed and completed such kammas, on the dissolution of the body, after death, he reappears in a happy destination... If instead he comes to the human state, he is influential wherever he is reborn. This is the way that leads to influence, that is to say, not to be envious, not to envy, begrudge or harbour envy about others' gain, honour, veneration, respect, salutations and offerings.

13. "Here, student, some woman or man is not a giver of food, drink, cloth, sandals, garlands, perfumes, unguents, bed, roof and lighting to monks or brahmans. Due to having performed and completed such kamma, on the dissolution of the body, after death, he reappears in a state of deprivation... If instead he comes to the human state, he is poor wherever he is reborn. This is the way that leads to poverty, that is to say, not to be a giver of food, drink, cloth, sandals, garlands, perfumes, unguents, bed, roof and lighting to monks and brahmans.

14. "But here some woman or man is a giver of food, drink, cloth, sandals, garlands, perfumes, unguents, bed, roof and lighting to monks and brahmans. Due to having performed and completed such kamma, on the dissolution of the body, after death, he reappears in a happy destination... If instead he comes to the human state, he is rich wherever he is reborn. This is the way that leads to riches, that is to say, to be a giver of food, drink, cloth, sandals, garlands, perfumes, unguents, bed, roof and lighting to monks and brahmans.

15. "Here, student, some woman or man is obdurate and haughty; he does not pay homage to whom he should pay homage, or rise up for whom he should rise up, or give a seat to whom he should give a seat, or make way for whom he should make way, or worship him who should be worshipped, or respect him who should be respected, or revere him who should be revered, or

honour him who should be honoured. Due to having performed and completed such kammas, on the dissolution of the body, after death, he reappears in a state of deprivation... If instead he comes to the human state, he is low-born wherever he is reborn. This is the way that leads to low birth, that is to say, to be obdurate and haughty, not to pay homage to whom he should pay homage, nor rise up for..., nor give a seat to..., nor make way for..., nor worship..., nor respect..., nor revere..., nor honour him who should be honoured.

16. "But here some woman or man is not obdurate or haughty; he pays homage to whom he should pay homage, rises up for whom he should rise up, gives a seat to whom he should give a seat, makes way for whom he should make way, worships him who should be worshipped, respects him who should be respected, reveres him who should be revered, honours him who should be honoured. Due to having performed and completed such kammas, on the dissolution of the body, after death, he reappears in a happy destination... If instead he comes to the human state, he is high-born wherever he is reborn. This is the way that leads to high birth, that is to say, not to be obdurate or haughty, to pay homage to whom he should pay homage, to rise up for..., to give a seat to..., to make way for..., to worship..., respect..., revere..., honour him who should be honoured.

17. "Here, student, some woman or man when visiting a monk or brahman, does not ask: 'What is wholesome, venerable sir? What is unwholesome? What is blameable? What is blameless? What should be cultivated? What should not be cultivated? What, by my doing it, will be long for my harm and suffering? Or what, by my doing it, will be long for my welfare and happiness?' Due to having performed and completed such kammas, on the dissolution of the body, after death, he reappears in a state of deprivation... If instead he comes to the human state, he will be stupid wherever he is reborn. This is the way that leads to stupidity, that is to say, when visiting a monk or brahman, not to ask: 'What is wholesome?... Or what, by my doing it, will be long for my welfare and happiness?'

18. "But here some woman or man when visiting a monk or brahman, asks: 'What is wholesome, venerable sir?... Or what, by my doing it, will be long for my welfare and happiness?' Due to

having performed and completed such kammas, on the dissolution of the body, after death, he reappears in a happy destination... If instead he comes to the human state, he is wise wherever he is reborn. This is the way that leads to wisdom, that is to say, when visiting a monk or brahman, to ask: 'What is wholesome, venerable sir?... Or what, by my doing it, will be long for my welfare and happiness?'

19. "So, student, the way that leads to short life makes people short-lived, the way that leads to long life makes people long-lived; the way that leads to sickness makes people sick, the way that leads to health makes people healthy; the way that leads to ugliness makes people ugly, the way that leads to beauty makes people beautiful; the way that leads to insignificance makes people insignificant, the way that leads to influence makes people influential; the way that leads to poverty makes people poor, the way that leads to riches makes people rich; the way that leads to low birth makes people low-born, the way that leads to high birth makes people high-born; the way that leads to stupidity makes people stupid, the way that leads to wisdom makes people wise.

20. "Beings are owners of kammas, student, heirs of kammas, they have kammas as their progenitor, kammas as their kin, kammas as their homing-place. It is kammas that differentiate beings according to inferiority and superiority."

21. When this was said, Subha the student, Todeyya's son, said to the Blessed One: "Magnificent, Master Gotama! Magnificent, Master Gotama! The Dhamma has been made clear in many ways by Master Gotama, as though he were turning upright what had been overthrown, revealing the hidden, showing the way to one who is lost, holding up a lamp in the darkness for those with eyes to see forms.

22. "I go to Master Gotama for refuge, and to the Dhamma and to the Sangha of bhikkhus. From today let Master Gotama accept me as a lay follower who has gone to him for refuge for life."

Majjhima Nikāya 136: The Great Exposition of Kamma (Mahākammavibhaṅga Sutta)

Introduction

This celebrated sutta shows some of the complexities of kamma and its results. Beginning with a strange view expressed by a confused wanderer and a confused answer given by a bhikkhu, the Buddha then gives his Great Exposition of Kamma, which is based upon four "types" of people:

1. the evil-doer who goes to hell (or some other low state of birth),
2. the evil-doer who goes to heaven,
3. the good man who goes to heaven, and
4. the good man who goes to hell (or other low birth).

The Buddha then shows how wrong views can arise from only partial understanding of truth. One can see the stages of this: (1) a mystic "sees" in vision an evil-doer suffering in hell, (2) this confirms what he had heard about moral causality, (3) so he says, "evil-doers always go to hell", and (4) dogma hardens and becomes rigid when he says (with the dogmatists of all ages and places), "Only this is true; anything else is wrong." The stages of this process are repeated for each of the four "persons," after which the Buddha proceeds to analyse these views grounded in partial experience and points out which portions are true (because verifiable by trial and experience) and which are dogmatic superstructure which is unjustified. Finally, the Buddha explains his Great Exposition of Kamma in which he shows that notions of invariability like "the evil-doer goes to hell" are much too simple. The minds of people are complex and they make many different kinds of kamma even in one lifetime, some of which may influence the last moment when kamma is made before death, which in turn is the basis for the next life.

The Sutta

1. Thus have I heard. On one occasion the Blessed One was living at Rājagaha, in the Bamboo Grove, the Squirrels' Feeding Place. Now on that occasion the venerable Samiddhi was living in a forest hut.

Then the wanderer Poṭaliputta, walking and wandering for exercise, came to the venerable Samiddhi and exchanged greetings with him, and when the courteous and amiable talk was finished, he sat down at one side. When he had done so, he said to the venerable Samiddhi:

2. "I heard and learned this, friend Samiddhi, from the monk Gotama's lips: 'Bodily kammas are vain, verbal kammas are vain, only mental kammas are true.' But there is actually that attainment having entered upon which nothing (of result of kammas) is felt at all."

"Not so, friend Poṭaliputta, do not say thus, do not misrepresent the Blessed One; it is not good to misrepresent the Blessed One; the Blessed One would not say so: 'Bodily kammas are vain, verbal kammas are vain, only mental kammas are true.' And there is actually that attainment having entered upon which nothing (of result of kammas) is felt at all."

"How long is it since you went forth, friend Samiddhi?"

"Not long, friend, three years."

"There now, what shall we say to the elder bhikkhus, when the young bhikkhu fancies the Master is to be defended thus? After doing intentional kamma, friend Samiddhi, by way of body, speech or mind, what does one feel (of its result)?"

"After doing an intentional kamma, friend Poṭaliputta, by way of body, speech or mind, one feels suffering (as its result)."

Then neither agreeing nor disagreeing with the words of the venerable Samiddhi, the wanderer Poṭaliputta got up from his seat and went away.

3. Soon after the wanderer Poṭaliputta had gone, the venerable Samiddhi went to the venerable Ānanda and exchanged greetings with him, and when the courteous and amiable talk was finished, he sat down at one side. When he had done so, he told the venerable Ānanda all his conversation with the wanderer Poṭaliputta.

When this was said, the venerable Ānanda told him: "Friend Samiddhi, this conversation should be told to the Blessed One. Come, let us go to the Blessed One, and having done so, let us tell him about this. As he answers, so we shall bear it in mind."

"Even so, friend," the venerable Samiddhi replied.

Then they went together to the Blessed One, and after paying homage to him, they sat down at one side. When they had done so, the venerable Ānanda told the Blessed One all the venerable Samiddhi's conversation with the wanderer Poṭaliputta.

4. When this was said, the Blessed One told the venerable Ānanda:

"I do not even know the wanderer by sight, Ānanda. How could there have been such a conversation? The wanderer Poṭaliputta's question ought to have been answered after analysing it, but this misguided man Samiddhi answered it without qualification."[5]

When this was said, the venerable Udāyin said to the Blessed One: "But, venerable sir, supposing when the venerable Samiddhi spoke, he was referring to this, namely, 'Whatever is felt is suffering.'"[6]

5. Then the Blessed One addressed the venerable Ānanda: "See, Ānanda, how this misguided man Udāyin interferes. I knew, Ānanda, that this misguided man Udāyin would unreasonably interfere now. To begin with it was the three kinds of feeling that were asked about by the wanderer Poṭaliputta. If, when this misguided man Samiddhi was asked, he had answered the wanderer Poṭaliputta thus: 'After doing an intentional kamma by way of body, speech and mind (whose result is) to be felt as pleasure, he feels pleasure; after doing an intentional kamma by way of body, speech and mind (whose result is) to be felt as pain, he feels pain; after doing an intentional kamma by way of body, speech and mind (whose result is) to be felt as neither-pain-nor-pleasure, he feels neither-pain-nor-pleasure'—by answering him thus, Ānanda, the misguided man Samiddhi would have given

5. These are two of the four ways of answering a question, the other two being: replying with a counter-question, and "setting aside" the question, i.e., replying with silence.

6. This is a quotation from the Buddha's words: see Saṃyutta Nikāya, Vedanā Saṃyutta, Rahogata-vagga Sutta 1.

the wanderer Poṭaliputta the right answer. Besides, Ānanda, who are the foolish thoughtless wanderers of other sects that they will understand the Tathāgata's Great Exposition of Kamma? (But) if you, Ānanda, would listen to the Tathāgata expounding the Great Exposition of Kamma (you might understand it)."[7]

"This is the time, Blessed One, this is the time, Sublime One, for the Blessed One to expound the Great Exposition of Kamma. Having heard it from the Blessed One, the bhikkhus will bear it in mind."

"Then listen, Ānanda, and heed well what I shall say."

"Even so, venerable sir," the venerable Ānanda replied. The Blessed One said this:

6. "Ānanda, there are four kinds of persons existing in the world. What four?

(i) "Here some person kills living beings, takes what is not given, misconducts himself in sexual desires, speaks falsehood, speaks maliciously, speaks harshly, gossips, is covetous, is ill willed and has wrong view.[8] On the dissolution of the body, after death, he reappears in the states of deprivation, in an unhappy destination, in perdition, in hell.

(ii) "But here some person kills living beings... and has wrong view. On the dissolution of the body, after death, he reappears in a happy destination, in the heavenly world.

(iii) "Here some person abstains from killing living beings, from taking what is not given, from misconduct in sexual desires, from false speech, from malicious speech, from harsh speech, from gossip, he is not covetous, is not ill willed and has right view.[9] On the dissolution of the body, after death, he reappears in a happy destination, in the heavenly world.

(iv) "But here some person abstains from killing living beings... and has right view. On the dissolution of the body, after death, he reappears in the states of deprivation, in an unhappy destination, in perdition, in hell.

7. (i) "Here, Ānanda, in consequence of ardour, endeavour, devotion, diligence and right attention, some monk or brahman

7. This is an addition necessary for understanding this sentence.

8. These are the ten unwholesome courses of kamma.

9. These are the ten wholesome courses of kamma.

attains such concentration of mind that, when his mind is concentrated, he sees with the heavenly eyesight, which is purified and surpasses the human, that some person kills living beings here, takes what is not given, misconducts himself in sexual desires, speaks falsehood, speaks maliciously, speaks harshly, gossips, is covetous, is ill willed, has wrong view. He sees that on the dissolution of the body, after death, he has reappeared in the states of deprivation, in an unhappy destination, in perdition, in hell. He says: 'It seems that there are evil kammas and that there is the result of misconduct; for I have seen that a person killed living beings here... had wrong view. I have seen that on the dissolution of the body, after death, he had reappeared in the states of deprivation, in an unhappy destination, in perdition, in hell.' He says: 'It seems that one who kills living beings... has wrong view, will always, on the dissolution of the body, after death, reappear in the states of deprivation, in an unhappy destination, in perdition, in hell. Those who know thus know rightly; those who know otherwise are mistaken in their knowledge.' So he obstinately misapprehends what he himself has known, seen and felt; insisting on that alone, he says: 'Only this is true, anything else is wrong.'

8. (ii) "But here in consequence of ardour, endeavour, devotion, diligence and right attention, some monk or brahman attains such concentration of mind that, when his mind is concentrated, he sees with the heavenly eyesight, which is purified and surpasses the human, that some person kills living beings here... has wrong view. He sees that on the dissolution of the body, after death, he has reappeared in a happy destination, in the heavenly world. He says: 'It seems there are no evil kammas, there is no result of misconduct. For I have seen that a person killed living beings here... had wrong view. I have seen that on the dissolution of the body, after death, he has reappeared in a happy destination, in the heavenly world.' He says: 'It seems that one who kills living beings... has wrong view will always, on the dissolution of the body, after death, reappear in a happy destination, in the heavenly world. Those who know thus know rightly; those who know otherwise are mistaken in their knowledge.' So he obstinately misapprehends what he himself has known, seen and felt; insisting on that alone, he says: 'Only this is true, anything else is wrong.'

9. (iii) "Here in consequence of ardour, endeavour, devotion, diligence and right attention, some monk or brahman attains such concentration of mind that, when his mind is concentrated, he sees with the heavenly eyesight, which is purified and surpasses the human, that some person abstains from killing living beings here... has right view. He sees that, on the dissolution of the body, after death, he has reappeared in a happy destination, in the heavenly world. He says: 'It seems that there are good kammas, there is result of good conduct. For I have seen that a person abstained from killing living beings here... had right view. I saw that on the dissolution of the body, after death, he had reappeared in a happy destination, in the heavenly world.' He says: 'It seems that one who abstains from killing living beings... has right view will always, on the dissolution of the body, after death, reappear in a happy destination, in the heavenly world. Those who know thus know rightly; those who know otherwise are mistaken in their knowledge.' So he obstinately misapprehends what he himself has known, seen and felt; insisting on that alone, he says: 'Only this is true; anything else is wrong.'

10. (iv) "But here in consequence of ardour, endeavour, devotion, diligence and right attention, some monk or brahman attains such concentration of mind that, when his mind is concentrated, he sees with the heavenly eyesight, which is purified and surpasses the human, that some person abstains from killing living beings here... has right view. He sees that on the dissolution of the body, after death, he has reappeared in the states of deprivation, in an unhappy destination, in perdition, in hell. He says: 'It seems that there are no good kammas, there is no result of good conduct. For I have seen that a person abstained from killing here... had right view. I saw that on the dissolution of the body, after death, he had reappeared in the states of deprivation, in an unhappy destination, in perdition, in hell.' He says: 'It seems that one who abstains from killing living beings... has right view, will always, on the dissolution of the body, after death, reappear in the states of deprivation, in an unhappy destination, in perdition, in hell. Those who know thus know rightly; those who know otherwise are mistaken in their knowledge.' So he obstinately misapprehends what he himself has known, seen and felt; insisting on that alone, he says: 'Only this is true; anything else is wrong.'

11. (i) "Now, Ānanda, when a monk or brahman says thus: 'It seems that there are evil kammas, there is the result of misconduct,' I concede that to him.

"When he says thus: 'For I have seen that some person killed living beings... had wrong view. I saw that on the dissolution of the body, after death, he had reappeared in states of deprivation, in an unhappy destination, in perdition, in hell,' I concede that to him.

"When he says thus: 'It seems that one who kills living beings... has wrong view, will always, on the dissolution of the body, after death, reappear in the states of deprivation, in an unhappy destination, in perdition, in hell,' I do not concede that to him.

"When he says thus: 'Those who know thus know rightly; those who know otherwise are mistaken in their knowledge,' I do not concede that to him.

"When he obstinately misapprehends what he himself has known, seen and felt; and insisting on that alone, he says: 'Only this is true; anything else is wrong,' I do not concede that to him.

"Why is that? The Tathāgata's knowledge of the Great Exposition of Kamma is different.

12. (ii) "Now when a monk or brahman says thus: 'It seems that there are no evil kammas, there is no result of misconduct,' I do not concede that to him.

"When he says thus: 'For I have seen that a person killed living beings... had wrong view. I saw that on the dissolution of the body, after death, he had reappeared in a happy destination, in the heavenly world,' I concede that to him.

"When he says thus: 'It seems that one who kills living beings... has wrong view, will always, on the dissolution of the body, after death, reappear in a happy destination, in the heavenly world,' I do not concede that to him.

"When he says thus: 'Those who know thus know rightly; those who know otherwise are mistaken in their knowledge,' I do not concede that to him.

"When he obstinately misapprehends what he himself has known, seen and felt; and insisting on that alone, he says: 'Only this is true; anything else is wrong,' I do not concede that to him.

"Why is that? The Tathāgata's knowledge of the Great Exposition of Kamma is different.

13. (iii) "Now when a monk or brahman says thus: 'It seems that there are good kammas, there is a result of good conduct,' I concede that to him.

"When he says thus: 'For I have seen that a person abstained from killing living beings here... had right view. I saw that on the dissolution of the body, after death, he had reappeared in a happy destination, in the heavenly world,' I concede that to him.

"When he says: 'It seems that one who abstains from killing living beings... has right view will always, on the dissolution of the body, after death, reappear in a happy destination, in the heavenly world,'[10] I do not concede that to him.

"When he says: 'Those who know thus know rightly; those who know otherwise are mistaken in their knowledge,' I do not concede that to him.

"When he obstinately misapprehends what he himself has known, seen and felt; and insisting on that alone he says: 'Only this is true: anything else is wrong,' I do not concede that to him.

"Why is that? The Tathāgata's knowledge of the Great Exposition of Kamma is different.

14. (iv) "Now when a monk or brahman says thus: 'It seems that there are no good kammas, there is no result of good conduct,' I do not concede that to him.

"When he says thus: 'For I have seen that a person abstained from killing living beings here... had right view. I saw that on the dissolution of the body, after death, he had reappeared in the states of deprivation, in an unhappy destination, in perdition, in hell,' I concede that to him.

"When he says thus: 'One who abstains from killing living beings... has right view will always, on the dissolution of the body, after death, reappear in the states of deprivation, in an unhappy destination, in perdition, in hell,' I do not concede that to him.

"When he says thus: 'Those who know thus know rightly; those who know otherwise are mistaken in their knowledge,' I do not concede that to him.

---

10. This amounts to the belief in theistic religions where virtue and faith (= whatever is held to be right view) are supposed to guarantee salvation.

"When he obstinately misapprehends what he himself has known, seen and felt; and insisting on that alone, he says: 'Only this is true; anything else is wrong,' I do not concede that to him.

"Why is that? The Tathāgata's knowledge of the Great Exposition of Kamma is different.

The Great Exposition of Kamma

15. (i) "Now, Ānanda, there is the person who has killed living beings here... has had wrong view. And on the dissolution of the body, after death, he reappears in the states of deprivation, in an unhappy destination, in perdition, in hell.[11] But (perhaps) the evil kamma producing his suffering was done by him earlier, or the evil kamma producing his suffering was done by him later, or wrong view was undertaken and completed by him at the time of his death.[12] And that was why, on the dissolution of the body, after death, he reappeared in the states of deprivation, in an unhappy destination, in perdition, in hell. But since he has killed living beings here... has had wrong view, he will feel the result of that here and now, or in his next rebirth, or in some subsequent existence.

16. (ii) "Now there is the person who has killed living beings here... has had wrong view. And on the dissolution of the body, after death, he reappears in a happy destination, in the heavenly

---

11. Devadatta, for instance, who persuaded prince Ajātasattu to murder his father (who was a stream-winner), three times attempted to murder the Buddha and once succeeded in wounding him, and caused a schism in the Sangha; the last two actions are certain to lead to birth in hell.

12. This series of three phrases appears to mean: *earlier,* either earlier in life before he undertook either the wholesome or unwholesome courses of kamma, or in some previous life; *later,* later in that very life, for even if a person does much evil kamma, usually he will also make some good kamma occasionally; *wrong view... time of his death,* this kind of wrong view will be of the type, "there is no kamma, no results of kamma, no evil, no results of evil," and so on. The next birth actually depends on the object of the last moments of a dying person's consciousness. At that time one should recollect all one's good kamma: generosity, loving kindness, compassion, pure precepts and so on. Evil should not be thought of then, though heavy evil kamma done previously may force itself into the mind and make recollection of one's generosity and virtue in keeping the precepts difficult or impossible.

world.[13] But (perhaps) the good kamma producing his happiness was done by him earlier, or the good kamma producing his happiness was done by him later, or right view was undertaken and completed by him at the time of his death. And that was why, on the dissolution of the body, after death, he reappeared in a happy destination, in the heavenly world. But since he has killed living beings here... has had wrong view, he will feel the result of that here and now, or in his next rebirth, or in some subsequent existence.[14]

17. (iii) "Now there is the person who has abstained from killing living beings here... has had right view. And on the dissolution of the body, after death, he reappears in a happy destination, in the heavenly world.[15] But (perhaps) the good kamma producing his happiness was done by him earlier, or the good kamma producing his happiness was done by him later, or right view was undertaken and completed by him at the time of his death. And that was why, on the dissolution of the body, after death, he reappeared in a happy destination, in the heavenly world. But since he has abstained from killing living beings here... has had right view, he will feel the result of that here and now, or in his next rebirth, or in some subsequent existence.

18. (iv) "Now there is the person who has abstained from killing living beings here... has had right view. And on the dissolution of the body, after death, he reappears in the states of deprivation, in an unhappy destination, in perdition, in hell.[16] But

13. A good example of this is the story of "Coppertooth," the public executioner who, after a career of murder as a bandit, then as the killer of his own bandit comrades and subsequently executioner of all criminals for fifty years, was taught by venerable Sāriputta Thera and his mind eased of the heavy weight of evil kamma so that he attained heavenly rebirth. See Dhammapada Commentary, ii, 203–209.

14. Though such a person attained a heavenly rebirth the evil kamma made will still mature sooner or later; he has not escaped its results.

15. King Pasenadi of Kosala, for instance.

16. This was what happened to Queen Mallikā, wife of King Pasenadi, who had led a good life, generous, keeping the Five Precepts, and the Eight Precepts on Uposatha days and so on, but once she did evil, having sexual relations with a dog. This unconfessed evil weighed heavily on her mind and she remembered it when dying. As a result she spent seven days in hell.

(perhaps) the evil kamma producing his suffering was done by him earlier, or the evil kamma producing his suffering was done by him later, or wrong view was undertaken and completed by him at the time of his death. And that was why, on the dissolution of the body, after death, he reappeared in the states of deprivation, in an unhappy destination, in perdition, in hell. But since he has abstained from killing living beings here... has had right view, he will feel the result of that here and now, or in his next rebirth, or in some subsequent existence.[17]

19. "So, Ānanda, there is kamma that is incapable (of good result) and appears incapable (of good result); there is kamma that is incapable (of good result) and appears capable (of good result); there is kamma that is capable (of good result) and appears capable (of good result); there is kamma that is capable (of good result) and appears incapable (of good result)."[18]

This is what the Blessed One said. The venerable Ānanda was satisfied and he rejoiced in the Blessed One's words.

Her power of goodness from the doing of many good kammas then gave her rebirth in a heavenly world. See Dhammapada Commentary, iii, 119–123.

17. Though this virtuous and good person has obtained a low rebirth through the power of previously done evil kamma, still the good kamma made by him will mature sooner or later, when it gets a chance.

18. This final terse paragraph may have been clear to the venerable Ānanda Thera, or he may have asked for an explanation, as we require and find in the Commentary, which says:

i. A strong unwholesome kamma (incapable of good result), the result of which will come before the results of weaker unwholesome kammas.
ii. Wholesome kamma (which appears capable of good result) is followed by unwholesome death-proximate kamma which makes the former incapable of good result immediately.
iii. A strong wholesome kamma will mature even before much accumulated unwholesome kamma.
iv. Unwholesome kamma (which appears incapable of good result) is followed by wholesome death-proximate kamma which will mature first and is capable of good results.

Majjhima Nikāya 41: The Brahmans of Sāla (Sāleyyaka Sutta)

Introduction

The brahmans of this discourse, intelligent people, asked a question about the causality of rebirth—why is one reborn in the states of deprivation (the hells, animals, and ghosts) while others make it to the heaven worlds?

The Buddha then analyses what kind of kamma will take one to a low rebirth. You see any of your own actions here? Then you know what to do about it, for if one makes any of these ten courses of unwholesome kamma strong in oneself, a result can be expected at least "on the dissolution of the body, after death," if not in this life.

The ten courses of wholesome kamma follow. They should be strengthened in oneself, repeated frequently so that they become habitual. If one recognises any of one's own actions among them, then just guard against the conceit: "I am good."

The last part of the sutta deals with the aspirations which one may have for rebirth at the time of death. Of course, one's previously made kamma must be such that it will support such aspirations. A miser might aspire to riches but his kamma will give him poverty. If a person has kept the Uposatha and generally all the precepts and been generous and truthful as well, this is the passport to heavenly birth (from the gods of the Four Kings up to the gods that Wield Power over others' Creations). Beyond this, it is necessary also to be proficient in jhāna and one will gain rebirth among the Brahmās (from the Divinity's Retinue to the Very Fruitful gods) according to proficiency in this. For the next five Brahmā-planes, the state of non-returning is required, while for the last four, one must have gained the formless attainments. Finally, one may aspire to no rebirth: to arahatship, but of course the aspiration alone is not sufficient—practise and sufficient insight-wisdom are needed.

The Sutta

1. Thus have I heard. On one occasion the Blessed One was wandering in the Kosalan country with a large Sangha of bhikkhus, and eventually he arrived at a Kosalan brahman village called Sāla.

2. The brahman householders of Sāla heard: "A monk called Gotama, it seems, a son of the Sakyans who went forth from a Sakyan clan, has been wandering in the Kosalan country with a large Sangha of bhikkhus and has come to Sāla. Now a good report of Master Gotama has been spread to this effect: 'That Blessed One is such since he is an arahat and Fully Enlightened, perfect in true knowledge and conduct, sublime, knower of worlds, incomparable teacher of men to be tamed, teacher of gods and humans, enlightened, blessed. He describes this world with its gods, its Māras, and its (Brahmā) Divinities, this generation with its monks and brahmans, with its kings and its people, which he has himself realised through direct knowledge. He teaches a Dhamma that is good in the beginning, good in the middle and good in the end with (the right) meaning and phrasing, he affirms a holy life that is utterly perfect and pure.' Now it is good to see such arahats."

3. The brahman householders of Sāla went to the Blessed One; and some paid homage to the Blessed One and sat down at one side; some exchanged greetings with him, and when the courteous and amiable talk was finished, sat down at one side; some raised hands palms together in salutation to the Blessed One and sat down at one side; some pronounced their name and clan in the Blessed One's presence and sat down at one side; some kept silence and sat down at one side.

4. When they were seated, they said to the Blessed One: "Master Gotama, what is the reason, what is the condition, why some beings here, on the dissolution of the body, after death, reappear in states of deprivation, in an unhappy destination, in perdition, even in hell; and what is the reason, what is the condition, why some beings here, on the dissolution of the body, after death, reappear in a happy destination, even in the heavenly world?"

5. "Householders, it is by reason of conduct not in accordance with the Dhamma, by reason of unrighteous conduct, that beings here on the dissolution of the body, after death, reappear in states of deprivation, in an unhappy destination, in perdition,

even in hell. It is by reason of conduct in accordance with the Dhamma, by reason of righteous conduct, that some beings here on the dissolution of the body, after death, reappear in a happy destination, even in the heavenly world."

6. "We do not understand the detailed meaning of this utterance of Master Gotama's spoken in brief without expounding the detailed meaning. It would be good if Master Gotama taught us the Dhamma so that we might understand the detailed meaning of Master Gotama's utterance spoken in brief without expounding the detailed meaning."

"Then, householders, listen and heed well what I shall say."

"Yes, venerable sir," they replied. The Blessed One said this:

7. "Householders, there are three kinds of bodily conduct not in accordance with the Dhamma, unrighteous conduct. There are four kinds of verbal conduct not in accordance with the Dhamma, unrighteous conduct. There are three kinds of mental conduct not in accordance with the Dhamma, unrighteous conduct.

8. "And how are there three kinds of bodily conduct not in accordance with the Dhamma, unrighteous conduct? Here someone is a killer of living beings: he is murderous, bloody-handed, given to blows and violence, and merciless to all living beings. He is a taker of what is not given: he takes as a thief another's chattels and property in the village or in the forest. He is given over to misconduct in sexual desires: he has intercourse with such (women) as are protected by the mother, father (mother and father), brother, sister, relatives, as have a husband, as entail a penalty, and also with those that are garlanded in token of betrothal. That is how there are three kinds of bodily conduct not in accordance with the Dhamma, unrighteous conduct.

9. "And how are there four kinds of verbal conduct not in accordance with the Dhamma, unrighteous conduct? Here someone speaks falsehood: when summoned to a court or to a meeting, or to his relatives' presence, or to his guild, or to the royal family's presence, and questioned as a witness thus, 'So, good man, tell what you know,' then, not knowing, he says 'I know,' or knowing, he says 'I do not know,' not seeing, he says 'I see,' or seeing, he says 'I do not see'; in full awareness he speaks falsehood for his own ends or for another's ends or for some trifling worldly end. He speaks maliciously: he is a repeater

elsewhere of what is heard here for the purpose of causing division from these, or he is a repeater to these of what is heard elsewhere for the purpose of causing division from those, and he is thus a divider of the united, a creator of divisions, who enjoys discord, rejoices in discord, delights in discord, he is a speaker of words that create discord. He speaks harshly: he utters such words as are rough, hard, hurtful to others, censorious of others, bordering on anger and unconducive to concentration. He is a gossip: as one who tells that which is unseasonable, that which is not fact, that which is not good, that which is not the Dhamma, that which is not the Discipline, and he speaks out of season speech not worth recording, which is unreasoned, indefinite, and unconnected with good. That is how there are four kinds of verbal conduct not in accordance with the Dhamma, unrighteous conduct.

10. "And how are there three kinds of mental conduct not in accordance with the Dhamma, unrighteous conduct? Here someone is covetous: he is a coveter of another's chattels and property thus: 'Oh, that what is another's were mine!' Or he has a mind of ill will, with the intention of a mind affected by hate thus: 'May these beings be slain and slaughtered, may they be cut off, perish, or be annihilated!' Or he has wrong view, distorted vision, thus: 'There is nothing given, nothing offered, nothing sacrificed, no fruit and ripening of good and bad kammas, no this world, no other world, no mother, no father, no spontaneously (born) beings,[19] no good and virtuous monks and brahmans that have themselves realised by direct knowledge and declare this world and the other world.'[20] That is how there are three kinds of mental conduct not in accordance with the Dhamma, unrighteous conduct.

"So, householders, it is by reason of conduct not in accordance with the Dhamma, by reason of unrighteous conduct, that some beings here, on the dissolution of the body, after death, reappear

19. Beings who appear due to the force of past action (kamma) in some states of birth: all gods and divinities, ghosts, inhabitants of hells; see Majjhima Nikāya Sutta 12 (Mahāsīhanāda Sutta).

20. For an explanation of these views held by some teachers in the Buddha's time, and which were a rejection of all moral values, see Ledi Sayādaw, *The Eightfold Path and Its Factors Explained* (BPS Wheel No. 245/247).

in states of deprivation, in an unhappy destination, in perdition, even in hell.

11. "Householders, there are three kinds of bodily conduct in accordance with the Dhamma, righteous conduct. There are four kinds of verbal conduct in accordance with the Dhamma, righteous conduct. There are three kinds of mental conduct in accordance with the Dhamma, righteous conduct.

12. "And how are there three kinds of bodily conduct in accordance with the Dhamma, righteous conduct? Here someone, abandoning the killing of living beings, becomes one who abstains from killing living beings; with rod and weapon laid aside, gentle and kindly, he abides compassionate to all living beings. Abandoning the taking of what is not given, he becomes one who abstains from taking what is not given; he does not take as a thief another's chattels and property in the village or in the forest. Abandoning misconduct in sexual desires, he becomes one who abstains from misconduct in sexual desires: he does not have intercourse with such women as are protected by mother, father (mother and father), brother, sister, relatives, as have a husband, as entail a penalty, and also those that are garlanded in token of betrothal. That is how there are three kinds of bodily conduct in accordance with the Dhamma, righteous conduct.

13. "And how are there four kinds of verbal conduct in accordance with the Dhamma, righteous conduct? Here someone, abandoning false speech, becomes one who abstains from false speech: when summoned to a court or to a meeting or to his relatives' presence or to his guild or to the royal family's presence, and questioned as a witness thus, 'So, good man, tell what you know,' not knowing, he says 'I do not know,' or knowing, he says 'I know,' not seeing he says 'I do not see,' or seeing, he says 'I see'; he does not in full awareness speak falsehood for his own ends or for another's ends or for some trifling worldly end. Abandoning malicious speech, he becomes one who abstains from malicious speech: as one who is neither a repeater elsewhere of what is heard here for the purpose of causing division from these, nor a repeater to these of what is heard elsewhere for the purpose of causing division from those, who is thus a reuniter of the divided, a promoter of friendships, enjoying concord, rejoicing in concord, delighting in concord, he becomes a speaker of words

that promote concord. Abandoning harsh speech, he becomes one who abstains from harsh speech: he becomes a speaker of such words as are innocent, pleasing to the ear and lovable, as go to the heart, are civil, desired of many and dear to many. Abandoning gossip, he becomes one who abstains from gossip: as one who tells that which is seasonable, that which is factual, that which is good, that which is the Dhamma, that which is the Discipline, he speaks in season speech worth recording, which is reasoned, definite and connected with good. That is how there are four kinds of verbal conduct in accordance with the Dhamma, righteous conduct.

14. "And how are there three kinds of mental conduct in accordance with the Dhamma, righteous conduct? Here someone is not covetous: he is not a coveter of another's chattels and property thus: 'Oh, that what is another's were mine!' He has no mind of ill will, with the intention of a mind unaffected by hate thus: 'May these beings be free from enmity, affliction and anxiety, may they live happily!' He has right view, undistorted vision, thus: 'There is what is given and what is offered and what is sacrificed, and there is fruit and ripening of good and bad kammas, and there is this world and the other world and mother and father and spontaneously (born) beings, and good and virtuous monks and brahmans that have themselves realised by direct knowledge and declared this world and the other world.' That is how there are three kinds of mental conduct in accordance with the Dhamma, righteous conduct.

"So, householders, it is by reason of conduct in accordance with the Dhamma, by reason of righteous conduct, that some beings here, on the dissolution of the body, after death, reappear in a happy destination, even in the heavenly world.

15. "If a householder who observes conduct in accordance with the Dhamma, righteous conduct, should wish: 'Oh, that on the dissolution of the body, after death, I might reappear in the company of the warrior-nobles of great property!' it is possible that on the dissolution of the body, after death, he may do so. Why is that? Because he observes conduct that is in accordance with the Dhamma, righteous conduct.

16. "If a householder who observes conduct in accordance with the Dhamma, righteous conduct, should wish: 'Oh, that on the dissolution of the body, after death, I might reappear in the company of the brahmans of great property!' it is possible...

17. "If a householder who observes conduct in accordance with the Dhamma,... '... I might reappear in the company of householders of great property!' it is possible...

18. "If a householder who observes conduct in accordance with the Dhamma, righteous conduct, should wish: 'Oh, that on the dissolution of the body, after death, I might reappear in the company of the gods of the Four Kings!' it is possible that on the dissolution of the body, after death, he may do so. Why is that? Because he observes conduct in accordance with the Dhamma, righteous conduct.

19. "...of the gods of the Realm of the Thirty-three...[21]

20. "...of the gods that have Gone to Bliss...

21. "...of the Contented gods...

22. "...of the gods that Delight in Creating...

23. "...of the gods that Wield Power over others' Creations...

24. "...of the gods of Brahmā's Retinue...

25. ...of the Radiant gods...

26. "...of the gods of Limited Radiance...

27. "...of the gods of Measureless Radiance...

28. "...of the gods of Streaming Radiance...

29. "...of the Glorious gods...

30. "...of the gods of Limited Glory...

31. "...of the gods of Measureless Glory...

32. "...of the gods of Refulgent Glory...

33. "...of the Very Fruitful gods...

34. "...of the gods Bathed in their own Prosperity...

35. "...of the Untormenting gods...

36. "...of the Fair-to-see gods...

37. "...of the Fair-seeing gods...

38. "...of the gods who are Junior to None...

39. "...of the gods of the base consisting of the infinity of space...

---

21. The rendering of the various gods' names are based on the commentary to the *Hadaya-vibhaṅga* (in the *Vibhaṅga,* second book of the Abhidhamma: see *The Book of Analysis,* P.T.S. Translation Series).

40. "...of the gods of the base consisting of the infinity of consciousness...

41. "...of the gods of the base consisting of nothingness...

42. "If a householder who observes conduct in accordance with the Dhamma, righteous conduct, should wish: 'Oh, that on the dissolution of the body, after death, I might reappear in the company of the gods of the base consisting of neither-perception-nor-non-perception!' it is possible that, on the dissolution of the body, after death, he may do so. Why is that? Because he observes conduct in accordance with the Dhamma, righteous conduct.

43. "If a householder who observes conduct in accordance with the Dhamma, righteous conduct, should wish: 'Oh, that by realisation myself with direct knowledge, I may here and now enter upon and abide in the deliverance of the heart and the deliverance by wisdom that are taint-free with exhaustion of taints!' it is possible that, by realisation himself with direct knowledge, he may here and now enter upon and abide in the deliverance of the heart and the deliverance by wisdom that are taint-free with exhaustion of taints. Why is that? Because he observes conduct in accordance with the Dhamma, righteous conduct."

44. When this was said, the brahman householders of Sāla said to the Blessed One:

"Magnificent, Master Gotama! Magnificent, Master Gotama! The Dhamma has been made clear in many ways by Master Gotama, as though he were turning upright what had been overthrown, revealing the hidden, showing the way to one who was lost, holding up a lamp in the darkness for those with eyes to see forms.

45. "We go to Master Gotama for refuge, and to the Dhamma, and to the Sangha of bhikkhus. From today let Master Gotama accept us as followers who have gone to him for refuge for life."

Concept and Meaning

Two Essays

by

C.F. Knight

and

Carlo Gragnani

WHEEL PUBLICATION NO. 250

The Delusive Concept

C. F. Knight

Few people realize to how great an extent their whole lives and thought processes are dominated by concepts. The concept is a general notion or idea arising through one or more of the senses, which is then reduced to terms of language after a mental classification.

We are confronted with a phenomenon, and through one or more of the senses it is noticed as an object. The mind receives the sense-impression, proceeds to investigate it, and comes to a decision in regard to it which may lead to impulsive non-volitional action, or to deliberate volitional action, and then the incident is registered as a memory and sinks down into the subconscious—and so a concept is born. In future, a word or words will be used to describe the experience.

Suppose that in our travels we come upon a mass of water confined by its banks. The senses react to the object. Through visual-consciousness its presence is impressed on the mind. The mind investigates it visually, and if it is flowing, we say it is a river, or if so surrounded by its banks that it cannot flow, we say it is a pond. Both "river" and "pond" are conceptual expressions to convey our sense impressions and experience, and to differentiate between flowing water and confined water. "River" and "pond" have become concepts of a mass of water under different conditions, and imply a permanently fixed identity of that particular phenomenon. Even when during drought the "river" no longer flows, the concept of "river" still holds good—it is not a "pond" or a "waterhole."

But the concept is superficial and has no relation to reality. It is at best delusive, deceptive, unreal, and disappointing, in the light and knowledge of reality. As an enduring, unchanging, entity the "river" is non-existent! You might say: "What about the Nile? It has been there for thousands of years." But the Nile of today is not the Nile of yesterday, let alone the Nile of the Pharaohs. It is ever in the process of arising and passing away. Its banks are eroding here and building up elsewhere. Its bed is being scoured out here and shallows formed there. Its waters change from moment to moment. The concept of "the River Nile" is reduced to a convenient conversational phrase empty of reality—its name no more than a label given to a part of a process which is in a continual state of flux and impermanency.

Even the names we give to our concepts are merely designations in common use amongst our particular language group. Our senses register a phenomenon and we say "I saw a cat," or "I saw a cow," "I bought a vegetable-marrow," or "I ate a banana." If we were to ask a Japanese, a German, a Malay, or Hindu, what they were, none would reply with our conceptual label. Each would have their own label for the same phenomenon common to all.

A child might have a Meccano set and today so assemble the bits and pieces as to build a crane. Again, we get a concept from the arrangement of the parts which we label "a crane." Tomorrow, with the same bits and pieces, he assembles them in the form of a building, and we say he has built a "house," another conceptual label for a different arrangement of the parts that yesterday we called a crane. Next he assembles them as a table and chairs—more labels. While the toy was a crane it was neither a house nor furniture. While it was a house it was neither a crane nor furniture. While it was a table and chairs it was neither a crane nor a house. The concept and name only apply to the form of the moment, and have no relationship to reality—in this case a box of links and ties. Spread them out on the table and they are neither crane, house, nor furniture.

At one time an inquirer who was troubled as to the reality of past and future lives asked of the Buddha if past, present, and future personalities were all real to a man, or only one of them. The Buddha questioned him: "If people were to ask you thus: 'Were you in the past? Will you be in the future? Are you now?'—how would you answer them?"

"I would say I was in the past; I shall be in the future; I am now", said Citta.

The Buddha continued: "If they rejoined, 'Well, that past personality that you had, is that real to you, and the future and present unreal?' (and so with the other two variations), how would you answer?"

"I would say that the past personality was real to me at the time when I had it, and the others unreal, and so also with the other two cases," replied Citta.

"Just so, Citta, when any one of the three modes of personality is going on, then it does not come under the category of the other two.

"Just as from a cow, comes milk, from milk curds, from curds butter, from butter ghee. When it is milk it is not called curds, butter, or ghee, and when it is called curds, it is not called by any other name.

"Just so when any one of the three modes of personality is going on, it is not called by the name of the other. These are merely names, expressions, turns of speech, designations in common use in the world, and of these the Tathāgata makes use indeed, but *is not led astray by them.*"

To Citta the concept of personality, past, present, or future, was real, or would be real, at the time he had it, but it was no more stable as a reality than milk, curds, butter, or ghee. To speak of "personality," whether past, present, or future, is merely a designation in common use in the world, a name to be used for conventional purposes when referring to the particular part of a process of arising and passing away of an unstable flux. The Buddha was not led astray by such terms or expressions, he even used them at times for conventional purposes, knowing them for what they were—merely turns of speech.

However, unlike the Buddha, many *are* led astray by them, failing to see the reality behind the appearance, for appearances are proverbially deceptive. That this should be so is rather remarkable in the sense that we readily accept the progressive concepts of a baby, a child, a youth, a young man, an old man, and finally a corpse. Yet, denying the evidences of our senses and lacking in insight, we persist in the concept of "personality" as an ego-entity, a stable reality. To revert to our concept of a river, and use it as an analogy, we would stop its flow and create a pond!

So then, our concepts of material and physical phenomena obscure the reality underlying them. We are deceived by either the rapidity, or the imperceptibility of the constant change they are undergoing, but at least the river, the pond, the crane, the house, the table and chairs, or the human body have the *appearance* of stability, which lays the basis for incorrectly assuming their permanency.

When we come to concepts of a mental or abstract nature, however, we are more than ever prone to be deceived, for these are of our own mental construction. They have, as it were, a built-in pattern of our own making, and man is loathe to admit self-deception.

We arrive at some of these concepts by a method of deduction. Morality and immorality, happiness and sorrow, good and evil, actions which are worthy or unworthy, characteristics to be proud or ashamed of, are to a great extent very personal concepts. Apart from early training and instruction we each have our own concept of what is "right" and what is "wrong", of what will bring us happiness and what will bring us sorrow, and so on. Morals are very largely geographical, and what would pass for conventional behaviour in one place or country has a different moral value in another. Few individuals subscribe entirely to any set pattern of behaviour common to their community. We deduce from the resultant sense-pleasure or dissatisfaction as to whether a thing is right or wrong, and our concept of happiness is based on our concept of the cause of happiness. That these concepts can be illusions is well illustrated by the failure of most people to realize the all-pervasiveness of Dukkha. To such the pursuit of sense-pleasures is the ultimate happiness, and the true serenity that comes with detachment has no appeal for them. Their concept of happiness is an illusion as time proves.

Then again, man has been endowed with the faculty of imagination—another prolific source of concepts. Imagination is a creative faculty of the mind enabling it to form images not present to the senses, and having no real existence, but assumed to exist for a special purpose. Gods and devils, heavens and hells, are concepts created by imagination, endowed with suppositional powers for a specific purpose. Not understanding the natural phenomena of nature, such as thunder and lightning, earthquakes and hurricanes, eclipses of the sun and moon, etc., man conceived a supernatural being as the author or agency responsible for the phenomena, to be appeased or supplicated in times of need or distress. From this concept grew up a multitude of other concepts. There was the benign god and the malicious devil. There were their respective abodes, heaven or hell under different names and of different conceptual structure. John of Patmos in the *Book of Revelation* gives a detailed conception of the Christian heaven, which is as different from the Norse abode of Wodan as it in turn is from the Paradise of the Moslem, but all of them are mental concepts assumed to exist, but born of the imagination of man. In time the faculties and functions of the god gradually became personified concepts, and the result was trinities and an expansion to a pantheon of lesser gods and goddesses—all on a no more substantial basis than the fertile imagination of man. Thus we have concept on concept, and concepts of concepts!

The most persistent concept that lingers on when many others have disappeared under the light of science and reason is the concept of the "soul." With the conceptual creation of gods and heavens, devils and hells, it was a natural progression to the conceptual creation of a disembodied spirit to reap the rewards and punishments according to its deserts. Here again the concepts are as varied as the religions which hold to the existence of a "soul," and its origin is equally wrapped in mystery. Of all the concepts of a "soul" the ancient Indian concept of it being a spark or fragment of the Godhead, from which it came and to which it eventually returned, was the most plausible. The least plausible, that held by many, that an indestructible eternal "something" is "created"—having a beginning but no end! Perhaps it is for these reasons that many Westerners who have rejected orthodoxy have turned to Vedanta, therein finding a more logical basis on which to build their concept of a "soul."

However, again, once more, in the Indian belief we come up against the concept of a "soul" or supramundane "self" being derived from the concept of a Godhead—as before, one concept giving birth to another concept.

In the third volume of the Saṃyutta-Nikāya there are many extracts from the Buddha's teachings where he is at great pains to make clear that the aggregates of existence—that is, the body, feelings, perception, mental activities, and consciousness—are impermanent and liable to suffering. Of them he says:

"What is impermanent, that is suffering. What is suffering, that is not the Self. What is not the Self, that is not mine, that am I not, that is not the Self of me." The translators give us "Self" with a capital "S," inferring "soul" or "ego-entity."

Of the untaught, undiscerning, unskilled, and untrained, the Buddha says, such regard the body as the Self; or maybe regard the Self as possessing body; or the body as being in the Self; or the Self as being in the body; or he regards the feelings, perceptions, mental activities, and consciousness in the same four ways; or regards the Self as existing separate and apart from the aggregates of existence.

But, says the Buddha, suffering still exists, and what is suffering cannot be the Self. "But whosoever holds not views of this sort about the impermanent body, the sorrow-fraught, the unstable, feelings, perceptions, activities, and consciousness, what are they but seers of what really is." They are those who have destroyed the concept of a "Self" or soul, and through insight, see things as they really are.

In the Dīgha-Nikāya is the story of Poṭṭhapāda. He had been listening to learned Brahmins discussing and disagreeing as to the how, when, and whereabouts of this soul in which they believed, and Poṭṭhapāda had his own concept regarding what he regarded as his soul. The Buddha gave him a lengthy discourse in refutation of the opinions of the Brahmins, some of whom had contended that it was consciousness that was a man's soul. At last Poṭṭhapāda, who apparently had not fully understood the Buddha when he had shown that consciousness could not be the soul, asks whether, then, consciousness is one thing and the soul another, for the Brahmins held that when the soul comes into a man he becomes conscious, and when his soul leaves him he becomes unconscious.

There is almost a note of exasperation in the Buddha's rejoinder: "But then, Poṭṭhapāda, do you really fall back on the soul?" (after all that I have just explained).

Poṭṭhapāda assures the Buddha that he does have the concept of a material soul, which he takes for granted.

"But if there were such a soul, Poṭṭhapāda, then even so your consciousness would be one thing and your soul another. Suppose you did have a soul, some ideas and states of consciousness would arise and others pass away, so that consciousness which is impermanent must be one thing and the soul another."

Poṭṭhapāda changes his ground and hypothesis, or concept. If he has not a material soul, maybe he has a soul made of mind. The Buddha reminds him that mind, too, is impermanent, and therefore it cannot be the soul.

For the third time Poṭṭhapāda postulates a soul, this time a soul with form made of consciousness, and again the Buddha replies that the same previous arguments would apply.

In final desperation Poṭṭhapāda asks if it is possible for him to ever understand the soul, and the Buddha replies:

"Hard it is for you, Poṭṭhapāda, to grasp this matter, holding as you do different views, other things approving themselves to you, setting different aims before yourself, striving after a different perfection, trained in a different system of doctrine!"

And that brings us right up to date with many people in the West who know "Where the Buddha erred," or where the many millions of his followers have failed to understand his doctrine of "no-Self" (*anattā*). These products of a different system of doctrine, holding different views, maybe even striving after a different perfection, have a closed mind to any doctrine that threatens their concept of a soul. To them their concept is a reality, and no one is going to be allowed to shake their faith in its existence. When even the Buddha was defeated by Poṭṭhapāda's inability, or unwillingness, to see any view but the one in which he was trained, we can take heart and realize that until such people are ready to let go of their preconceived concepts, and open their minds to the Dhamma, argument or discussion will be of no avail. We can but offer the Dhamma, as did the Buddha, hoping that some point made some day will destroy the false concept and lead them to being "seers of what really is."

In the Saṃyutta-Nikāya the Buddha has this to say:

"This world usually bases its views on two things: on existence and non-existence. Everything exists: this is one extreme. Nothing exists: this is the other extreme. Overcoming these two extremes the Tathāgata teaches you the Doctrine of the Middle Way." This is a continual becoming and passing away. Where all is changing from becoming to passing, no constant entities can be found.

Once more referring to the Scriptures, this time to the Majjhima-Nikāya, the Buddha is discoursing on false views, and says:

"An ordinary uninstructed person who takes no account of the wise teachers, unskilled and untrained in the Dhamma, lives with his mind obsessed by a false view as to 'own body,' overcome by it he does not comprehend the escape, as it really is, from the false view that has arisen. That false view of his, resistant, not dispelled, is a fetter binding him to the hither shore. He lives with his mind obsessed by perplexity, obsessed by clinging to rites and customs, obsessed by attachment to sense-pleasures, obsessed by malevolence. These are fetters binding him to the hither shore.

"And what is the way, what the course for getting rid of these five fetters? By aloofness from clinging, by getting rid of the unskilled states of mind, by allaying every bodily impropriety, aloof from pleasures of the sense, aloof from unskilled states of mind, he enters and abides in the first meditation which is accompanied by initial thought and discursive thought, is rapturous and joyful. Whatever there is of material shape, feeling, perception, mental activities, and consciousness—he beholds these things as impermanent, suffering, a misfortune, an affliction, as decay, empty and not-self. He turns his mind from these things. He focuses his mind on the deathless element, thinking: 'This is real, this is the excellent, the tranquillizing of all the activities, the casting out of all clinging, the destruction of craving, dispassion, stopping, Nibbāna.'"

Ānanda, to whom the Buddha had been speaking, then asked:

"If this is the way, revered sir, the course for getting rid of the five fetters, then how is it that some there are who have found freedom through knowledge, and others there are who have found freedom through intuitive wisdom?"

The Buddha replied: "As to this, Ānanda, I say there is a difference in their faculties."

This closing statement of the Buddha's is most interesting, for there are some who claim that insight can only be won by meditation. It is true that learning cannot take the place of insight, because learning affords only more concepts and still more concepts, but learning can lead to knowledge, and knowledge can lead to perceiving the unreality of the concept. Nevertheless, of primary importance is the purifying of the mind if insight is to be won. Then there must be the desire for knowledge of reality. There also must be the preparation of the mind in order to gain insight, and there must be the patient and persistent endeavour to analyse the concept till its unreality is perceived by initial, or original, and discursive thought.

If we are to become "seers of what really is," then we must destroy the false concepts that are blinding us, must see them as figments of our own most fertile imagination behind and beyond which Reality exists.

The Search for Meaning

Carlo Gragnani

> Man is dominated neither by the will-to-pleasure (Freud) nor by the will-to-power (Adler) but by the will-to-meaning.
>
> (Victor Frankl)

I look into the distance, I can see something, but what is it? It seems that I cannot be satisfied with the "it" that I can see: I want to know the "what," that is to say, the meaning. The knowledge of the meaning puts a stop to my curiosity; at least temporarily, since meanings are fathomless; there is always a deeper meaning.

But what is, really, a meaning? Whatever it is, it belongs to a constellation in which concepts, ideas, objects, words participate.

A concept is a group of elements which particular entities have in common—chair, table, pain, pleasure, honour, democracy, and what not, are concepts. "Chair" for instance evokes an infinite number of objects, each one having distinctive features which make it unique, nevertheless sharing with all others, common characteristics.

Concepts allow man to think and to talk in general without making reference to any single object. If concepts did not exist, I couldn't even ask for a steak in a restaurant. It is true that sometimes the waiter brings me something which barely resembles a steak; and this is tantamount to saying that frequently concepts have no well-defined boundaries. But it would be stretching the point too far if, having ordered a steak, I found the sole of a shoe on my plate.

The group of elements which certain objects have in common, and which constitute a concept, points to the fundamental, to the basic use these objects are put to. For example, the fundamental use of certain types of objects called chairs is to sit on them. Certainly, I can sit on many other objects, on the step of a stair, for instance. But in these cases I would not utilize these objects for the main purpose they have been made for. In their turn, chairs, although made to sit on, may be used for a variety of purposes, even for hanging oneself.

Now, to say fundamental *use* is tantamount to saying fundamental *meaning*. The meaning is nothing else than the use we put things to. A gift I received recently was meaningless as long as I was unable to discover its usefulness; eventually I found out that it was a pepper-grinder (in disguise) and immediately it became meaningful for me.

We have seen that objects may have other uses apart from the fundamental one, that is to say, that an object may have many meanings; the fundamental meaning of a car is to be a means of transportation—to be fit for transporting people or goods is what is required from an object in order to be classified under the concept *car*. But the car of Mr. Brown has for him also the meaning to create envy in his neighbours. And this meaning may be so important as to override the fundamental one. He may even go so far as to buy a second- or third-hand car, very imposing, although barely mobile, just to display it, highly polished, in front of his house.

Another aspect of "meanings" is that they may exist in the abstract or in the concrete. They exist in the abstract when we think or talk about them without any object being present (void meanings). We may have a conversation about music, democracy, love, religion in general. But for a meaning to exist in concrete, an object must be present: a melody to be heard, a house to be seen ... The meaning is fulfilled, so to speak, by the presence of the object.

The fulfillment of a meaning asks for conditions. To experience a melody it is necessary that the succession of sounds be neither too fast, nor too slow. Besides, the hearer has to be at an appropriate distance from the source of the sounds. Similarly, to see a house, one should be neither too near nor too distant from it. Space and time conditions are therefore necessary, or, in other words, one must be in focus for a concrete meaning to appear.

Even when the object of a meaning is as intangible as a feeling, one must be in focus for the meaning to appear. For an insulting word to be *concretely* insulting to me, I have, so to speak, to be attuned to this. If I am not in a receptive mood, the word misses the target, that is actual offence.

Concepts, objects, meanings do not need words to exist. They are present even at the pre-verbal level. Words are not necessary in order to come into contact with objects and meanings. A dog knows very well what is the meaning of signs, as forerunners of events. However, words are necessary to convey concepts, meanings, to talk about them in the abstract, in general.

But the function of words goes far beyond their being a means of communication: they also make concepts and meanings much more determined, articulated. They isolate, and cut into the flux of reality much more distinctly than it is possible to do at the preverbal level: they go much further in the process of solidification and abstraction. In fact, this process may be realized in different degrees. To be sure, even in a perception I crystallize the very rapid succession of visual sensations into an object—let us say a tree. But when I think or say the word "tree" as a void-meaning, I realize the most abstract and remote solidification, because I am really disconnected from any sensory impression.

So, words fix what is instantaneous, fugacious, into something clear, articulate, rational, understandable, communicable, but highly abstract. The lived process is transcended and transformed at the topmost level. Let us take as an example the following words: "the battle of Waterloo." I can make any sort of reasoning about that: the meaning of the battle, its causes, its effects, how it put an end to an historical era, and so on and so forth. But in fact the so-called battle of Waterloo was nothing else than a conglomeration of single, atomic events; a congeries of people running and shooting. The real battle of Waterloo was probably what Fabrizio Del Dongo (the hero of *La Chartreuse de Parme* by Stendhal) saw of it: a series of episodes having neither head nor tail. Only, we give them unity; we organize them.

Certainly we are bound to use words if we want to communicate. I have just written many words—I cannot do otherwise. Man seems to be condemned to meanings, as Merleau-Ponty used to say.

Nevertheless, if words solidify, they may also have the contrary function. There are words which do not define, rationalize, indicate clear-cut entities, but allude, evoke, stimulate, suggest. We can see this particularly in poetry, where words lose their corporeality, creating between-the-lines fluid "moods of the soul". This is also the function of religious words, sacred words, magic words.

To consider words only in their capacity of communicating concepts, ideas, meanings, is certainly a great limitation. Words are the most common but also the most mysterious things in life. They characterize the human species. But to deal with words in general is not the purpose of this article.

Reverting to the connection between words, on the one hand, concepts and meanings, on the other, it is to be noticed that meanings expressed by words are, generally, stable, but not invariable. Probably we would not recognize as tables or chairs what centuries ago were known under these names. Some time ago I was attracted by the title of an article in a daily paper; it read: "The Defence of the Territory." Being born in a period of intense nationalism, this title evoked in me army problems, menaces of war, and the like. Since these questions did not seem to be topical, I started reading the article with curiosity. Then I realized that pollution was its subject. Until the 15th century, the word "courtesan" meant a dignified lady living at the court of a king. Some change in the meaning has intervened since those days!

Meanings change not only in time, but in space. Eastern democracy is not the same as Western democracy. The fact is that *meanings are social entities*, they have social utility. It is not by chance that Eskimos have thirty odd names to denote what we, more generically, call "snow." Besides, single meanings do not stand by themselves. A meaning is related to many other meanings, each one influencing the others. The meaning of "marriage," for instance, is different according to whether in a particular social setting there is or is not the possibility of "divorce." In the latter case, "marriage" alludes to an indissoluble link; in the former, this characteristic is not present.

The meaning of a word depends also on that of similar words that the speaker or the writer has not selected. If among a series of synonyms I choose one of them, the meaning of the chosen one can be negatively defined as not being that of the words I have discarded.

If I say: "That actress in that film is very pretty" the meaning of pretty is established indirectly by my having discarded such synonyms as "lovely," "beautiful," "attractive," "delightful," "pleasing," "charming"...

She is pretty (and *not* lovely or beautiful, etc.).

Besides, a meaning is a sediment of previous meanings. As said before, meanings change through time, but in this historical process, something of the old meanings remains in the new ones. We receive meanings from preceding generations, charged with various strata of significances. Before we reach the age of reason, words are already there, centuries old. So, if meanings are the work of Man, Man is also the work of meanings. We are hardly aware of all the meanings of the words we use. This is why, as often as not, what we say is not exactly what we have the intention to say. Sometimes our own words reveal new meanings, even to us. This is particularly the case of the works of art, where more is found than the artist has consciously put into them.

(If, at this point, the reader asks himself in desperation "but what is the meaning of this meaningless talk about meaning?" he would have a glaring, on-the-spot evidence of the strength of his drive towards meaning.)

So we are constantly looking for meanings. More precisely, we are not satisfied with any meaning, but we try to pass from—so to speak—less meaningful meanings to more meaningful ones. What is that I can see from afar? It is a big dark spot (which is a meaning, after all).

But I do not stop at that; I approach that dark spot until I recognize a tree (a meaning much more articulated than "a dark spot"). What is it that I now hear? A noise (poor meaning); I approach and I can hear the voices of two people having a conversation (more articulated meaning); I get nearer and I can hear what they say (still more articulated meaning). And so on.

We spend our life in search of meanings, including the meaning of life itself.

Meanings are the furniture of the mind. Or, if you like, they are tools we have inherited from our predecessors. Old things, although we have modernized them occasionally. And with these old tools we try to deal with the new—what is going on here and now.

Being in contact with symbols, man is in contact with what is far, and not with what is near. For instance, when man has a desire, he is having a contact with the object of his desire, and not with the desire itself, which after all, is the only present reality. If I stretch out my arm to get something, the stretching of my arm passes unnoticed, my attention being focused on the object to be attained, or even further, on the state of happiness I expect to emerge from the possession of the object.

So man is bent forwards towards a more and more distant future, less and less defined. In the meantime, he does not know where he is putting his feet.

Suppose we pay attention to where we put our feet. Suppose we are aware of the "here" instead of the "there"; of the "it" and not of the "what." Suppose we have an inquisitive mind about the living flux, as it presents itself. Suppose we succeed in letting the past be the past, and the future be the future. Suppose we stop trying to solidify what is not solid. Suppose we see the present as such, and not as a creation of the past or an anticipation of the future. Wouldn't we feel less the need for security? Wouldn't we speculate less about what will come next in this or another life? Wouldn't we know a bit more about reality? Wouldn't we be less "we"? Then the "it" of "what is it?" would not be overlooked while searching for its "what," of its meaning. We would not be condemned to the proliferation of meanings which are prisons of our own making. But, alas, the most insurmountable barriers are those which do not exist. As long as we voluntarily accept to be the victims of ourselves, there is no salvation. Who or what binds us? What prevents us from being attentive to what we are doing? Why do we not watch our steps?

Being attentive to what we are doing, watching our steps are—the reader would have discovered by now—only metaphors standing for Buddhist meditation.

Reduced to its essentials (and perhaps simplifying the matter too much) meditation can be defined as *mindfulness* applied to the *that* which happens *now.*

It may be worthwhile to dwell a little on these three words.

To be mindful is to be full of mind, awake, aware, attentive to a presence: the *that*; it is noticing the *that,* acknowledging the *that,* and not speculating on it. It is simply feeling, tasting, savouring it; to be alert on how it arises, stays, and disappears giving rise to something else.

The *that* is what happens in the *now*, and these two refer to one another, since the *now* points to the *that* which happens at that very moment.

Of course the *now* is the only time which can be lived. Our life is a succession of *nows.* I can breathe only the *now*—breathing and not any breathing before or after that. To be sure I can think of my yesterday-breathing and my (presumed) tomorrow-breathing. But this, of course, is not breathing now; it is remembering now and foreseeing now. So, if I pay attention to the now, to each now, it becomes easy for me to come in contact with the correlative *that*; I cannot be mistaken about the *that* (which is very often the case if the *now* is neglected). For instance, if I am fearful of an atomic war, the *now* tells me that what is present is fear and not the war itself.

But the *now* is paradoxical; in fact, on the one hand, we cannot live but in the *now*; on the other hand, the *now* has no temporal thickness; the present moment slides easily into the past and projects itself into the future. Every meditator knows by experience how difficult it is to catch the immediate present. In fact it is never caught. Just because one tries to catch it, one cannot. The moment one stops trying...

But it is not for these "technical" difficulties that meditation does not come easily.

In fact, the reluctance to meditate is to be found in our disliking to contact the *now* and the connected *that.*

We do not like to be aware of the inescapable fact that we cannot live but in the present. We live in the *now*, of course, but we avoid to be aware of that. The Ego, from its point of view, has all the reasons for escaping the *now,* which reveals that reality is impermanent, unsatisfactory, and devoid of self. The life of the Ego is a continuous escape from *that*; an unsuccessful escape, to be sure, but an attempt always renewed. And this is the case not only when the *that* is suffering (in the common, empirical sense), but also when it is (supposed) to be agreeable. The Ego is incapable to enjoy anything; as soon as a desired goal is attained, either the pleasure is undermined by the fear of losing the object or the latter becomes duller and duller.

We live our life waiting for something to be over or, like Mr. Micawber, for something to turn up. We would like the present moment to stay (and it doesn't) or to be non-existent (but here it is).

King Midas couldn't eat because everything he touched was immediately turned into gold. Similarly, man has the greatest difficulties in being aware of the most immediate reality; as soon as his senses come into touch with it, he glides over it, or better, he transforms it into concepts, ideas, something which has a meaning. His primary experiences are, in this way, crystallized, solidified. Man succeeds in making even movement immobile by freezing it into fixed algebraic formulae. Surrounded by rigidities of his own making, man makes himself rigid too. Solidity, rigidity are not only space characteristics: they imply also a temporal connotation, since what is solid is usually durable.

This process does not go without inconveniences, because neither man nor what is around him are stable entities. And it is not easy to fix a flux, nor to make durable what is perishable. If, nevertheless, this feat (doomed to failure) is attempted, there must be some serious reasons. They are nothing else than the desire for security. Security asks for solidity and duration in the widest sense of the words: something to lean on, materially or spiritually.

I would not feel secure in a kaleidoscopic world where nothing would repeat itself. I want to recognize things, I want to identify people and myself too; I want to be sure that what I believe in is true, the Absolute Truth. In short, I want to be an "I," since only under these conditions there is an "I."

The "I" is desire to exist; therefore the "I" is careful to protect itself and it fears to be annihilated. So I worry. Yes; I exist now, but what about tomorrow? In this way I project myself forwards, oblivious of the present, bent on the future, running towards death; the death which I would like to avoid, but nevertheless anticipate, in leading such a deadly existence.

The "I" dislikes death. Would the "I" be happy with an endless time at its disposal? Sometimes it seems that this is the case. But it is because it does not consider the implication of it. If it did, it would be even more appalled at the prospect than at its destiny to be a mortal being.

So, not pleased with either prospect, man believes in another life. A life much better than, but not so very different from this one as to become a "life of another."

A life, therefore, not too much disembodied, not too much angelic, in a place where we would meet our parents, relatives, friends, who, however, would be much nicer than they were here. A life without quarrels, without negative feelings, a life which it is better to leave in the vague. If we tried to outline its features in detail, we would run the risk of seeing boredom appear in the background.

So man believes, hopes... But he who hopes, doubts, suffers. What a pretty predicament! It seems that man is his own problem: an impossible problem with a strong desire to solve it; and that goes on and on until he discovers the real nature of desire, never satisfied, never extinguished, promising Paradise, leading to Hell.

We have seen what is the meaning of meanings, concepts, words; how man utilizes all these "tools" (or language at large) in order to satisfy his impossible desire to be lasting, durable, amongst other lasting, solid, durable entities; how he can discover and be aware of his delusion and why he encounters resistance on the way of this discovery.

From all that we should not jump to the hasty and unarticulated conclusion that language is the demon which keeps man ignorant, whereas the wise man is untainted by that evil.

Against this exceedingly simplified version of reality, it is to be said that language is one of the essential prerogatives of a human being. Language, in all its articulations, such as thinking, categorizing, distinguishing, is obviously unavoidable in any however primitive human life. Even certain animals have memory, recognize, distinguish this from that, in a word possess a kind of rudimental thinking.

But it is true that under the influence of desire, man, through language, sees reality in a distorted way; in a way which conforms to what he would like it to be.

When reality is properly experienced as in meditation (including awareness of any event which manifests itself in daily life) reality speaks for itself. Then man listens. He listens with all his being, so to speak. He may feel an unpleasant aspect of that reality. But he must accept the LAW which is beyond or above himself. Accepting the LAW is understanding the LAW in the full sense of the word.

Of course, meditation is not thinking, in the sense of being involved in a chain of thoughts. It is awareness. If, for instance, the *that* in the *now* is a bodily pain, to be aware of *that* is to attend, to feel that sensation and also to acknowledge it by a mental notation: this is "pain"; or simply: "pain" (whereby naming, categorizing, thinking, language in short, come into play). That means to stay with pain as long as pain stays with you, to follow its ups and downs. But it is frequent that one goes off at a tangent and thinks: "I have always suffered during my life; how unhappy I have been!" However, supposing that this thought comes into the mind, he who exercises awareness does not indulge in it or try to chase it away, but, instead, he acknowledges the appearance of a thought, noticing its mental essence, the connected feelings and so on.

Such are the complex interconnections among meditation, awareness, and language.

One can name truth or phantasms. Words can be faithful symbols or deceptive ones.

But words of truth are not awareness of truth. Reciting the Four Noble Truths and the Law of Dependent Origination is not to perceive them in one's innermost, not to be penetrated by them, which is the matter of awareness.

To say that existence is characterized by impermanence, unsatisfactoriness, and absence of self is to express ideas, concepts, meanings, to put words into use. This is not necessarily tantamount to live accordingly. But for him who lives in accordance with them, those words, concepts, ideas, emerge from reality as he experiences it.

So, the problem is not to be for or against language. This is a false dilemma; false because crude. There is much more to be said on that. And if the wise man is silent, that is because the foolish man is too often talkative. And still there are plenty of Suttas! And how many meanings, concepts, words in them!

The Roots of Good and Evil

Buddhist Texts Translated from the Pali

With Comments and Introduction
by
Nyanaponika Thera

WHEEL PUBLICATION NO. 251/252/253

Introduction

The Buddha has taught that there are three roots of evil: greed, hatred and delusion. These three states comprise the entire range of evil, whether of lesser or greater intensity, from a faint mental tendency to the coarsest manifestations in action and speech. In whatever way they appear, these are the basic causes of suffering.

These roots have their opposites: non-greed, non-hatred and non-delusion. These are the three roots of good: of all acts of unselfishness, liberality and renunciation; of all expressions of loving kindness and compassion; of all achievements in knowledge and understanding.

These six mental states are the roots from which everything harmful and beneficial sprouts. They are the roots of the Tree of Life with its sweet and bitter fruits.

Greed and hatred, maintained and fed by delusion, are the universal impelling forces of all animate life, individually and socially. Fortunately, the roots of good also reach into our world and keep the forces of evil in check, but the balance is a precarious one needing to be preserved by constant watchfulness and effort. On the level of inanimate nature, too, we find counterparts to greed and hatred in the forces of attraction and repulsion, kept in their purposeless reactive movement by inherent nescience which cannot provide a motive for cessation of the process. Thus, through an unfathomable past, the macrocosm of nature and the microcosm of mind have continued their contest between attraction and repulsion, greed and hatred; and unless stopped by voluntary effort and insight, they will so continue for aeons to come. This cosmic conflict of opposing energies, unsolvable on its own level, is one aspect of *dukkha* (unsatisfactoriness): the ill of restless, senseless movement as felt by a sensitive being.

On the human level, too, we see that man, who proudly believes himself to be a “free agent”—the master of his life and even of nature—is in his spiritually undeveloped state actually a passive patient driven about by inner forces he does not recognize. Pulled by his greed and pushed by his hatred, in his blindness he does not see that the brakes for stopping these frantic movements are in his reach, within his own heart. The brakes are the roots of good themselves, which can be cultivated to such a degree that greed, hatred and delusion are utterly destroyed.

Though we have spoken of the six roots as being "roots of good and evil," our use of the terms "good" and "evil" is provisional, a simplification chosen to introduce this teaching by familiar terms. In the Buddhist texts they are called the roots of the wholesome (*kusala-mūla*) and the roots of the unwholesome (*akusala-mūla*). And thus we, too, shall generally call them.

This differentiation of terms marks an important distinction, for the "spread" of the mental states called roots is much wider and deeper than the moral realm to which the words "good" and "evil" refer. The distinction may be defined as follows. An intentional action performed by body or speech is immoral—an evil or a "sin"—when it is motivated by the unwholesome roots and is *intentionally and directly harmful to others*. This constitutes *socially* significant immorality, for which it is the criterion. Such actions are termed *unwholesome bodily* or *verbal kamma*. Thoughts associated with these unwholesome roots, wishing the harm of others, constitute *individually* significant immorality, for which they are the criterion. They include thoughts such as those of injury, murder, theft, fraud and rape, and also false ideologies leading to the harm of others or condoning such harm. Whether or not these thoughts are followed by deeds or words, they constitute *unwholesome mental kamma*.

When greed, hatred and delusion, in any degree, do *not* cause intentional harm to others, they are not evil or immoral in the strict sense of our definition. However, they are still kammically unwholesome in that they maintain bondage and lead to unpleasant results. Similarly, the term "wholesome" extends beyond socially significant morality to comprise also what is individually beneficial, such as acts of renunciation and attempts to understand the nature of reality.

The recent crisis of theistic faith which has taken hold in the West has brought in its trail a moral crisis as well. For many, belief in God has been shattered, and often those who lose their belief in God fail to see any convincing reason for morality without a divine sanction coming down from above. Left without a sound foundation for ethics, they either accept materialistic political ideologies or allow their conduct to be guided by self-interest. Yet we also find today a growing number of people seeking better alternatives. To them the Buddha's teaching on the wholesome and unwholesome roots provides a criterion of good and evil that is neither theological nor authoritarian but experiential, one with a sound psychological basis offering an autonomous pragmatic motivation for avoiding evil and choosing the good.

The social and political motivations for moral conduct proposed to modern man may not openly contradict the basic sentiments of morality, but as their structures are bound to specific historical conditions and reflect the varying self-interests and prejudices of the dominant social group, the values they propose are highly relative, lacking universal validity. In contrast, Buddhist ethics, being based on psychological fact and not on external contingencies, provides a core of moral principles inherently free from relativistic limitations, valid for all time and under all circumstances. By introspection and observation, we can understand that the unwholesome roots are undesirable mental states, productive of suffering for ourselves and others; and since it is our common nature to avoid suffering and to desire happiness, we can understand that it serves our own long-range interest as well as the good of others to restrain actions born of these roots and to act in ways motivated by their wholesome opposites. A brief survey of the evil roots will make this clear.

Greed is a state of lack, need and want. It is always seeking fulfilment and lasting satisfaction, but its drive is inherently insatiable, and thus as long as it endures it maintains the sense of lack.

Hatred, in all its degrees, is also a state of dissatisfaction. Though objectively it arises in response to undesired people or circumstances, its true origins are subjective and internal, chiefly frustrated desire and wounded pride. Buddhist psychology extends the range of hatred beyond simple anger and enmity to include a variety of negative emotions—such as disappointment, dejection, anxiety and despair—representing misguided reactions to the impermanence, insecurity and imperfection inherent in all conditioned existence.

Delusion, taking the form of ignorance, is a state of confusion, bewilderment and helplessness. In its aspect of false views, delusion issues in dogmatism; it takes on a fanatical, even obsessive character, and makes the mind rigid and encapsulated.

All three unwholesome roots lead to inner disharmony and social conflict. In Tibetan paintings they are depicted at the very hub of the Wheel of Life,[1] symbolically represented by a cock, a pig and a snake, turning round and round, catching each other's tails. The three unwholesome roots, indeed, produce and support each other.

The root of greed gives rise to resentment, anger and hatred against those who obstruct the gratification of desire or compete in the chase to gain the desired objects—whether sensual enjoyment, power, dominance or fame. In this way greed leads to conflict and quarrels. When frustrated, instead of producing enmity and aversion, greed may bring about grief, sadness, despair, envy and jealousy—states which also come under the heading of hatred. The pain of deprivation and frustration again sharpens the keenness of desire, which then seeks an escape from pain by indulging in other kinds of enjoyment.

Both greed and hatred are always linked with delusion. They are grounded upon delusion and, on their part, produce still more delusion as we pursue the objects we desire or flee from those we dislike. Both love and hate blind us to the dangers besetting our pursuits; they lead us away from our true advantage. It is the delusion beneath our love and hate that really blinds us, delusion that leads us astray.

The basic delusion, from which all its other forms spring, is the idea of an abiding self: the belief in an ego. For the sake of this illusory ego men lust and hate; upon this they build their imagination and pride. This ego-belief must first be clearly comprehended as a delusive viewpoint. One must pierce through the illusion of self by cultivating right understanding through penetrative thought and meditative insight.

Though the wholesome and unwholesome roots are individual mental states, their manifestations and repercussions have the greatest social significance. Each individual in society rises up at once to protect himself, his loved ones, his property, security and freedom, from the greed, hatred and delusions of others. His own greed, hatred and ignorance may in turn arouse

---

1. See *The Wheel of Birth and Death*, Bhikkhu Khantipālo (Wheel No. 147/149), p. 16.

others to anxious concern and resentment, though he may not be aware of this or care about it. From all this there results an intricate interlocking of suffering—suffering caused to others and suffering experienced oneself. Hence the Buddha repeatedly said that the unwholesome roots cause harm both to oneself and to others, while the wholesome roots are sources of benefit for both the individual and society (see Texts 18–22).

The wholesome and unwholesome roots are of paramount human concern on all levels. As the originating causes of *kamma*, our life-affirming and rebirth-producing intentional actions, they are the motive powers and driving forces of our deeds, words and thoughts. They mould our character and our destiny and hence determine the nature of our rebirth. Being dominant features in the structure of the mind, the unwholesome roots are used in the Abhidhamma Piṭaka for the classification of unwholesome consciousness and also for a typology of temperaments. All the stages of the path to deliverance are closely concerned with the wholesome and unwholesome roots. At the very beginning, the coarsest forms of greed, hatred and irresponsible ignorance have to be abandoned through virtue (*sīla*), while in the advanced stages the aids of meditation (*samādhi*) and wisdom (*paññā*) have to be applied to a deeper-reaching removal of the unwholesome roots and to the cultivation of the wholesome ones. Even Arahatship and Nibbāna—the consummation of the great quest—are both explained in terms of the roots: as the extinction of greed, hatred and delusion.

This wide-ranging significance of the Buddha's teaching on the roots places it at the very core of the Dhamma. Showing the distinct marks of a fully enlightened mind, it is a teaching simple as well as profound, and hence accessible on many levels. The fact that greed, hatred and delusion, in their extreme forms, are the root causes of much misery and evil should be painfully obvious to every morally sensitive person. Such an initial understanding, open to commonsense, may well grow into full comprehension. It may then become the insight that moves one to enter the path to deliverance—the eradication of greed, hatred and delusion.

Within the framework of the Buddha's teaching, the Roots of Good and Evil have found their place in a great variety of contexts. To illustrate this by an ample selection of Buddhist texts—almost entirely taken from the discourses of the Buddha—is the intention of the following pages.

May progress on that Path prevail and may there be a steady growth of the Roots of Good.

Homage to Him who has seen the Roots of All Things!

Greed is the root of heedlessness,
A cause of strife is greed.
Greed into enslavement drags.
A hungry ghost one will in future be.
The Buddha who greed's nature fully knows
I worship Him, the Greed-free One.

Namo te mūla-dassāvī.
Pamādamūlako lobho, lobho vivādamūlako,
dāsabyakārako lobho, lobho paramhi petiko.
Taṃ lobhaṃ parijānantaṃ vande' haṃ vītalobhakaṃ.

Hate is the root of turbulence,
And ugliness results from hate.
Through hatred much destruction comes,
To an infernal world one will in future go.
The Buddha who hate's nature fully knows
I worship Him, the Hate-free One.

Vihaññamūlako doso, doso virūpakārako,
vināsakārako doso, doso paramhi nerayo.
Taṃ dosaṃ parijānantaṃ vande' haṃ vītadosakaṃ.

Delusion is the root of all this misery,
Creator of all ills is ignorant delusion.
Mind's blindness from delusion stems,
As a dumb animal one will in future live.
The Buddha who delusion's nature fully knows
I worship Him, the Undeluded One.

Sabbāghamūlako moho, moho sabbītikārako,
sabbandhakārako moho, moho paramhi svādiko.
Taṃ mohaṃ parijānantaṃ vande' haṃ vītamohakaṃ.

(A traditional devotional Pali text from Sri Lanka. Source unknown.)

For a Long Time

Often, O monks, should one reflect upon one's own mind thus: "For a long time has this mind been defiled by greed, by hatred, by delusion." Mental defilements make beings impure, mental cleansing purifies them...

Mind is more multi-featured than a multi-figured painting...

Mind is more variegated than the varieties of animals... Therefore, O monks, should one often reflect upon one's own mind thus: "For a long time has this mind been defiled by greed, by hatred, by delusion." Mental defilements make beings impure, mental cleansing purities them.

SN 22:10

I. Basic Explanations

1. Definitions

There are three roots of the unwholesome: greed, hatred and delusion; and there are three roots of the wholesome: non-greed, non-hatred and non-delusion.

DN 33 (Saṅgīti Sutta)

Comment

These two sets of three are, respectively, the roots of unwholesome and wholesome volitional action (*kamma*), by way of deeds, words or thoughts.

The term "root" (*mūla*), the commentaries explain, has the sense of firm support, cause, condition and producer. The figurative character of the term suggests that the roots can also be taken as conveyors of the "nourishing sap" of the wholesome or unwholesome. They convey this sap to the mental factors and functions existing simultaneously with themselves, as well as to the wholesome or unwholesome actions in which they issue. They are *producers* by being productive of rebirth.

The words "unwholesome" and "wholesome," as used here, are renderings of the Pali terms *akusala* and *kusala*, respectively.

Alternative renderings used by other translators are, for the wholesome: profitable, skilful; for the unwholesome: unprofitable, unskilful. The terms "wholesome" and "unwholesome" comprise all volitional actions that bind living beings to *saṃsāra*, the round of rebirth and suffering. The actions having these roots may, therefore, be called *kammically* wholesome or unwholesome. Hence the range of the unwholesome is wider than that of the immoral, as it includes forms of the root-defilements which are not immoral in the strict sense explained above. The wholesome, as dealt with here and in most, though not all, of the following texts, is that of the mundane type. The wholesome of the supramundane type is not productive of *kamma* and therefore does not result in rebirth (see Text 17).[2]

The commentators to the Pali scriptures explain *kusala*, the wholesome, as a healthy state of mind (*ārogya*), as morally faultless (*anavajja*) and as having favourable or pleasant *kamma*-results (*sukha-vipāka*). Another connotation of *kusala*, "dexterous" or "skilful," according to the commentators, does not apply in this context. Yet kammically wholesome actions may also be described as skilful insofar as they lead to happiness in the present and future, and to progress on the path to liberation.

Akusala, the unwholesome, has the opposite characteristics: it is an unhealthy or sickly state of mind (*gelañña*), morally faulty and blameworthy (*sāvajja*), and has unpleasant *kamma*-results (*dukkha-vipāka*). For all these reasons, unwholesome actions in thoughts, words and deeds can also be said to be unskilful responses to life.

Of these commentarial explanations, two are derived from a discourse called "The Mantle" (Bāhitika Sutta, Majjhima Nikāya, 88): namely, "morally faulty" or "faultless" (*sāvajjo, anavajjo*), and "having unhappy or happy *kamma*-results" (*dukkha-, sukha-vipāka*). The discourse adds that the unwholesome brings affliction and harm (*sabyāpajjo*), while the wholesome is free from affliction

2. Mundane (*lokiya*) are all those states of consciousness—arising in the worldling as well as in noble ones (*ariya*)—which are not associated with the supramundane paths and fruitions of stream-entry, etc. The supramundane (*lokuttara*) type of the wholesome signifies the four paths and the four fruitions of the stream-enterer, once-returner, non-returner and the Arahant.

and harm (*abyāpajjo*). This corresponds to the commentarial description of the unwholesome as an unhealthy state of mind, and of the wholesome as a healthy one.

1. The Range of the Six Roots

(a) *The Unwholesome.* The three unwholesome roots are not restricted to the strong manifestations suggested by the English terms greed, hatred and delusion. To understand their range it is important to know that in the Pali these three terms stand for all degrees of intensity, even the weakest, of the three defilements, and for all varieties in which these appear. In their weak degrees their unwholesome influence on character and kammic consequences is, of course, not as grave as that of their stronger forms. But even weak forms may carry the risk of either growing stronger or of making a person's character more susceptible to their graver manifestations. A fuller view of the various forms the unwholesome roots assume may be gained from a list of their synonyms, partly taken from the Dhammasaṅgaṇī, the first book of the Abhidhamma Piṭaka.

Greed: liking, wishing, longing, fondness, affection, attachment, lust, cupidity, craving, passion, self-indulgence, possessiveness, avarice; desire for the five sense objects; desire for wealth, offspring, fame, etc.

Hatred: dislike, disgust, revulsion, resentment, grudge, ill-humour, vexation, irritability, antagonism, aversion, anger, wrath, vengefulness.

Delusion: stupidity, dullness, confusion, ignorance of essentials (e.g., the Four Noble Truths), prejudice, ideological dogmatism, fanaticism, wrong views, conceit.

(b) *The Wholesome.* Though formulated negatively, the three wholesome roots signify positive traits:

Non-greed: unselfishness, liberality, generosity; thoughts and actions of sacrifice and sharing; renunciation, dispassion.

Non-hatred: loving kindness, compassion, sympathy, friendliness, forgiveness, forbearance.

Non-delusion: wisdom, insight, knowledge, understanding, intelligence, sagacity, discrimination, impartiality, equanimity.

2. *The Commentarial Definitions of the Unwholesome Roots*

Greed has the characteristic of grasping an object, like birdlime (lit. "monkey-lime"). Its function is sticking, like meat put in a hot pan. It is manifested as not giving up, like the dye of lamp-black. Its proximate cause is seeing enjoyment in things that lead to bondage. Swelling with the current of craving, it should be regarded as carrying beings along with it to states of misery as a swift-flowing river does to the great ocean.

Hatred has the characteristic of savageness, like a provoked snake. Its function is to spread, like a drop of poison, or its function is to burn up its own support, like a forest fire. It is manifested as persecuting like an enemy that has got his chance. Its proximate cause is the grounds for annoyance (*āghāta-vatthu*). It should be regarded as being like stale urine mixed with poison.

Delusion has the characteristic of blindness, or it has the characteristic of unknowing. Its function is non-penetration, or its function is to conceal the true nature of an object. It is manifested as the absence of right view,[3] or it is manifested as darkness. Its proximate cause is unwise (unjustified) attention. It should be regarded as the root of all that is unwholesome.

Vism XIV, 162, 171

3. *The Commentarial Definitions of the Wholesome Roots*

Non-greed has the characteristic of the mind's lack of desire for an object, or it has the characteristic of non-adherence, like a water drop on a lotus leaf. Its function is not to lay hold (or not to grasp), like a liberated bhikkhu. It is manifested as not treating (the desire-evoking object) as a shelter (or non-cleaving), as a man who has fallen into filth (will not cling to it).

Non-hatred has the characteristic of lack of savagery, or the characteristic of non-opposing, like a congenial friend. Its function is to remove annoyance, or its function is to remove fever, as sandalwood does. It is manifested as agreeableness, like the full moon.

Non-delusion has the characteristic of penetrating (things) according to their true nature, or it has the characteristic of sure penetration, like the penetration of an arrow shot by a skilful

3. Comy.: absence of knowledge concerning (the truth of) suffering, etc.

archer. Its function is to illuminate the objective field, like a lamp. It is manifested as non-bewilderment, like a forest guide. The three should be regarded as the roots of all that is wholesome.

Vism XIV, 143

4. *The Nature of the Wholesome Roots*

Non-greed is opposed to the taint of avarice; non-hatred to the taint of immorality; non-delusion to an undeveloped state of wholesome qualities.

Non-greed is a condition of giving (*dāna*); *non-hatred* is a condition of virtue (*sīla*); *non-delusion* is a condition of mental development (or meditation; *bhāvanā*).

Through *non-greed* one does not overrate (an attractive object), as the lustful person does. Through *non-hatred* one does not underrate or deprecate (an unattractive or disagreeable object), as the hater does. Through *non-delusion* one has an undistorted view of things, while one who is deluded conceives things in a distorted way.

With *non-greed* one will admit an existing fault (in an attractive object) and will behave accordingly, while a greedy or lustful person will hide that fault. With *non-hatred* one will admit an existing virtue (in a disagreeable or hostile object) and will behave accordingly, while the hater will disparage that virtue. With *non-delusion* one will admit facts as they are and behave accordingly, while a deluded person holds the true for false (the factual for non-factual) and the false for true (the non-factual for factual).

With *non-greed* one does not have suffering through separation from the beloved; but the greedy and lustful person identifies himself with the beloved and hence cannot bear separation from him. With *non-hatred* one does not have suffering through association with the unbeloved; but the hater identifies himself with (his aversion against) the unbeloved and cannot bear association with him. With *non-delusion* one does not have suffering through not obtaining what one wishes, because the undeluded person will be able to reflect in this way: "How can it be possible that what is subject to decay should not enter into decay?"

With *non-greed* one does not encounter the suffering of birth, because *non-greed* is the opposite of craving, and craving is at the root of the suffering of birth. With *non-hatred* the suffering of ageing is not felt (strongly, or prematurely); because it is one harbouring strong hate who ages quickly. With *non-delusion* there is no suffering in dying; because it is dying with a confused or deluded mind that is suffering, but this does not happen to one who is undeluded.

Non-greed makes for a happy life among lay people (who often quarrel about property). *Non-delusion* makes for a happy life among ascetics and monks (who often quarrel about opinions). *Non-hatred* makes for happy living with all.

Through *non-greed* there is no rebirth in the realm of the famished ghosts (*peta*); because generally beings are reborn there through their craving, and *non-greed* (unselfishness, renunciation) is opposed to craving. Through *non-hatred* there is no rebirth in the hells; for it is through hate and a fierce temperament that beings are reborn in hell, which is congenial to hate; but *non-hate* (loving kindness) is opposed to hate. Through *non-delusion* there is no rebirth in the animal world, for it is generally through delusion that beings are reborn as animals who are always deluded; but *non-delusion* (wisdom) is opposed to delusion.

Among these three, *non-greed* prevents approach in lust, *non-hatred* prevents alienation through hate, *non-delusion* prevents the loss of equipoise (or impartiality) due to delusion.

Furthermore, to these three roots, in the order given, correspond the following sets of three perceptions: the perception of renunciation, of good will, and of non-violence; and also the perception of bodily foulness, of boundless love and compassion, and of the elements.

Through *non-greed* the extreme of sense-indulgence is avoided; through *non-hatred* the extreme of self-mortification; through *non-delusion* a middle course is practised.

Non-greed breaks the bodily bondage of covetousness, *non-hatred* breaks the bodily bondage of ill-will, and *non-delusion* breaks the other two bondages (i.e., that of clinging to rites and rituals, and of dogmatic fanaticism).

By virtue of the first two wholesome roots, the practice of the first two foundations of mindfulness (i.e., body and feelings) will succeed; by virtue of the third wholesome root (*non-delusion*), the practice of the last two foundations of mindfulness (state of mind and contents of mind) will succeed.

Non-greed is a condition of health, because one who is not greedy will not partake of something unsuitable, even if it is tempting, and hence he will remain healthy. *Non-hatred* is a condition of youthfulness, because one who is free from hate is not consumed by the fires of hate that cause wrinkles and grey hair, and thus he remains youthful for a long time. *Non-delusion* is a condition of longevity, because one who is undeluded will know what is beneficial and what is harmful, and by avoiding the harmful and resorting to the beneficial he will have a long life.

Non-greed is a condition of the boon of wealth, because one who is not greedy will obtain wealth through his liberality (as its kammic result). *Non-hatred* is a condition of the boon of friendship, because through loving kindness one will win friends and not lose them. *Non-delusion* is a condition of the boon of self-development, because he who is undeluded and does only what is beneficial will perfect himself.

Through *non-greed* one has detachment to persons and things belonging to one's own group; because even in the case of their destruction, one will not feel the suffering that is caused by strong attachment. With *non-hatred,* the same will hold true in the case of persons and things belonging to a hostile group; because one who is free of hatred will have no thoughts of enmity even towards those who are hostile. With *non-delusion*, the same holds true concerning persons and things belonging to a neutral group; because in one who is undeluded there is no strong attachment to anybody or anything.

Through *non-greed* one will understand impermanence; for a greedy person, in his longing for enjoyment, will not see the impermanence of transitory phenomena. Through *non-hatred* one will understand suffering; for one inclined to *non-hate*, in comprehending the grounds of annoyance discarded by him, sees phenomena as suffering. Through *non-delusion* one will understand not-self; for one who is undeluded is skilled in grasping the nature of reality, and he knows that the five aggregates are without an internal controller. Just as the understanding of impermanence, etc., is effected by *non-greed*, etc., so are also *non-greed*, etc. produced by the understanding of impermanence, etc. Through the understanding of impermanence arises *non-greed*; through the understanding of suffering arises *non-hatred*; through the understanding of non-self arises *non-delusion*. For who will allow attachment to arise for something which he fully well knows is impermanent? And, when knowing phenomena to be suffering, who would produce the additional and exceedingly pungent suffering of anger? And, when knowing phenomena as void of self, who would again plunge into confusion of mind?

From the *Atthasālinī* (commentary to the *Dhammasaṅgaṇī* of the Abhidhamma Piṭaka), pp. 127 ff.

5. The Diversity of the Unwholesome Roots

There may be outsiders, O monks, who will ask you: "There are, friends, three states of mind: greed, hatred and delusion. What is their distinction, their diversity, their difference?"

Questioned thus, O monks, you may explain it to those outsiders in this way:

"Greed is a lesser fault and fades away slowly; hatred is a great fault and fades away quickly; delusion is a great fault and fades away slowly."

AN 3:68 (extract)

Comment

The statements in this text about greed being a lesser fault, and so on, have to be taken in a relative sense. The commentary explains: "Greed (or lust) is a lesser fault in a twofold way: (1) in public opinion (*loka*; i.e., in the 'eyes of the world'), and (2) with regard to *kamma*-result (*vipāka*), i.e., the rebirth resulting from the *kamma* (impelled by greed).

"(1) If, for instance, parents give their children in marriage, according to the standards of worldly life no fault is involved (though greed enters into the parents' affection and sexuality in marriage).

"(2) If in marriage one is satisfied with one's own marriage-partner (and thus observes the third precept), there is thereby no rebirth in the lower worlds. Thus greed or lust can be a lesser fault in regard to *kamma*-result. Greed, however, is 'slow in fading away,' being as hard to remove as oily soot. Greed for particular objects or sensual lust for a certain person may persist throughout life. It may even continue for two or three existences without disappearing."

Thus, relative to hatred and delusion, greed is a lesser evil. For if it remains within the bounds of basic morality, and does not entail a violation of the five precepts, it will not exclude a favourable rebirth caused by good *kamma*. Greed, however, is very hard to overcome entirely. Its fine hair-roots reach deep into our nature, and it may clad itself in many alluring garments, assuming subtle disguises and sublime forms of beauty. As "lust for life" or "the will to live" it is the very core of existence. As life-affirming craving it is the origin of suffering.

"Hatred," according to the commentary, "may lead to wrong-doings towards parents, brothers, sisters, ascetics (i.e., people of religious calling), etc. Wherever such an offender goes, blame and bad reputation will follow him. If, through hatred, he even commits one of the heinous offences (*ānantariya-kamma*), such as parricide, etc., he will suffer in hell for aeons.[4] In that way, hatred is a great fault both in public opinion and by its *kamma*-result. Yet hatred may quickly fade away; for soon after committing an offence out of hatred or anger one may repent, ask those whom one has wronged for forgiveness, and if that is granted, the act is atoned for (as far as the offender's state of mind is concerned)."

Hatred is a disruptive and antisocial factor, a source of untold misery for individuals and all human groups. One would thus expect society to regard it as a "great fault," as the great enemy of societal welfare, and make every effort to weaken and eliminate it. But on the contrary we find that human institutions, large and small, have often promoted hate for their own selfish ends, or have fostered deeds, words and thoughts of hate motivated by delusive ideologies. Throughout history, leaders seeking the support of the masses have always found it easier to unite people by means of a common hate than by a common love.

On the individual level, hatred in all its degrees is often roused by conflicting self-interests and by other kinds of egocentric

4. The Buddhist scriptures speak of five "heinous offences"—parricide, matricide, killing an Arahant, wounding a Buddha, and maliciously causing a schism in the Sangha.

antagonism. Hatred can grow as obsessive as lustful passion, but it is generally more destructive for both the hater and his victim. It can take deep roots in the mind, be it in the form of smouldering resentment or the enjoyment of outbursts of violence. Through hatred, man's mind may sink to a subhuman level, and thus for the hater there is always the risk of being reborn in a subhuman realm of existence.

Yet for one who does not identify himself with all his states of mind, but sees the need and has the will to transform himself—for such a one it will not be difficult to control his hatred or anger before it grows stronger. Hatred causes irritation, tension and distress; and since human beings are basically "desirous of happiness and averse to unhappiness," those who do understand the consequences of hatred will normally wish to get rid of it.

"Delusion," according to the commentary, "is a great fault for both reasons, that is, in the eyes of public opinion and with regard to its unhappy *kamma*-result (in the same ways as mentioned above for hatred). If an action is done under the impact of delusion, such action will set one free only very slowly; it can be likened to a bear skin, which will not become bright even if washed seven times."

If unrestrained acts of unlawful greed or lust are performed without a feeling of guilt, but are, on the contrary, justified by such prejudiced views as the claim that might makes right, such deluded greed will obviously not be easy to eliminate. It will not be given up even under the impact of repeated failures to satisfy it, which may only strengthen the greed through frustration and resentment. There are also forms of deluded greed supported by a religious (or pseudo-religious) sanction (see Comment to Text 17). All these forms of deluded greed can be eliminated only when the delusive false views and principles are discarded. But even in cases where greed is not backed by wrong theory, when self-indulgence has the uninhibited innocence of ignorance or when the delusive view involved is just the naive belief that "this is the right and natural thing to do"—in these cases, too, our bondage by such deluded greed will be hard to break.

It is similar when delusion instigates hatred and keeps it alive with wrong views or attitudes. If, for instance, due to delusive views, people regard others belonging to certain races, classes or religions as legitimate objects of hate, this will be a much stronger bondage than any impassioned but temporary outburst of anger having only the normal admixture of delusion.

Without the presence of delusion, no greed or hatred can arise. The unwholesome roots of greed and hatred always occur associated with delusion. Delusion, however, may occur by itself and can be a very powerful source of evil and suffering. In view of that omnipresence of delusion in the unwholesome, the Dhammapada says that there is no entanglement equal to the widespread net of delusion (v. 251), and that ignorance (a synonym of delusion) is the greatest taint of the mind (v. 243). Hence the Buddha declares: "All unwholesome states have their root in ignorance, they converge upon ignorance, and by the abolishing of ignorance, all the other unwholesome states are abolished" (SN 20:1).

Ignorance, of course, does not mean a mere lack of information about this or that subject of worldly knowledge. It is, rather, the lack of right understanding concerning the Four Noble Truths: namely, the ignorance (or wilful ignoring) of the full range and depth of suffering, of its true cause, of the fact that there can be an end of suffering and of the path that leads to the end of suffering.

The truth of suffering is hidden by the four distortions of reality (*vipallāsa*), the four great illusions of seeing permanence in the impermanent, happiness in what is truly suffering, selfhood in what is void of a self, and beauty in the unbeautiful. These distortions, powerful universal manifestations of ignorance and delusion, shut out an understanding of the truth of suffering, and thereby obscure the other truths, too. The four may appear on any of three levels: at the level of quite ordinary misperceptions (*saññā-vipallāsa*), or as wrong ways of thinking (*citta-vipallāsa*), or as expressed in definite wrong ideas and theories (*diṭṭhi-vipallāsa*). Tenaciously held wrong views can forge the strongest chain fettering beings to pain-fraught *saṃsāra*. If these views go so far as to deny the moral relevance of any action, they will lead in the next existence to a "fixed destiny" of rebirth in a world of misery.[5]

Sheer stupidity is, of course, also a form of delusion, and it can stultify a person's inner growth throughout life and for many lives to come. But there can be an escape from it, if that dull person's

5. On "wrong views with fixed result" (*niyata-micchā-diṭṭhi*), see Apaṇṇaka Sutta (Wheel No. 98/99), p. 23.

good roots of non-greed (selflessness) and non-hate (kindness, compassion) are strong enough to become active.

The most deep-rooted and powerful aspect of delusion, and the most consequential of wrong views, is personality-belief. Personality-belief is the belief in an abiding self or soul, with its attendant conceits and conceptions. The belief may be naive and unreflective, or supported by definite theories and convictions. But however it is held, this personality-belief makes delusion a barrier hard to overcome and slow to fade away, while the moral implications of egocentricity make it a "great fault."

Considering the wide range and universal influence of delusion, it is understandable that, under the name of ignorance, it appears as the first factor in the chain of dependent origination (*paṭicca-samuppāda*). As the chief impelling force that keeps the wheel of existence in rotation, delusion is indeed "a great fault and slow to fade away."

II. General Texts

6. Overcoming Birth and Death

If three things were not found in the world, the Perfect One, the Holy One who is fully enlightened, would not appear in the world, nor would his teaching and discipline shed their light over the world.

What are these three things? They are birth, old age and death. Because these three are found in the world, the Perfect One, the Holy One who is fully enlightened, has appeared in the world, and his teaching and discipline shed their light over the world.

It is, however, impossible to overcome birth, old age and death without overcoming another three things, namely: greed, hatred and delusion.

AN 10:76

7. Bondage and Freedom

There are two things:[6] seeing enjoyment in things that can fetter,[7] and seeing dissatisfaction[8] in things that can fetter.

He who lives seeing enjoyment in things that can fetter cannot give up greed, hatred and delusion; and without giving them up he will not be freed from birth, old age and death, not from sorrow, lamentation, pain, grief and despair; he will not be freed from suffering, this I declare. But he who lives seeing dissatisfaction in things that can fetter will give up greed, hatred and delusion; and by giving them up he will be freed from birth, old age and death, from sorrow, lamentation, pain, grief and despair; he will be freed from suffering, this I declare.

AN 2:6

---

6. Or two kinds of outlook.
7. *Saṃyojaniyesu dhammesu assādānupassitā.* Comy.: things which are conditions for the ten fetters (*saṃyojana*).
8. Or revulsion, disgust; *saṃyojaniyesu dhammesu nibbidānupassitā.*

8. Barbs

Greed is a barb, hatred is a barb, and delusion is a barb. Hence, monks, you should abide without (these) barbs, abide free from (these) barbs. Without (such) barbs are the Arahats, free from (such) barbs are the Arahats.

AN 10:72

Comment

The Pāli word for "barb" is *kaṇṭaka*, literally "a thorn." A similar figurative expression, that of a dart (*salla*), occurs in the Suttanipāta:

I saw what is so hard to see,
the dart embedded in the heart—
the dart by which afflicted we
hurry on in all directions.
If once this dart has been removed,
one will not hurry, will not sink.

vv. 938–939

9. From the Mahā-Vedalla Sutta

Greed is a producer of limitations, hatred is a producer of limitations, delusion is a producer of limitations.*

Greed is something burdensome, hatred is something burdensome, delusion is something burdensome.**

Greed is a maker of (tainted) marks, hatred is a maker of (tainted) marks, delusion is a maker of (tainted) marks.*** All these are given up by the taint-free Arahat; they are cut off at the root, made barren like a palm-stump, brought to non-existence, no longer liable to arise again in the future.

MN 43

Comments

* "Producer of limitations" (*pamāṇa-karaṇa*). The three roots of evil limit man's outlook, place limitations on his vision of things as they really are, and limit his potential freedom of choice. As the subcommentary says, they make for a "shallow and narrow mentality" (*uttāno paritta-cetaso*).

The commentary explains differently, saying that the manifestations of the three unwholesome roots provide a standard or criterion (*pamāṇa*) for judging whether people are unliberated worldlings (*puthujjana*) or noble persons (*ariya*). But as this text later contrasts this term with *appamāṇa-cetovimutti*, the "boundless liberation of the mind," the interpretation chosen here appears more probable.

** "Something burdensome" (*kiñcana*). The Pāli word *kiñcana* means "something." In another passage of the same text (not reproduced here), this is contrasted with *ākiñcañña-cetovimutti*, the "liberation of mind through (the meditative state of) nothingness." The commentary, however, relates the word to a verb *kiñchati*, "to crush, press down, oppress." Greed, hatred and delusion are certainly a heavy burden, pressing man down by "something or other" that evokes his passions and clouds his vision. The term *kiñcana* sometimes also has the meaning of property or possessions.

*** "Maker of (tainted) marks" (*nimitta-karaṇa*). The three unwholesome roots impress, as it were, their marks upon the objects of sense perception; hence these objects are habitually identified as attractive and repulsive, or as bases evoking confusion and wrong views. The roots also attach to "self and world" the delusive marks of permanence, happiness, selfhood and beauty instead of the true marks of impermanence, liability to suffering, not-self and impurity.

10. Māra's prisoner[9]

He who has not abandoned greed, hatred and delusion is called Māra's prisoner, captured in Māra's snares, subject to the Evil One's will and pleasure.

But he who has abandoned greed, hatred and delusion is no longer Māra's prisoner; he is freed from Māra's snares, no longer subject to the Evil One's will and pleasure.

It 68

9. Māra: the personification of the forces antagonistic to enlightenment.

11. Crossing the Ocean

A monk or a nun who has not abandoned greed, hatred and delusion, such a one has not crossed the ocean (of *saṃsāra*), with its waves and whirlpools, monsters and demons.

But a monk or a nun who has abandoned greed, hatred and delusion, such a one has crossed the ocean (of *saṃsāra*), with its waves and whirlpools, monsters and demons, has traversed it and gone to the other shore (Nibbāna), standing on firm ground as a true saint.

It 69

12. The Three Fires

There are three fires: the fire of lust, the fire of hatred and the fire of delusion.

The fire of lust burns lustful mortals
Who are entangled in the sense-objects.
The fire of hate burns wrathful men
Who urged by hate slay living beings.
Delusion's fire burns foolish folk
Who cannot see the holy Dhamma.

Those who delight in the embodied group[10]
Do not know this triple fire.
They cause the worlds of woe to grow:
The hells, and life as animal,
The ghostly and demoniac realms;
Unfreed are they from Māra's chains.

But those who live by day and night
Devoted to the Buddha's law,
They quench within the fire of lust
By seeing the impurity of body.

They quench within the fire of hate
By loving kindness, loftiest of men.

---

10. The term "embodied group" (*sakkāya*) refers to the transient personality consisting of the five aggregates: body, feeling, perception, mental formations and consciousness.

Delusion's fire they also quench
By wisdom ripening in penetration.[11]
When they extinguish these three fires,
Wise, unremitting day and night,
Completely they are liberated,
Completely they transcend all ill.

Seers of the holy realm,[12]
Through perfect knowledge[13] *wise,*
By direct vision ending all rebirth,
They do not go to any new existence.

It 93

From the Commentary by Bhadantācariya Dhammapāla

Because greed, when it arises, burns and consumes living beings, it is called a fire; and so it is with hatred and delusion. Just as a fire consumes the fuel through which it has arisen, and grows into a vast conflagration, similarly it is with greed, hatred and delusion: they consume the life-continuity in which they have arisen and grow into a vast conflagration that is hard to extinguish.

Innumerable are the beings who, with hearts ablaze with the fire of lust, have come to death through the suffering of unfulfilled desire. This is greed's burning power. For the burning power of hatred, a special example is the "deities ruined by their angry minds" (*manopadosika-devā*), and for delusion, the "deities ruined by their playful pleasures" (*khiḍḍapadosika-devā*).[14] In their delusion, the latter become so forgetful that they miss their meal-time and die. This is the burning power of greed, hatred and delusion, as far as the present life is concerned. In future lives these three are still more terrible and hard to endure, insofar as greed, etc., may cause rebirth in the hells and the other worlds of woe.

---

11. Literally, "leading to the piercing" (*nibbedha-gāminī*). This refers to the piercing, or destroying, of the mass of defilements.

12. The "holy realm" is Nibbāna.

13. "Through perfect knowledge" (*sammad-aññāya*). *Aññā* is the highest knowledge, or gnosis, attained by Arahatship.

14. The former die and fall away from their heaven because of anger, the latter because of their negligence. See the Brahmajāla Sutta (DN 1).

13. Three Inner Foes

There are three inner taints, three inner foes, three inner enemies, three inner murderers, three inner antagonists. What are these three? Greed is an inner taint.... Hatred is an inner taint.... Delusion is an inner taint, an inner foe, an inner enemy, an inner murderer, an inner antagonist.

Greed is a cause of harm,
Unrest of mind it brings.
This danger that has grown within,
Blind folk are unaware of it.

A greedy person cannot see the facts,
Nor can he understand the Dhamma.
When greed has overpowered him,
In complete darkness he is plunged.

But he who does not crave and can forsake
This greed and what incites to greed,
From him quickly greed glides off
Like water from a lotus leaf.

Hate is a cause of harm,
Unrest of mind it brings.
This danger that has grown within,
Blind folk are unaware of it.

A hater cannot see the facts,
Nor can he understand the Dhamma.
When hate has overpowered him,
In complete darkness he is plunged.

But he who does not hate and can forsake
This hatred and what incites to hate,
From him quickly hatred falls off
As from a palm tree falls the ripened fruit.

Delusion is a cause of harm,
Unrest of mind it brings.
This danger that has grown within,
Blind folk are unaware of it.

He who is deluded cannot see the facts,
Nor can he understand the Dhamma.
If a man is in delusion's grip,
In complete darkness he is plunged.

But he who has shed delusion's veil
Is undeluded where confusion reigns;
He fully scatters all delusion,
Just as the sun dispels the night.

It 88

Comment

Greed, hatred and delusion strong enough to lead to subhuman rebirth are abandoned by the first path, that of stream-entry. Sensual desire and hatred, in their coarse forms, are abandoned by the second path (of once-return), and in their subtle forms by the third path (of non-return). All remaining greed and delusion, along with their associated defilements, are abandoned by the fourth path—that of Arahatship.

III. The Roots and Kamma

14. The Causes of Action

There are, O monks, three causes for the origin of action (*kamma*): greed, hatred and delusion.

From greed, O monks, no greedlessness will arise; it is greed that arises from greed. From hatred no hatelessness will arise; it is hatred that arises from hatred. From delusion no non-delusion will arise; it is delusion that arises from delusion.

Due to actions born of greed, born of hatred, born of delusion, neither divine beings will appear, nor humans, nor any other kind of happy existence.[15] Rather the hells, the animal kingdom, the realm of ghosts or some other kind of woeful existence will appear due to actions born of greed, hatred and delusion.

These are, O monks, three causes for the origin of action.

There are, O monks, three other causes for the origin of action: non-greed, non-hatred and non-delusion.

From non-greed, O monks, no greed will arise; it is non-greed that arises from non-greed. From non-hatred no hatred will arise; it is non-hatred that arises from non-hatred. From non-delusion no delusion will arise; it is non-delusion that arises from non-delusion.

Due to actions born of non-greed, non-hatred and non-delusion, neither the hells will appear, nor the animal kingdom, nor the realm of ghosts, nor any other kind of woeful existence. Rather divine beings, humans or some other kind of happy existence will appear due to actions born of non-greed, non-hatred and non-delusion.

These are, O monks, three other causes for the origin of action.

AN 6:39

Comment

In this text the Buddha implicitly rejects the maxim that "the end justifies the means"—a doctrine widely followed in politics and sometimes even by religious institutions. Our text further

---

15. By way of rebirth.

declares as groundless the hope of those who apply this maxim in the belief that they will be rewarded in a future life for serving their cause by unrighteous means in this life, or in the case of non-religious application, that a future generation will reap the reward of present violence and repression in an ideal society or "paradise on earth."

Our text further negates the notion that lustful passion, or actions usually regarded as immoral or sinful, need not be obstacles to liberation or salvation, and can even aid their attainment. Such ideas, in varying formulations, have been mooted in the antinomian sects belonging to several of the world's great religions.[16] The notion that the end justifies the means occurs also in the basic principle of the intentional theory of ethics: "Whatever is done with the intention of doing good to the world is right or virtuous." All such notions, the Buddha's statement implies, are untenable, undermined by the deep psychological connections of the roots.

15. The Ten Ways of Action

If a noble disciple knows what is unwholesome and knows the root of the unwholesome; if he knows what is wholesome and knows the root of the wholesome—he is then, to that extent, one of right understanding; he is one whose understanding is correct, who has firm confidence in the teaching, and has arrived at (the core of) the good Dhamma.

And what is unwholesome? Killing is unwholesome, taking what is not given is unwholesome, sexual misconduct is unwholesome; lying is unwholesome, tale-bearing is unwholesome, harsh language is unwholesome, vain talk is unwholesome; covetousness is unwholesome, ill-will is unwholesome, wrong views are unwholesome.

And what is the root of the unwholesome? Greed is a root of the unwholesome, hatred is a root of the unwholesome, delusion is a root of the unwholesome.

And what is wholesome? Abstaining from killing is wholesome, abstaining from taking what is not given is wholesome,

16. For a fuller repudiation of this thesis in the Buddha's own time, see *The Snake Simile* (MN 22), tr. by Nyanaponika Thera (Wheel No. 48/49), pp. 13, 16, 39.

abstaining from sexual misconduct is wholesome; abstaining from lying ... from tale-bearing ... from harsh language ... from vain talk is wholesome; non-covetousness is wholesome, non-ill-will is wholesome, right view is wholesome.

And what is the root of the wholesome? Non-greed is a root of the wholesome, non-hatred is a root of the wholesome, non-delusion is a root of the wholesome.

MN 9

Comment

In this discourse, spoken by the venerable Sāriputta, the unwholesome and the wholesome are explained by the "ten ways of unwholesome and wholesome action" (*akusala-kusala-kammapatha*), which extend to deeds, words and thoughts. They are also called the ten bad and ten good ways of conduct.

This explanation of the unwholesome enumerates ten cases of definite immoral behaviour. Even the last three items, referring to unwholesome *mental kamma*, have in this context an immoral character. As ways of unwholesome mental action, they signify the covetous desire to appropriate others' property; the hateful thoughts of harming, hurting or killing others; and those wrong views which deny moral causality and thus give room and justification for immoral acts.

These ten, however, do not exhaust the range of the term *unwholesome*. As mentioned earlier, the range of the unwholesome is wider than that of the immoral. It is not restricted to violations of the ten bad courses, but comprises all deeds, words and thoughts motivated by any degree of greed, hatred and delusion.

To give a few examples: fondness for good food, music or physical comfort is not immoral, but as an attachment which binds us to the world of sense experience, it is kammically unwholesome. The same holds true for sexual acts, words and thoughts directed to one's marriage partner. These, too, according to the moral code of lay society, are not immoral. Yet as strong manifestations of craving, they fall under the unwholesome root "greed." One's personal stupidity, narrowness of view, ignorance of what is truly beneficial and similar limitations of mind are not immoral and need not have immediate immoral consequences. Yet they are great impediments to the acquisition of liberating wisdom and bind one firmly to *saṃsāra*. Therefore, they too are unwholesome, being forms of the unwholesome root "delusion."

16. The Roots of the Ten Unwholesome Ways

Killing, I declare, O monks, is of three kinds: motivated by greed, motivated by hatred, motivated by delusion.

Also the taking of what is not given, sexual misconduct, lying, tale-bearing, harsh language, vain talk, covetousness, ill-will and wrong views—all these, I declare, are of three kinds: motivated by greed, motivated by hatred, motivated by delusion.

Thus, O monks, greed is an originator of the *kamma*-concatenation, hatred is an originator of the *kamma*-concatenation, delusion is an originator of the *kamma*-concatenation. But by the destruction of greed, hatred and delusion, the *kamma*-concatenation comes to an end.

AN 10:174

17. Rebirth and Its Cessation

I

There are, O monks, three causes for the origin of action: greed, hatred and delusion.

An action performed out of greed, born of greed, caused by greed, originating in greed;

an action performed out of hatred, born of hatred, caused by hatred, originating in hatred;

an action performed out of delusion, born of delusion, caused by delusion, originating in delusion—

such an action will ripen wherever the individual is reborn; and wherever the action ripens, there the individual will reap the fruit thereof, be it in this life, in the next or in future lives.

It is as with seeds that are undamaged and unspoiled, unimpaired by wind and heat, capable of sprouting, sown well in a good field, planted in well-prepared soil. If there is plentiful rain, these seeds will come to growth, increase and reach full development. Similarly, an action performed out of greed, hatred or delusion will ripen wherever the individual is reborn; and wherever the action ripens, the individual will reap the fruit thereof, be it in this life, in the next life or in future lives.

II

There are three other causes for the origin of action: non-greed, non-hatred and non-delusion.

If an action is performed out of non-greed, born of non-greed, caused by non-greed, originating in non-greed, and if greed has entirely gone;

if performed out of non-hatred, born of non-hatred, caused by non-hatred, originating in non-hatred, and if hatred has entirely gone;

if performed out of non-delusion, born of non-delusion, caused by non-delusion, originating in non-delusion, and if delusion has entirely gone—

such an action is thereby given up, cut off at its root, made (barren) like a palm-stump, brought to non-existence and is no longer liable to arise in the future again.

It is as with seeds that are undamaged and unspoiled, unimpaired by wind and heat, capable of sprouting, sown well in a good field. If now a man were to burn them, reduce them to ashes and then scatter the ashes in a strong wind or throw them into a stream's rapid current which carried them away—then these seeds would have been utterly destroyed, made unable to sprout again.

Similarly, if an action is performed out of non-greed, non-hatred and non-delusion, and if greed, hatred and delusion have entirely gone—such an action is thereby given up, cut off at its root, made (barren) like a palm-stump, brought to non-existence and is no longer liable to arise in the future again.

AN 3:33

Comment on Section II

Greed and delusion in their weaker forms are entirely eliminated on attaining Arahatship, while hatred down to its weakest form is fully abandoned at the stage of the non-returner. Section II of our text applies, therefore, only to actions performed at these stages of final emancipation. Only then are these actions finally "given up" so that they can no longer lead to a future rebirth. It is thus only at Arahatship that all three unwholesome roots are "entirely gone," though they are decisively weakened at the earlier three stages of emancipation.

The Arahat's action, as no longer productive of rebirth, occurs also as the fourth item in a fourfold division of *kamma*:

Dark action that brings dark results;
bright action that brings bright results;
partly bright and partly dark action which brings partly bright and partly dark results;
action neither bright nor dark which brings neither bright nor dark results and leads to the exhaustion of action.

AN 4:232; MN 57

The text explains that this last type of action is the volition of giving up all acts of kammic formation, that is, the volition present in the states of consciousness pertaining to the four paths of emancipation. But this fourth type can also be understood as the actions an Arahat performs in ordinary life, for these do not lead him into kammic involvement or bind him to a future rebirth. His good actions may appear quite similar to the moral deeds of noble (though unliberated) worldlings, but the Arahat's actions are not motivated by the slightest trace of craving and ignorance. In the Arahat's mind there is no greed (craving) by way of wishing that his virtue be recognized and appreciated, no delusion (ignorance) by way of a proud satisfaction in "being good," no illusionary expectations as to the result of these good actions; nor is there any other self-reference in any form whatever. An Arahat's good actions are a spontaneous outflow of a fully purified mind and heart, responding without hesitation to situations where help is needed and possible. But though his actions may be inspired by sympathy and compassion, beneath them there is detachment and deep serenity instead of emotional involvement. As long as the momentum of his life-force lasts, the Arahat lives on as an embodiment of wisdom and compassion. But as the Arahat's mind no longer clings to anything, not even to the results of his actions, there is no potentiality left for any future rebirth. The life-nourishing sap conveyed by the roots has ceased to flow, and the roots of continued existence themselves are cut off.

IV. The Social Significance of the Roots

18. From the Kālāma Sutta

"What do you think, Kālāmas? When greed, hatred and delusion arise in a person, is it for his benefit or harm?"—"For his harm, venerable sir."—"Kālāmas, a person who is greedy, hating and deluded, overpowered by greed, hatred and delusion, his thoughts controlled by them, will take life, take what is not given, indulge in sexual misconduct, and tell lies; he will also prompt others to do likewise. Will that conduce to his harm and his suffering for a long time?"—"Yes, venerable sir."

"What do you think, Kālāmas? Are these things wholesome or unwholesome?"—"Unwholesome, venerable sir."—"Blamable or blameless?"—"Blamable, venerable sir."—"Censured or praised by the wise?"—"Censured, venerable sir."—"Undertaken and practised, do these things lead to harm and suffering, or not? Or how is it in this case?"—"Undertaken and practised, these things lead to harm and suffering. So does it appear to us in this case."

"Therefore, Kālāmas, did we say: Do not go upon repeated hearing (of orally transmitted religious tradition), nor upon a linear succession (of teachers), nor upon hearsay, nor upon the authority of scriptures, nor upon speculative and logical grounds, nor upon thought-out theories, nor upon preference for views pondered upon, nor upon another's seeming competence, nor upon the consideration that 'The monk is our teacher.'

"But when you yourselves know: 'These things are unwholesome, blamable, censured by the wise, and if undertaken and practised they will lead to harm and suffering,' then give them up."

AN 3:65

19. Why Give Up the Roots of Evil?

Once a wandering ascetic, Channa by name, visited the venerable Ānanda and spoke to him as follows:

"You, friend Ānanda, teach the giving up of greed, hatred and delusion, and we, too, teach it. But, friend Ānanda, what disadvantage have you seen in greed, hatred and delusion that you teach that they ought to be given up?"

"Friend, a person who is greedy, hating and deluded, overpowered by greed, hatred and delusion, his thoughts controlled by them, aims at his own harm, aims at others' harm, aims at the harm of both, and he suffers pain and grief in his mind. But when greed, hatred and delusion are given up, he will not aim at his own harm, nor at the harm of others, nor at the harm of both, and he will not suffer pain and grief in his mind.

"A person who is greedy, hating and deluded, overpowered by greed, hatred and delusion, his thoughts controlled by them, leads an evil way of life in deeds, words and thoughts; he does not know his own true advantage, nor that of others, nor that of both. But when greed, hatred and delusion are given up, he will not lead an evil way of life in deeds, words and thoughts; and he will understand his own true advantage, that of others and that of both.

"Greed, hatred and delusion, friend, make one blind, unseeing and ignorant; they destroy wisdom, are bound up with distress and do not lead to Nibbāna.

"Because we have seen these disadvantages in greed, hatred and delusion, therefore, friend, do we teach that they ought to be given up.

"This Noble Eightfold Path, namely: right understanding, right thought, right speech, right action, right livelihood, right effort, right mindfulness and right concentration—this, friend, is the path, the way to the giving up of greed, hatred and delusion."

AN 3:71

20. The Visible Teaching

"People speak of the 'visible teaching.' In how far, Lord, is the teaching visible here and now, of immediate result, inviting to come and see, onward-leading, to be directly experienced by the wise?"

"A person who is greedy, hating and deluded, overpowered by greed, hatred and delusion, aims at his own harm, at others' harm, at the harm of both, and he suffers pain and grief in his mind. He also leads an evil way of life in deeds, words and thoughts, and he does not know his own true advantage, that of others and that of both.

"But when greed, hatred and delusion are given up, he will not aim at his own harm, at others' harm, at the harm of both, and he will not suffer pain and grief in his mind. He will not lead an evil life and he will understand his own true advantage, that of others and that of both.

"In that sense is the teaching visible here and now, of immediate result, inviting to come and see, onward-leading, to be directly experienced by the wise."

AN 3:53

Comment

The description of the teaching (Dhamma) as being "visible here and now" and so forth, is the same as in the traditional text of homage to the Dhamma.

The Dhamma taught by the Buddha is the Four Noble Truths. If that Dhamma is here identified with the teaching on the unwholesome roots and their abandonment, we may understand the connection thus: the presence of greed, hatred and delusion corresponds to the truths of suffering and its origin, their abandonment to the truths of the path and its goal, Nibbāna, the cessation of suffering.

When, through earnest effort in practising the Dhamma, one succeeds in weakening the evil roots, the truth of the teaching becomes clearly visible. The Dhamma indeed yields immediate results. Having accepted its invitation to "come and see," one has tested it and seen its benefits for oneself. Encouraged by these partial results, one will be led onwards towards the goal—the final eradication of greed, hatred and delusion. But the experience has to be personal—gone through by each one himself, alone, through wisdom and energy devoted to the work of liberation.

21. Four Types of People

There are four types of people in the world. One who works for his own good, but not for the good of others; one who works for the good of others, but not for his own good; one who works neither for his own good nor for the good of others; and one who works for his own good as well as for the good of others.

And which is the person who works for his own good, but not for the good of others? It is he who strives for the abolishing of greed, hatred and delusion in himself, but does not encourage others to abolish greed, hatred and delusion.

And which is the person who works for the good of others, but not for his own good? It is he who encourages others to abolish greed, hatred and delusion, but does not strive for the abolishing of greed, hatred and delusion in himself.

And which is the person who works neither for his own good nor for the good of others? It is he who neither strives for the abolishing of greed, hatred and delusion in himself, nor encourages others to abolish greed, hatred and delusion.

And which is the person who works for his own good as well as for the good of others? It is he who strives for the abolishing of greed, hatred and delusion in himself, and also encourages others to abolish greed, hatred and delusion.

AN 4:76

22. The Roots of Violence and Oppression

There are, O monks, three roots of the unwholesome: greed, hatred and delusion.

Greed, hatred and delusion of every kind are unwholesome. Whatever *kamma* a greedy, hating and deluded person heaps up, by deeds, words or thoughts, that, too, is unwholesome.[17] Whatever suffering such a person, overpowered by greed, hatred and delusion, his thoughts controlled by them, inflicts under false pretexts[18] upon another—by killing, imprisonment, confiscation of property, false accusations or expulsion, being prompted in this by the thought, "I have power and I want power"—all this is unwholesome too. In this manner, there arise in him many evil unwholesome states of mind, born of and originating from

17. The verb *abhisaṅkharoti*, "heaps up," refers to kammic accumulation through the volitional *kamma*-formations (*saṅkhāra*), which are here of an unwholesome character. The commentary emphasizes the fact that greed, hatred and delusion are not only unwholesome in themselves, but also roots of future unwholesome evil conditions.

18. *Asatā*: lit. falsely, untruthfully.

greed, hatred and delusion, caused and conditioned by greed, hatred and delusion.

AN 3:69

Comment

As our text vividly shows, the three roots of evil have dreadful repercussions on society, as causes of cruelty and the infliction of suffering. The Buddha speaks of the three as motives for the unrestrained use of power, and the examples given in the text make it clear that he refers to political power: a ruler's abuse of power whether in time of war against his country's enemy, or in peacetime towards its own population. During his lifetime, the Buddha must have observed many cases of violence and oppression. He also must have known that the false pretexts justifying such abuses of power are used in war as well as in peace. False propaganda against a country's enemy, and slander of the chosen victims in the ruler's own country, obviously existed even 2500 years ago. In fact, all those instances of violence and oppression mentioned by the Buddha have quite a familiar ring today. And, of course, the driving forces behind them are still the same: greed, hatred and delusion. In modern history, however, the central role has shifted towards delusion, which runs beneath various aggressive ideologies of a religious, political or racial character.

The Buddha may have been recalling his life as a prince at his father's court when he spoke those moving verses opening the sutta called "The Use of Violence" (Attadaṇḍa Sutta):

The use of violence breeds terror:
See the nation embroiled in strife!
How this has moved my heart,
How I was stirred, I shall now tell.

Seeing the crowds in frantic movement,
Like swarms of fish when the pond dries up;
Seeing how people fight each other,
By fear and horror I was struck.

Sn vv. 935–36

Only rarely did the Buddha speak about those darker sides of contemporary society, but these few texts show that he was a keen and compassionate observer.

Generally, all three roots of evil operate in those acts of violence and oppression which our text mentions. But in specific cases any of the three might be dominant, though an element of delusion, or ignorance, will always be present. In war, rulers might be motivated chiefly by greed for territory, wealth, economic dominance or political supremacy; but to make the war popular among their own people, they will employ hate-propaganda to whip up their will to fight. Delusion was a prominent motive in the religious wars of the past, and in our present time it still crops up in ideological wars and revolutions, as well as in religious, political and racial persecutions within a country. In all these cases, delusion produces hate, with greed too often lurking in the background. Oppressive regimes, in their acts directed against sections of their own people, share the same motive. The interaction of the roots is sometimes quite complex, as they grow in strength by feeding each other.

The Buddha understood well the psychology of the mighty, which basically has not changed through the millennia. All those wrongful acts, from killing down to expulsion of innocent victims, are committed out of the lust for power—the enjoyment of power, the wish to secure it and the drive to expand its range. This power craze is, of course, an obsessive delusion intricately bound up with authority. It threatens to overcome all those who exercise authority over others, from the old-style monarchs to the modern dictator. Even the petty bureaucrat does not escape: he too delights in wielding his own little share of power and displaying his stamp of authority.

V. The Removal of the Unwholesome Roots

23. The Triple Gem and the Abandoning of the Evil Roots

Once the venerable Ānanda was staying in Kosambī, at Ghosita's monastery. At that time a certain householder, a lay devotee of the Ājīvaka ascetics, went to see the venerable Ānanda. Having arrived, he saluted him and sat down at one side. So seated, he said this to the venerable Ānanda:

"How is it, revered Ānanda: Whose doctrine is *well-proclaimed*? Who are those who live *well-conducted* in the world? Who are the *blessed ones* in the world?"[19]

"Now, householder, I shall ask you a question on this matter, and you may answer as you think fit. What do you think, householder: as to those who teach a doctrine for the abandoning of greed, hatred and delusion, is their doctrine well-proclaimed or not? Or what do you think about this?"

"I think their doctrine is well-proclaimed, revered sir."

"Then, householder, what do you think: those whose conduct is directed to the abandoning of greed, hatred and delusion, do they live well-conducted in this world or not? Or what do you think about this?"

"I think they are well-conducted, revered sir."

"And further, householder, what do you think: those in whom greed, hatred and delusion are abandoned, cut off at the root, made (barren) like a palm-stump, brought to non-existence, no longer liable to arise in the future again—are they the blessed ones in the world or not? Or what do you think about this?"

---

19. The words used here, "well-proclaimed" (*svākkhāta*), "well-conducted" (*supaṭipanna*) and "blessed ones" (*sugata*) are key words in the well-known formula of homage to the Dhamma, Sangha and the Buddha (in our text, in this sequence). The term *sugata*, "well-farer," was perhaps pre-Buddhist usage for a saintly person and was later on increasingly applied to the Buddha as one of his epithets. In Medieval India, the Buddhists were known as *Saugata*, the followers of the Sugata.

"Yes, I do think, revered sir, that these are the blessed ones in the world."

"So, householder, you have admitted this: Well-proclaimed is the creed of those who teach a doctrine for the abandoning of greed, hatred and delusion. Those are well-conducted whose conduct is directed to the abandoning of greed, hatred and delusion. And the blessed ones are those who have abandoned greed, hatred and delusion and have totally destroyed it in themselves."

"Wonderful, revered sir! Marvellous, revered sir! There was no extolling of your creed, nor a disparaging of another's creed. Just by keeping to the subject matter, the doctrine was explained by you. Only facts were spoken of and no selfish reference was brought in.

"It is excellent, revered sir, very excellent. It is as if one were to set aright what was overturned, reveal what was hidden, point the way to those who have lost it, hold up a light in the darkness so that those who have eyes may see what is visible. Thus was the teaching in diverse ways explained by the worthy Ānanda.

"I now go for refuge to that Exalted One, to his Teaching, and to the Order of monks. May master Ānanda accept me as a lay follower from this day onwards as long as life shall last. May he regard me as one who has thus taken refuge."

AN 3:71

Comment

This text introduces us to an unnamed lay follower of the Ājīvakas, a sect of naked ascetics contemporary with the Buddha. The questioner must have been a person of sensitivity, and was obviously disgusted with the self-advertisement he may have found in his own sect and among other contemporary religious teachers. So he wanted to test a disciple of the Buddha to see if they too indulged in self-praise. He even laid a trap for the venerable Ānanda, by phrasing his questions in terms of the well-known Buddhist formula of homage to the Triple Gem. Perhaps he expected that the venerable Ānanda would answer thus: "These are the very words we use, and we claim these achievements for our doctrine, for our monks and for our Buddha." But the venerable Ānanda's reply, being free from self-praise and blame of others, came as a happy surprise to him. And as the questioner was perceptive, he immediately grasped the profound significance of the venerable Ānanda's words connecting the Three Gems with the abandonment of the unwholesome roots. Moved to admiration for both the speaker and his teaching, the inquirer declared on the spot his dedication to the Triple Gem.

This dialogue between a non-Buddhist and a Buddhist monk suggests that the teaching on the three roots can be immediately convincing to anyone with an open mind and heart. It offers an eminently practical, non-creedal approach to the very core of the Dhamma, even for those reluctant to accept its other tenets. It is for this reason that the awareness of those three roots and their significance is elsewhere called a directly "visible teaching" (Text 20) and a doctrine that can be grasped without recourse to faith, tradition or ideologies (Text 33). It can be easily seen that greed, hatred and delusion are at the root of all individual and social conflict. Those who still hesitate to accept the Buddha's teaching on the truths of suffering and its origin in their entire range of validity may not be ready to admit that *all* degrees and varieties of greed, hatred and delusion are roots of suffering. Yet even if they only understand the more extreme forms of those three states to be the root causes of evil and unhappiness, such understanding, practically applied, will be immensely beneficial to themselves and to society.

From such an initial understanding and application, it may not be too difficult for an honest searching mind to proceed to the conclusion that even the very subtle tendencies towards greed, hatred and delusion are harmful—seeds from which their most destructive forms may grow. But the Dhamma is a gradual teaching: the extension of that initial understanding should be left to the natural growth of the individual's own insight and experience without being forced upon him. This was the very attitude which the Enlightened One himself observed in his way of teaching.

Following the example of the venerable Ānanda, it will be profitable also in the present day if, for various levels of understanding, the practical message of the Dhamma is formulated in terms of the wholesome and unwholesome roots. In its simplicity as well as its profundity, this teaching carries the distinct seal of Enlightenment. It is a teaching that will directly affect everyday life, and will also reach to the very depth of existence, showing the way to transcend all suffering.

24. The Purpose of the Teaching

Sīha, a general and formerly a disciple of the Nigaṇṭhas (Jains), once questioned the Buddha about various accusations levelled against him. One of them was that the Buddha taught a destructive doctrine and was a nihilist, a destroyer. The Buddha replied:

> "There is one way, Sīha, in which one might rightly speak of me as a destroyer, as one who teaches his doctrine with a destructive purpose: because I teach Dhamma for the purpose of destroying greed, hatred and delusion; for the destroying of manifold evil and unwholesome states of mind do I teach Dhamma."

AN 3:12

25. It Can Be Done

Abandon what is unwholesome, O monks! One *can* abandon the unwholesome, O monks! If it were not possible, I would not ask you to do so.

If this abandoning of the unwholesome would bring harm and suffering, I would not ask you to abandon it. But as the abandoning of the unwholesome brings benefit and happiness, therefore I say, "Abandon what is unwholesome!"

Cultivate what is wholesome, O monks! One *can* cultivate the wholesome, O monks! If it were not possible, I would not ask you to do so.

If this cultivation of the wholesome would bring harm and suffering, I would not ask you to cultivate it. But as the cultivation of the wholesome brings benefit and happiness, therefore I say, "Cultivate what is wholesome!"

AN 2:19

Comment

This text proclaims, in simple and memorable words, man's potential for achieving the good, thus invalidating the common charge that Buddhism is pessimistic. But since man also has, as we know only too well, a strong potential for evil, there is as little ground for unreserved optimism about him and his future. Which of his potentialities becomes actual—that for good or that for evil—depends on his own choice. What makes a person a full human being is facing choices and making use of them. The range of man's choices and his prior awareness of them expand with the growth of his mindfulness and wisdom, and as mindfulness and wisdom grow, those forces that seem to "condition" and even to compel his choices into a wrong direction become weakened.

These hope-inspiring words of the Buddha about man's positive potential will be grasped in their tremendous significance and their full range if we remember that the words wholesome and unwholesome are not limited to a narrow moral application. The wholesome that can be cultivated comprises everything beneficial, including those qualities of mind and heart which are indispensable for reaching the highest goal of final liberation. The unwholesome that can be abandoned includes even the finest traces of greed, hatred and delusion. It is, indeed, a bold and heartening assurance—a veritable "lion's roar"—when the Buddha said, with such wide implications, that what is beneficial can be cultivated and what is harmful can be abandoned.

26. The Arising and Non-Arising of the Roots

There may be outsiders, O monks, who will ask you:

"Now, friends, what is the cause and condition whereby unarisen greed arises and arisen greed becomes stronger and more powerful?" "An attractive object," they should be told. In him who gives unwise attention to an attractive object, unarisen greed will arise, and greed that has already arisen will become stronger and more powerful.

"Now, friends, what is the cause and condition whereby unarisen hatred arises and arisen hatred becomes stronger and more powerful?" "A repulsive object," they should be told. In him who gives unwise attention to a repulsive object, unarisen hatred will arise, and hatred that has already arisen will grow stronger and more powerful.

"Now, friends, what is the cause and condition whereby unarisen delusion arises and arisen delusion becomes stronger and more powerful?" "Unwise attention," they should be told.

In him who gives unwise attention, unarisen delusion will arise, and delusion that has already arisen will grow stronger and more powerful.

"Now, friends, what is the cause and condition for unarisen greed not to arise and for the abandoning of greed that has arisen?" "A (meditation) object of impurity," they should be told. In him who gives wise attention to a (meditation) object of impurity, unarisen greed will not arise and greed that has arisen will be abandoned.

"Now, friends, what is the cause and condition for unarisen hatred not to arise and for the abandoning of hatred that has arisen?" "Loving-kindness that is a freeing of the mind," they should be told. In him who gives wise attention to loving kindness that is a freeing of the mind, unarisen hatred will not arise and hatred that has arisen will be abandoned.

"Now, friends, what is the cause and condition for unarisen delusion not to arise and for the abandoning of delusion that has arisen?" "Wise attention," they should be told. In him who gives wise attention, unarisen delusion will not arise and delusion that has arisen will be abandoned.

AN 3:68

Comment

This text shows the decisive role attention plays in the origination and eradication of the unwholesome roots. In the discourse "All Taints" (Sabbāsava Sutta, MN 2) it is said: "The uninstructed common man ... does not know the things worthy of attention nor those unworthy of attention. Hence he fails to give attention to what is worthy of it and directs his attention to what is unworthy of it." And of the well-instructed disciple the same discourse says that he knows what is worthy of attention and what is not, and that he acts accordingly.

The commentary to that discourse makes a very illuminating remark: "There is nothing definite in the nature of the things (or objects) themselves that makes them worthy or unworthy of attention; but there is such definiteness in the *manner* (*ākāra*) of attention. A manner of attention that provides a basis for the arising of what is unwholesome or evil (*akusala*), that kind of attention should not be given (to the respective object); but the kind of attention that is the basis for the arising of the good and wholesome (*kusala*), that manner of attention should be given."

It is this latter type of attention that in our present text is called "wise attention" (*yoniso manasikāra*). The former kind is "unwise attention" (*ayoniso manasikāra*), which elsewhere in the commentaries is said to be the proximate cause of delusion.

Things pleasant or unpleasant—that is, those potentially attractive or repulsive—are given to us as facts of common experience, but there is nothing compelling in their own nature that determines our reaction to them. It is our own deliberate attitude towards them, the "manner of attention," which decides whether we will react with greed to the pleasant and with aversion to the unpleasant, or whether our attention will be governed instead by right mindfulness and right understanding, resulting in right action. In some cases, it will also be possible and advisable to withdraw or divert attention altogether from an object; and this is one of the methods recommended by the Buddha for the removal of unwholesome thoughts. (See Text 27 and Comment.)

Our freedom of choice is present in our very first reaction to a given experience, that is, in the way we attend to it. But only if we direct *wise* attention to the object perceived can we make use of our potential freedom of choice for our own true benefit. The range of freedom can be further widened if we train ourselves to raise that wise attention to the level of right mindfulness.

27. Five Methods for Removing Unwholesome Thoughts

A monk who is intent on the higher consciousness (of meditation) should from time to time give attention to five items. What five?

1. When, owing to an object to which the monk has given (wrong) attention, there arise in him evil unwholesome thoughts connected with desire,[20] with hatred and with delusion, then that monk should give his attention to a different object, to one connected with what is wholesome. When he is doing so, those evil unwholesome thoughts connected with desire, hatred and delusion are abandoned in him and subside. With their abandonment, his mind becomes inwardly steady and settled, unified and concentrated....

20. Here, the Pali term used is *chanda*, not *rāga* (lust) or *lobha* (greed).

2. If, when giving attention to an object that is wholesome, there still arise in him evil unwholesome thoughts connected with desire, with hatred and with delusion, then the monk should reflect upon the danger in these thoughts thus: "Truly, for such and such reasons these thoughts are unwholesome, they are reprehensible and result in suffering!" When he is reflecting in this way, those evil unwholesome thoughts are abandoned in him and subside. With their abandonment, his mind becomes inwardly steady and settled, unified and concentrated....

3. If, when reflecting upon the danger in these thoughts, there still arise in him evil unwholesome thoughts connected with desire, with hatred and with delusion, he should try not to be mindful of them, not to give attention to them. When he is not giving attention to them, those evil unwholesome thoughts will be abandoned in him and subside. With their abandonment, his mind becomes inwardly steady and settled, unified and concentrated....

4. If, when he is not giving attention to these thoughts, there still arise in him evil unwholesome thoughts connected with desire, with hatred and with delusion, he should give attention to the removal of the source of these thoughts.[21] When he is doing so, those evil unwholesome thoughts are abandoned in him and subside. With their abandonment, his mind becomes inwardly steady and settled, unified and concentrated....

5. If, while he is giving attention to the removal of the source of these thoughts, these evil unwholesome thoughts still arise in him, he should, with teeth clenched and the tongue pressed against the palate, restrain, subdue and suppress mind by mind.[22] When he is doing so, those evil unwholesome thoughts are abandoned in him and subside. With their abandonment, his mind becomes inwardly steady and settled, unified and concentrated....

When those evil unwholesome thoughts connected with desire, hate and delusion, which have arisen owing to (wrong)

---

21. This rendering follows the sutta's commentary, which explains the word *saṅkhāra* (in the phrase *vitakka-saṅkhāra-saṇṭhāna*) by condition, cause or root. An alternative rendering of this phrase would be "quieting the thought formations."

22. That is, he has to restrain the unwholesome state of mind by a wholesome state of mind, i.e., by his efforts to remove those unwholesome thoughts.

attention given to an object, have been abandoned in a monk and have subsided (due to his applying these five methods), and when (due to that) his mind has become steady and settled, unified and concentrated—then that monk is called a master of the pathways of thoughts: he will think the thoughts he wants to think and will not think those he does not want to think. He has cut off craving, severed the fetter (to existence) and with the full penetration of conceit, he has made an end of suffering.

MN 20 (Vitakkasaṇṭhāna Sutta)[23]

Comment

This Discourse on the Removal of Unwholesome Thoughts was addressed by the Buddha to monks devoted to meditation, especially to the attainment of the meditative absorptions (*jhāna*), which constitute the higher consciousness (*adhicitta*) mentioned in the sutta. But the five methods for stopping unwholesome thoughts are not restricted to those engaged in strict meditative practice. They are also helpful when desire, aversion and delusion arise during less intensive contemplations undertaken by monks or lay people. Even in situations of ordinary life, when one is confronted with an onrush of unwholesome thoughts, these methods will prove effective, provided one can muster the presence of mind needed to promptly apply them. In applying them, one will be practising right effort, the sixth factor of the Noble Eightfold Path. For the attempt to overcome arisen unwholesome thoughts is one of the four great efforts (*sammappadhāna*), constituting the path factor of right effort.

By the *first* method one tries to replace harmful thoughts by their beneficial opposites. The discourse gives the simile of a carpenter removing a coarse peg with the help of a fine peg. The commentary explains as follows: when an unwholesome thought of desire for a living being arises, one should counter it by thinking of the impurity of the body; if there is desire for an inanimate object, one should consider its impermanence and its ownerless nature. In the case of aversion against a living being, one should

23. For a complete translation, including the commentary, see *The Removal of Distracting Thoughts*, tr. by Soma Thera (Wheel No. 21).

direct thoughts of loving kindness and friendliness towards that being; one should remove resentment against inanimate things or against adverse situations by thinking of their impermanence and impersonal nature. When deluded or confused thoughts arise, one should make an effort to clarify them and discern things as they are.

The sutta statement deals with the case of countering undesirable thoughts immediately on their arising. For sustained success in substantially reducing and finally abolishing them, one should strengthen the wholesome roots opposed to them whenever one meets the opportunity to do so. Non-greed should be enhanced by selflessness, generosity and acts of renunciation; non-hate by patience and compassion; non-delusion by cultivating clarity of thought and a penetrative understanding of reality.

The *second* method for removing unwholesome thoughts is that of evoking repugnance and a sense of danger with regard to them. The simile in the discourse is that of a well-dressed young man or woman who feels horrified, humiliated and disgusted when the carcass of an animal is slung around his or her neck. Calling to mind the unworthiness of evil thoughts will produce a sense of shame (*hiri*) and abhorrence. The awareness that these unwholesome thoughts are harmful and dangerous will produce a deterring "dread of consequences" (*ottappa*). This method of evoking repugnance may also serve as an aid for returning to the first method of "replacement by good thoughts," unless one has now become able to check the intruding thoughts through the second method. This method can be very effective when encounters in ordinary life call for quick restraint of the mind.

By the *third* method one tries to ignore undesirable thoughts by diverting one's attention to other thoughts or activities. Here the simile is that of closing one's eyes at a disagreeable sight or looking in another direction. If this method is applied during a session of meditation, it may require a temporary interruption of the meditation. For a diverting occupation, the commentary gives as examples recitation, reading or looking through the contents of one's bag (or pocket). Reciting or reading may be helpful outside meditative practice, too. Until those troublesome thoughts have subsided, one might also take up some little work that requires attention.

The *fourth* method is illustrated in the discourse by a man who runs fast and then asks himself: "Why should I run?" and he slows down; he then continues that process of calming his activity by successively standing still, sitting and lying down. This simile suggests that this method involves a sublimating and refining of the coarse unwholesome thoughts. But as this sublimation is a slow and gradual process, it may not be applicable to a meditative situation when a quicker remedial action is required. The commentarial interpretation seems, therefore, to be preferable: one traces unwholesome thoughts back to the thoughts or the situation which caused them to arise and then tries to remove that thought source from one's mind. This may often be easier than confronting directly the full-grown end-result. It will also help to divert the mind (according to the third method) from those unwholesome thoughts, which at this stage may be hard to dislodge. We may thus describe the fourth method as "tracing the thought source." But from the longer view of a continued endeavour to eliminate the harmful thoughts, interpreting this method as sublimation and gradual refinement need not be excluded. Such refinement can reduce the intensity and the immoral quality of the three unwholesome roots and even divert their energy into wholesome channels.

The *fifth* and last method is that of vigorous suppression. This method is to be applied when unwholesome thoughts have gained such a strength that they threaten to become unmanageable and to bring about situations of grave peril, practically and morally. The discourse illustrates this method by a strong-bodied man forcing down a weaker person by sheer physical strength.

If the application of these five methods is not neglected but is kept alive in meditative practice as well as in ordinary circumstances, one can expect a marked and progressive weakening of the three unwholesome roots, culminating in the perfect mastery of thoughts promised at the end of the sutta.

28. For One's Own Sake

For one's own sake, monks, vigilant mindfulness should be made the mind's guard and this for four reasons:

"May my mind not harbour lust for anything inducing lust!"—for this reason vigilant mindfulness should be made the mind's guard, for one's own sake.

"May my mind not harbour hatred toward anything inducing hatred!"—for this reason vigilant mindfulness should be made the mind's guard, for one's own sake.

"May my mind not harbour delusion concerning anything inducing delusion!"—for this reason vigilant mindfulness should be made the mind's guard, for one's own sake.

"May my mind not be infatuated by anything inducing infatuation!"—for this reason vigilant mindfulness should be made the mind's guard, for one's own sake.

When now, monks, a monk's mind does not harbour lust for lust-inducing things, because he is free from lust;

when his mind does not harbour hatred toward hate-inducing things, because he is free from hatred;

when his mind does not harbour delusion concerning anything inducing delusion, because he is free from delusion;

when his mind is not infatuated by anything inducing infatuation, because he is free from infatuation—then such a monk will not waver, shake or tremble; he will not succumb to fear, nor will he adopt the views of other recluses.[24]

AN 4:17

29. The Noble Power

Monks, it is good for a monk if, from time to time:

he perceives the repulsive in the unrepulsive,

if he perceives the unrepulsive in the repulsive,

if he perceives the repulsive in both the unrepulsive and the repulsive,

if he perceives the unrepulsive in both the repulsive and the unrepulsive,

if he avoids both the repulsive and the unrepulsive (aspects), and dwells in equanimity, mindful and clearly comprehending.

But with what motive should a monk perceive the repulsive in the unrepulsive? "May no lust arise in me for lust-inducing objects!"—it is with such a motive that he should perceive in this way.

24. That is, other religious or philosophical ideas.

With what motive should he perceive the unrepulsive in the repulsive? "May no hatred arise in me towards hate-inducing objects!"—it is with such a motive that he should perceive in this way.

With what motive should he perceive the repulsive in the unrepulsive as well as in the repulsive? "May no lust arise in me for lust-inducing objects nor hatred towards hate-inducing objects!"—it is with such a motive that he should perceive in this way.

With what motive should he perceive the unrepulsive in the repulsive as well as in the unrepulsive? "May no hatred arise in me towards lust-inducing objects nor lust for lust-inducing objects!"—it is with such a motive that he should perceive in this way.

With what motive should he avoid both the repulsive and the unrepulsive, and dwell in equanimity, mindful and clearly comprehending? "May lust for lust-inducing objects, hatred towards hate-inducing objects and delusion towards deluding objects never arise in me anywhere in any way!"—it is with such a motive that he should avoid both the repulsive and the unrepulsive, and dwell in equanimity, mindful and clearly comprehending.

AN 5:144

Comment

This fivefold method of mastering perception is called in Pali *ariya-iddhi*, a term which may be rendered as noble power, noble success or noble magic; or, alternatively, as the power, success or magic of the noble ones (*ariya*). In its perfection, this arduous practice can be ascribed only to Arahats, as several suttas and commentaries indicate. But, as our text shows at the beginning, the Buddha recommended this training to the monks in general, including those in whom the three unwholesome roots were still active. It is for eradication of these roots that is said to be the motivation for taking up this practice.

For applying this fivefold power, the following directions have been given in the Canon and commentaries.[25]

25. Compiled from the Paṭisambhidāmagga and commentaries to the Dīgha Nikāya and Aṅguttara Nikāya.

1. To perceive the repulsive in the unrepulsive, one pervades attractive living beings with the contemplation of the body's impurity; towards attractive inanimate objects one applies the contemplation of impermanence.

2. To perceive the unrepulsive in the repulsive, one pervades repulsive living beings with loving kindness and views repulsive inanimate objects as consisting of the four elements; but living beings too ought to be contemplated by way of the elements.

3. To perceive the repulsive in both the unrepulsive and the repulsive, one pervades both with the contemplation of impurity and applies to them the contemplation of impermanence. Or, if one has first judged a being to be attractive and later repulsive, one now regards it as unrepulsive throughout, i.e., from the viewpoint of impurity and impermanence.[26]

4. To perceive the unrepulsive in both the repulsive and the unrepulsive, one pervades both with loving kindness and views both as bare elements. Or, if one has first judged a being to be repulsive and later attractive, one now regards it as unrepulsive throughout; i.e., from the viewpoint of loving kindness and as consisting of elements.

5. Avoiding both aspects, one applies the six-factored equanimity of which it is said: "On perceiving (any of the six sense objects, including mental objects), he is neither glad nor sad, but keeps to equanimity and is mindful and clearly comprehending." He does not lust after a desirable object nor does he hate an undesirable one; and where others thoughtlessly allow delusion to arise, he does not give room to delusion. He remains equanimous towards the six objects, being equipped with the six-factored equanimity which does not abandon the pure natural state of the mind.

These five methods of applying the noble power have several applications. They are first for use during meditation, when images of repulsive and unrepulsive beings or things arise in the mind. At such a time one can overcome the attraction or aversion by dwelling on the counteractive ideas—such as loving kindness or

26. "Owing to a change in one's own attitude towards a person or due to a change in character (or behaviour) of that person." Sub. Comy. to Majjhima Nikāya.

analysis into elements—as long as required to dispel the defilements. Second, these methods can be used in the encounters of everyday life when the counteractive ideas must be tersely formulated and rapidly applied. This will require previous familiarity with them and alertness of mind. In encounters with repulsive people one may also think of their good qualities and of their common human nature, with its failings and sufferings. When meeting a physically attractive person, one may vividly visualize that person's body as subject to ageing and decay.

These five modes of perception, as perfected in the Arahat, reveal the high-point of the mind's sovereign mastery over the world of feelings and emotions. They show a state where the response to provocative objects, usually so habitually fixed, can be chosen at will. This approach differs from that used in the contemplation of feelings as shown below (Text 35). In the latter the feeling-values of experience are accepted as they are given, but by applying bare attention to them, one "stops short" at the feelings themselves without allowing them to grow into the passionate reactions of lust or aversion. However, in this method of the noble power, the meditator does not take the feeling-values for granted; he does not accept them as they present themselves. His response is to reverse the feeling-value (mode 1, 2), to equalize the response to the repulsive and the unrepulsive (mode 3, 4) and to transcend both by mindful equanimity (mode 5).

These fives modes thus constitute a subtle "magic of transformation" by which pleasant and unpleasant feelings, as they habitually arise, can be changed at will or replaced by equanimity. A mind that has gone through this training has passed the most severe test, indeed. Through that training, it obtains an increasing control over emotive reactions, and internal independence from the influence of habits and passions. It is said in the Satipaṭṭhāna Sutta, "He dwells independent and clings to nothing." These words conclude a statement recurring after each of the exercises given in the sutta. In the light of the above observations, it is significant that they also occur after the section on contemplation of feelings found in that sutta.

According to our text, the purpose for cultivating the noble power is the eradication of greed, hatred and delusion. In a mind disciplined in this radical training, the root defilements cannot find a fertile soil for growth. The training also provides the experiential basis for comprehending the true nature of feelings as being relative and subjective. This the five modes of the noble power demonstrate in a convincing way. The relativity of feelings and of the emotions roused by them was succinctly expressed by Āryadeva (2nd century CE):

By the same thing lust is incited in one, hate in the other, delusion in the next. Hence sense objects have no inherent value.

Catuḥ-Śataka, 8:177

Perfection in applying this noble power is the domain only of the truly noble ones, the Arahats, whose mastery of mind and strength of will are equal to the task of exercising it effortlessly. But also on much lower levels, an earnest endeavour to develop this noble power will be of great benefit. In the text here commented upon, the Buddha does not restrict the cultivation of the noble power to Arahats, but begins his exposition with the words: "It is good for a monk...." We may add: not only for a monk. Prior practice of right mindfulness (*satipaṭṭhāna*), however, will be indispensable. Of particular importance is the contemplation of feelings, by which one learns to distinguish between the feeling linked with a perception and the subsequent emotional reaction to it.

30. The Four Ways of Progress

There are four ways of progress: difficult progress with slow understanding, difficult progress with swift understanding, easy progress with slow understanding and easy progress with swift understanding.*

What is the difficult progress with slow understanding? There is one who naturally has strong greed, strong hatred and strong delusion, and caused by it he often suffers pain and grief. The five faculties, namely, faith, energy, mindfulness, concentration and wisdom,** appear in him only in a weak state; and due to their weakness he attains but slowly the immediate condition for the destruction of the taints.***

What is the difficult progress with swift understanding? There is one who naturally has strong greed, strong hatred and strong delusion, and caused by it he often suffers pain and grief. But the five faculties, namely, faith, energy, mindfulness, concentration and wisdom, appear in him in a very strong degree, and due to their strength he attains swiftly the immediate condition for the destruction of the taints.

What is the easy progress with slow understanding? There is one who naturally is without strong greed, strong hatred and strong delusion, and therefore he does not often suffer pain and grief, caused by them. The five faculties, however, appear in him only in a weak state; and due to their weakness he attains only slowly the immediate condition for the destruction of the taints.

What is the easy progress with swift understanding? There is one who naturally is without strong greed, strong hatred and strong delusion, and therefore he does not often suffer pain and grief, caused by them. The five faculties, namely, faith, energy, mindfulness, concentration and wisdom, appear in him in a very strong degree; and due to their strength he attains swiftly to the immediate condition for the destruction of the taints.

AN 4:162

Comments

* For the four ways of progress (*catasso paṭipadā*), see *The Path of Purification* (*Visuddhimagga*), pp. 87 ff. In the case of "difficult progress" (*dukkha-paṭipadā*), the term *dukkha* has three different connotations: (1) Difficult, (2) painful due to the presence of strong greed, etc., (3) "unpleasant" if progress is achieved with an unpleasant subject of meditation such as the foulness of the body. In the case of easy progress (*sukha-paṭipadā*), *sukha* refers: (a) to a relatively easy conquest of the passions, which thus do not cause much suffering; (b) to the happiness experienced during the meditative absorptions (*jhāna*), which likewise constitute the happy mode of progress.

** Well-balanced and strongly developed faculties (*indriya*) are the essential mental tools for successful insight meditation (*vipassanā*), culminating in Arahatship. On the faculties, see *The Way of Wisdom* by Edward Conze, Wheel No. 65/66.

*** "Immediate condition" (*ānantariyaṃ*), according to the commentary, refers to the concentration of mind associated with the path (of Arahatship; *magga-samādhi*). This concentration, lasting for a single moment, precedes the immediately following attainment to the fruition of Arahatship, where the destruction of the taints (*āsavānaṃ khaya*) reaches its consummation.

VI. Removal through Mindfulness and Insight

31. To Be Abandoned by Seeing

Which are the things, O monks, that can be abandoned neither by bodily acts nor by speech, but can be abandoned by wisely seeing them? Greed can be abandoned neither by bodily acts nor by speech; but it can be abandoned by wisely seeing it. Hatred can be abandoned neither by bodily acts nor by speech; but it can be abandoned by wisely seeing it. Delusion can be abandoned neither by bodily acts nor by speech; but it can be abandoned by wisely seeing it.

AN 10:23

Comment

"Wisely seeing," according to the commentary, refers here to the wisdom pertaining to the paths of emancipation along with the insight that culminates in the paths. From this explanation it follows that the term *abandoning* has to be understood here in its strict sense, as final and total elimination, effected by realization of the paths of emancipation (stream-entry, etc.).

Nevertheless, a weakening of the unwholesome roots can be effected also by body and speech, through curbing more and more their outward manifestations in deeds and words, motivated by greed, hatred and delusion.

The phrase "wisely seeing" may serve to emphasize the crucial importance of mindfully observing the presence or absence of the unwholesome roots within one's own mind flux. This repeated confrontation with them prepares the way to liberating insight.

32. From the Satipaṭṭhāna Sutta

And how, monks, does a monk dwell practising mind-contemplation on the mind?

Herein a monk knows the mind with lust as with lust; the mind without lust as without lust; the mind with hatred as with hatred; the mind without hatred as without hatred; the mind with delusion as with delusion; the mind without delusion as without delusion....

Thus he dwells practising mind-contemplation on the mind, internally, or externally, or both internally and externally. He dwells contemplating the states of origination in the mind, or he dwells contemplating the states of dissolution in the mind, or he dwells contemplating the states of both origination and dissolution in the mind. Or his mindfulness that "there is mind" is established in him to the extent necessary for knowledge and awareness. He dwells detached, clinging to nothing in the world.

MN 10

33. Beyond Faith

"Is there a way, O monks, by which a monk, without recourse to faith, to cherished opinions, to tradition, to specious reasoning or to preference for his preconceived views, may declare the final knowledge (of Arahatship), thus: 'Rebirth has ceased, the holy life has been lived, completed is the task and nothing remains after this'?

"There is such a way, O monks. And what is it?

"Herein, monks, a monk has seen a form with his eyes, and if greed, hatred and delusion are in him, he knows 'There is in me greed, hatred and delusion'; and if greed, hatred and delusion are absent in him, he knows 'There is no greed, hatred and delusion in me.'

"Further, monks, a monk has heard a sound, smelled an odour, tasted a flavour, felt a tactile sensation or cognized a mental object, and if greed, hatred and delusion are in him, he knows 'There is in me greed, hatred and delusion'; and if greed, hatred and delusion are absent in him, he knows 'There is no greed, hatred and delusion in me.'

"And if he thus knows, O monks, are these ideas such as to be known by recourse to faith, to cherished opinions, to tradition, to specious reasoning or to preference for one's preconceived views?"

"Certainly not, Lord."

"Are these not rather ideas to be known after wisely realizing them by experience?"

"That is so, Lord."

"This, monks, is a way by which a monk, without recourse to faith, to cherished opinions, to tradition, to specious reasoning or to preference for his preconceived views, may declare final knowledge (of Arahatship), thus: 'Rebirth has ceased, the holy life has been lived, completed is the task and nothing more remains after this.'"

SN 35:153

34. The Visible Teaching[27]

Once the venerable Upavāna went to the Exalted One, saluted him respectfully and sat down at one side. Thus seated he addressed the Exalted One as follows:

"People speak of the 'visible teaching.' In how far, Lord, is the teaching visible here and now, of immediate result, inviting to come and see, onward-leading, to be directly experienced by the wise?"

"Herein, Upavāna, a monk, having seen a form with his eyes, experiences the form and experiences desire for the form.[28] Of the desire for forms present in him, he knows: 'There is in me a desire for forms.' If a monk, having seen a form with his eyes, experiencing the form and experiencing desire for the form, knows that desire for forms is present in him—in so far, Upavāna, is the teaching visible here and now, of immediate result, inviting to come and see, onward-leading, to be directly experienced by the wise.

"It is similar if a monk experiences desire when he hears a sound with his ears, smells an odour with his nose, tastes a flavour with his tongue, feels a tangible with his body or cognizes an idea with his mind. If he knows in each case that desire is present in him—in so far, Upavāna, is the teaching visible here and now, of immediate result, inviting to come and see, onward-leading, to be directly experienced by the wise.

---

27. See also Text 20.

28. Though this text refers only to desire (*rāga*, "lust"), the statements in it are also valid for a reaction to the sixfold sense perception by hatred and delusion.

"Further, Upavāna, a monk, having seen a form with his eyes, experiences the form without experiencing desire for the form. Of the absent desire for form he knows: 'There is in me no desire for forms.' If a monk, having seen a form with his eyes, experiencing the form without experiencing desire for the form, knows that desire for forms is not present in him—in so far, too, Upavāna, is the teaching visible here and now, of immediate result, inviting to come and see, onward-leading, to be directly experienced by the wise.

"It is similar if a monk does not experience desire when he hears a sound with his ears, smells an odour with his nose, tastes a flavour with his tongue, feels a tangible with his body or cognizes an idea with his mind. If he knows in each case that desire is not present in him—in so far, Upavāna, is the teaching visible here and now, of immediate result, inviting to come and see, onward-leading, to be directly experienced by the wise."

SN 35:70

Comment on Texts 32–34

When thoughts connected with greed (desire, attraction), hatred (anger, aversion) or delusion (prejudices, false views) arise in an untrained mind, generally one reacts to them in one of two ways: either one allows oneself to be carried away by them or one tries to repress them. The first type of reaction is a full identification with the unwholesome roots; the second extreme is the attempt to ignore their presence, shirking a confrontation with them. In this latter case, one regards the defiled thoughts as a disreputable part of one's mind, harmful to one's self-esteem, and thus blots them out from one's awareness.

The approach through *bare attention,* as indicated in the above texts, is a middle way that avoids these two extremes. It involves neither passive submission nor anxious recoil, but a full awareness of the unwholesome thoughts while holding to the mental post of detached observation. These thoughts will then be seen simply as psychological events, as impersonal and conditioned mental processes, as "mere phenomena rolling on" (*suddhadhammā pavattanti*). When thus objectified, they will no longer initiate emotional reactions by way of attachment, aversion or fear. Bare attention empties these thoughts of self-reference and prevents the identification with them as a fictive ego. Thus the confrontation even with one's imperfections may give rise to a clear realization of egolessness. From that, again, there may emerge the state of mind described in the Satipaṭṭhāna Sutta: "He dwells detached, clinging to nothing." It will now be understood why, in Texts 32 and 34, it is said that even the awareness of the unwholesome in oneself can make the teaching "visible here and now."

This application of detached awareness can be said to belong to the first method of Text 27, replacing the arisen unwholesome thoughts by the wholesome ones of right mindfulness. Even if one does not fully succeed with this method, a sober, factual awareness of the inherent danger, according to the second method, may prove to be effective. If not, one may then be obliged to use the stronger emotional impact of repugnance to eliminate them.

35. Removal through the Contemplation of Feelings

In the case of pleasant feelings, O monks, the underlying tendency to lust should be given up; in the case of painful feelings the underlying tendency to resistance (aversion) should be given up; in the case of neutral feelings, the underlying tendency to ignorance should be given up.

If a monk has given up the tendency to lust in regard to pleasant feelings, the tendency to resistance in regard to painful feelings and the tendency to ignorance in regard to neutral feelings, then he is called one who is free of unwholesome tendencies, one who has the right outlook. He has cut off craving, severed the fetter to existence, and, through the full penetration of conceit, he has made an end of suffering.[29]

If one feels joy, but knows not feeling's nature,
Bent towards greed, one will not find deliverance.

If one feels pain, but knows not feeling's nature,
Bent towards hate, one will not find deliverance.

29. "Conceit" refers in particular to "self-conceit" (*asmi-māna*), on both the intellectual and emotional levels.

And even neutral feeling which as peaceful
The Lord of Wisdom has proclaimed,
If, in attachment, one should cling to it,
One will not be free from the round of ill.

But if a monk is ardent and does not neglect
To practise mindfulness and comprehension clear,
The nature of all feelings will he penetrate.

And having done so, in this very life
He will be free from cankers and all taints.
Mature in knowledge, firm in Dhamma's ways,
When once his life-span ends, his body breaks,
All measure and concepts he will transcend.

SN 36:3

Comment

In these three "underlying tendencies" (*anusaya*), we encounter the three unwholesome roots under different names. These tendencies are defilements which, by repeated occurrence, have become habitual responses to situations provoking greed, hate and delusion, and hence tend to appear again and again. They may also be called inherent propensities of the mind. Underlying the stream of consciousness in a state of latency, they are always ready to spring up when a stimulus incites them, manifesting themselves as unwholesome deeds, words or thoughts. By having grown into underlying tendencies, the three roots obtain a most tenacious hold on the mind. Even moral conduct (*sīla*) and concentration (*samādhi*), by themselves, cannot prevail against the tendencies; at best they can only check their outward manifestations. To uproot the tendencies at the level of depth, what is required is insight-wisdom (*vipassanā-paññā*), aided by virtue and concentration. The insight-wisdom needed to fully uproot the three must have the strength acquired at the two final stages of emancipation, non-return and Arahatship.[30]

The non-returner eliminates completely the tendency to resistance or aversion, i.e., the root "hatred"; the tendency to lust,

30. See *Manual of Insight*, Ledi Sayādaw (Wheel No. 31/32), pp. 81 ff.

i.e., the root "greed," he eliminates as far as it extends to desire for the five outer sense pleasures.

The Arahat eliminates the remaining tendency to lust, the desire for fine-material and immaterial existence, and also all tendencies to ignorance, the root "delusion."

Though not able to effect a final elimination of the underlying tendencies, moral restraint in bodily and verbal acts helps to reduce the active formation of *new* unwholesome tendencies, and concentration helps to control the *mental* source of such tendencies, at least temporarily. Insight-wisdom attained on levels lower than the noble paths and fruitions will provide the basis for gradual progress toward the full maturation of liberating wisdom.

The type of insight practice which is particularly efficacious in weakening and removing the underlying tendencies is the Satipaṭṭhāna method called the contemplation of feelings (*vedanānupassanā*). It is the uncontrolled reaction to feelings that produces and nourishes the tendencies. According to Buddhist psychology, the feelings one passively undergoes in sense experience are morally neutral. They are *results* of *kamma*, not creators of *kamma*. It is the reaction to feelings following the passive sense encounters that determines the wholesome or unwholesome quality of the responsive active states of consciousness. In the contemplation of feelings, one distinctly realizes that a pleasant feeling is not identical with lust and need not be followed by it; that an unpleasant feeling is not identical with aversion and need not be followed by it; that a neutral feeling is not identical with ignorant, deluded thoughts and need not be followed by them. In that practice, the meditator learns to stop at the bare experience of pleasant, painful and neutral feelings. By doing so, he makes a definite start in cutting through the chain of dependent origination at that decisive point where feeling becomes the condition for craving (*vedanāpaccayā taṇhā*). It will thus become the meditator's indubitable experience that the causal sequence of feeling and craving is not a necessary one, and that the Buddha's words of encouragement are true: "One *can* abandon the unwholesome! If it were not possible, I would not ask you to do so." (See Text 25.)

36. The Dart

An untaught worldling, O monks, experiences a pleasant feeling, he experiences a painful feeling or he experiences a neutral feeling. A well-taught noble disciple likewise experiences a pleasant feeling, a painful feeling or a neutral feeling. Now, what is the distinction, the diversity, the difference that obtains here between a well-taught noble disciple and an untaught worldling?

When an untaught worldling is touched by a painful feeling, he worries, grieves and laments, beats his breast, weeps and is distraught. He then experiences two kinds of feelings, a bodily and a mental feeling. It is as if a man were pierced by a dart, and following the first piercing, he is hit by a second dart. So he will experience feelings caused by two darts. It is similar with an untaught worldling: when touched by a painful (bodily) feeling, he worries and grieves; he laments, beats his breast, weeps and is distraught. So he experiences two feelings, a bodily and a mental feeling.

Having been touched by that painful feeling, he resists (and resents) it.[31] Then in him who so resists (and resents) that painful feeling, an underlying tendency of resistance against that painful feeling, comes to underlie (his mind).[32] Under the impact of that painful feeling he then proceeds to enjoy sensual happiness. And why does he do so? An untaught worldling, monks, does not know of any other escape from painful feelings except the enjoyment of sensual happiness. Then in him who enjoys sensual happiness, an underlying tendency to lust for pleasant feelings comes to underlie (his mind). He does not know, according to facts, the arising and ending of those feelings, nor the gratification, the danger and the escape connected with them. In him who lacks that knowledge, an underlying tendency to ignorance as to neutral feelings comes to underlie (his mind). When he experiences a pleasant feeling or a painful feeling or a neutral feeling, he feels it as one fettered by it. Such a one, O monks, is called an untaught worldling who is fettered by birth, by old age, by death, by sorrow, lamentation, pain, grief and despair. He is fettered to suffering, this I declare.

---

31. *Paṭighavā hoti.*

32. *Paṭighānusayo anuseti*: that is, the underlying tendency manifests itself at that time, and is also strengthened by that manifestation.

But in the case of a well-taught noble disciple, O monks, when he is touched by a painful feeling, he does not worry, nor grieve and lament, he does not beat his breast and weep, nor is he distraught. It is one feeling he experiences: a bodily one, but not a mental feeling. It is as if a man were pierced by a dart, but he was not hit by a second dart following the first one. So this person experiences feelings caused by a single dart only. It is similar with a well-taught noble disciple: when touched by a painful feeling, he does not worry, nor grieve and lament, he does not beat his breast and weep, nor is he distraught. He experiences one single feeling, a bodily one.

Having been touched by that painful feeling, he does not resist (and resent it). Then in him who does not resist (and resent) that painful feeling, no underlying tendency of resistance against that painful feeling comes to underlie (his mind). Hence, under the impact of the painful feeling he does not proceed to enjoy sensual happiness. And why not? As a well-taught noble disciple, he knows of an escape from painful feelings other than the enjoyment of sensual happiness. Then in him who thus does not proceed to enjoy sensual happiness, no underlying tendency to lust for pleasant feeling comes to underlie (his mind). He knows, according to facts, the arising and ending of those feelings, and the gratification, the danger and the escape connected with them. In him who knows thus, no underlying tendency to ignorance as to neutral feelings comes to underlie (his mind). When he experiences a pleasant feeling, or a painful feeling, or a neutral feeling, he feels it as one who is not fettered by it. Such a one, O monks, is called a well-taught noble disciple who is not fettered by birth, by old age, by death; not fettered by sorrow, lamentation, pain, grief and despair. He is not fettered to suffering, this I declare.

This, O monks, is the distinction, the diversity, the difference that obtains between a well-taught noble disciple and an untaught worldling.

SN 36:6

37. The Elimination of the Tendencies Arising from Sixfold Sense Perception

Dependent on eye and forms, eye-consciousness arises; dependent on ear and sounds, ear-consciousness arises; dependent on nose and smells, nose-consciousness arises; dependent on tongue and flavours, tongue-consciousness arises; dependent on body and tangibles, body-consciousness arises; dependent on mind and mental objects, mind-consciousness arises.

The meeting of the three is contact, and with contact as condition there arises what is felt as pleasant or painful or neutral. If, when touched by pleasant feeling, one does not enjoy it or affirm or accept it, then no underlying tendency to lust any longer underlies it. If, when touched by painful feeling, one does not worry, grieve and lament, does not beat one's breast and weep, and is not distraught, then no underlying tendency to resistance any longer underlies it. If, when touched by a neutral feeling, one understands, according to facts, the arising and ending of that feeling, and the gratification, danger and escape (connected with it), then no underlying tendency to ignorance any longer underlies it. Then, indeed, O monks, that one shall here and now make an end of suffering by abandoning the underlying tendency to lust for pleasant feelings, by eliminating the underlying tendency to resistance against painful feelings, and by abolishing the underlying tendency to ignorance in the case of natural feelings, having thus given up ignorance and produced true knowledge—this is possible.

MN 148

38. Non-returning

If you give up three things, O monks, I vouchsafe you the state of non-returning. What are these three things? They are greed, hatred and delusion.

The greed infatuated by which
beings go to evil destiny,
those of insight give it up
because they fully understand that greed;
and having thus discarded it,
they never return to this world.

The hate enraged by which
beings go to evil destiny,
those of insight give it up
because they fully understand that hate;
and having thus discarded it,
they never return to this world.

The delusion blinded by which
beings go to evil destiny,
those of insight give it up,
because they fully understand delusion;
and having thus discarded it,
they never return to this world.

Condensed from It 1–3

VII. The Goal

39. The Visible Nibbāna

When greed, hatred and delusion are abandoned, one neither aims at one's own harm, nor at the harm of others, nor at the harm of both, and one will not suffer pain and grief in one's mind. In that sense is Nibbāna visible here and now.

If one experiences the complete elimination of greed, the complete elimination of hatred, the complete elimination of delusion, in that sense is Nibbāna visible here and now, of immediate result, inviting to come and see, onward-leading, to be directly experienced by the wise.

AN 3:56

40. What Is Nibbāna?

A wandering ascetic, Jambukhādaka by name, approached the venerable Sāriputta and asked him the following question:

"One speaks about 'Nibbāna.' Now, what is that Nibbāna, friend?"

"It is the elimination of greed, the elimination of hatred, the elimination of delusion—this, friend, is called Nibbāna."

"But is there a way, is there a path, friend, for the realization of that Nibbāna?"

"Yes, friend, there is such a way, there is a path for the realization of that Nibbāna. It is the Noble Eightfold Path, namely, right understanding, right thought, right speech, right action, right livelihood, right effort, right mindfulness and right concentration."

SN 38:1

41. Two Aspects of Nibbāna

This was said by the Blessed One, spoken by the Holy One, and thus I have heard:

There are, O monks, two aspects of Nibbāna: the Nibbāna-element with the groups of existence still remaining (*sa-upādisesa-nibbānadhātu*), and the Nibbāna-element with no groups remaining (*anupādisesa-nibbānadhātu*).

What now is the Nibbāna-element with the groups of existence still remaining? In that case, O monks, a monk is an Arahat: he is taint-free, has fulfilled the holy life, accomplished his task, thrown off the burden, attained his goal, cast off the fetters of existence and is liberated through right wisdom. But there still remain with him (until his death) the five sense-organs that have not yet disappeared and through which he still experiences what is pleasant and unpleasant, as well as bodily ease and pain. The extinction of greed, hatred and delusion in him, this is called the Nibbāna-element with the groups of existence still remaining.

And what is the Nibbāna-element with no groups of existence remaining? In that case, O monks, a monk is an Arahat ... liberated through right wisdom. In him, all those feelings, no longer relished, will even here (at his death) come to extinction. This is called the Nibbāna-element with no groups of existence remaining.

It 44
(Adapted from the translation by
Ñāṇatiloka Mahāthera)

42. The Happiness of Liberation

He, the Arahat, knows this:

"Once there was greed, and that was evil; now that is no more, and so it is well. Once there was hatred, and that was evil; now that is no more, and so it is well. Once there was delusion, and that was evil; now that is no more, and so it is well."

Thus the Arahat lives, even during his lifetime, free of craving's hunger, stilled and cooled (of passion's heat), feeling happy, with his heart become holy.

AN 3:66

VIII. The Roots in the Abhidhamma

In the *Dhammasaṅgaṇī*, the first book of the Abhidhamma Piṭaka, the three unwholesome roots are used for a classification of unwholesome consciousness into twelve classes: eight "rooted in greed" (*lobha-mūla*), two "rooted in hatred" (*dosa-mūla*) and two "rooted in delusion" (*moha-mūla*). These names for the three divisions of unwholesome consciousness are used in the *Visuddhimagga*.[33] The names do not occur in the *Dhammasaṅgaṇī* itself, but the roots are clearly implied. Consciousness rooted in hate is described there as "associated with resentment" (or resistance, *paṭigha-sampayutta*).

The states of consciousness rooted in greed and hatred have delusion as a second root. Delusion, however, can also appear as a single root, without the presence of greed or hatred.

Both the good and the evil roots also occur, of course, in the lists of the mental concomitants (*cetasika*) of wholesome and unwholesome consciousness, respectively.

The wholesome roots, under the name of *hetu*, "root cause," serve also for a classification of rebirth consciousness.

Rebirth as a human being is always the result of good *kamma* (*kusala-vipāka*). As rebirth consciousness is a resultant of *kamma*, and not *kamma* in itself, the root causes accompanying it are "kammically indeterminate" (*abyākata-hetu*). In human rebirth consciousness, there may be either three accompanying root causes (*ti-hetuka-paṭisandhi*), or when lacking non-delusion, two (*dvi-hetuka-paṭisandhi*) or, in rare cases, none (*ahetuka-paṭisandhi*). In three-rooted rebirth, the strength or weakness of the roots may differ widely. In two-rooted rebirth, the absence of non-delusion, of course, does not mean the entire absence of intelligence, but a complete inability to understand reality and, especially, the Four Noble Truths. Rootless rebirth (*ahetuka-paṭisandhi*) occurs throughout the four lower worlds of misery (animals, ghosts,

---

33. In the medieval Abhidhamma manuals such as the *Abhidhammatthasaṅgaha*, the nomenclature is: *lobha-sahagata* (accompanied by greed), *paṭigha-sampayutta* (associated with resentment) and *momūha* (strongly delusive).

demons and hellish beings); among humans it is restricted to those born blind, deaf, crippled, mentally deficient, etc.

In almost every human being there is some potential for the good, as human rebirth is always the result of wholesome *kamma*. We said "almost," because for mentally deficient human beings this potential is greatly handicapped; but not necessarily so for other humans reborn without wholesome root causes (*ahetuka*), as for instance those born crippled, etc. Whether that potential for good is activated and strengthened, or weakened and even lost, depends to a great extent on the type of roots prevailing in the rebirth-producing *kamma* of the previous life. For this has a strong formative influence on the character tendencies of the present existence, as the following commentarial text will show.

43. The Exposition of Prevalence

In some beings greed is prevalent, in others hatred or delusion; and again in others, non-greed, non-hatred or non-delusion are prevalent. What is it that governs this prevalence? It is the root-cause in the previous life that governs the prevalence of roots in the present life.

There is differentiation at the very moment of the accumulating of *kamma*. In one person, at the moment of (rebirth-producing) *kamma*-accumulation, greed is strong and non-greed is weak, non-hatred and non-delusion are strong and hatred and delusion are weak; then his weak non-greed is unable to prevail over his greed, but non-hatred and non-delusion, being strong, can prevail over his hatred and delusion. Hence when a being is born through rebirth-linking caused by that *kamma*, he will be greedy, good-natured, not irascible, intelligent and having knowledge that can be likened to a lightning flash.

In another case, at the moment of *kamma*-accumulation, greed and hatred are strong, and non-greed and non-hatred are weak, but non-delusion is strong and delusion weak; then, in the way stated, that person will have both greed and hatred, but he will be intelligent and have flash-like knowledge like the Elder Dattābhaya.

When, at the moment of *kamma*-accumulation, greed, non-hatred and delusion are strong and the other roots are weak, then, in the way stated, that person will be greedy and dull-witted, but he will be good-natured and not irascible.

When, at the moment of *kamma*-accumulation, the three roots, greed, hatred and delusion are strong and non-greed, etc., are weak, then, in the way stated, that person will be greedy, given to hatred and given to delusion.

When, at the moment of *kamma*-accumulation, non-greed, hatred and delusion are strong and the others are weak, then, in the way stated, that person will have few (lustful) defilements, being unmoved even when seeing a heavenly sense-object; but he will be given to hatred and his understanding will be slow.

When, at the moment of *kamma*-accumulation, non-greed, non-hatred and delusion are strong, and the others weak, then, in the way stated, that person will not be greedy and will be good-natured, but he will be slow of understanding.

When, at the moment of *kamma*-accumulation, non-greed, hatred and non-delusion are strong, and the others weak, then, in the way stated, that person will not be greedy; he will be intelligent, but given to hatred and irascibility.

But when, at the moment of *kamma*-accumulation, the three (wholesome roots), non-greed, non-hatred and non-delusion, are strong, and greed, etc., are weak, then, in the way stated, he has no greed and no hate and he is wise, like the Elder Saṅgharakkhita.

From the *Atthasālinī*, pp. 267 f.

44. Root-Cause Condition (hetu-paccaya)

The roots of good and evil are also the constituents of the root-cause condition, or root-cause-relation, the first of the twenty-four modes of conditionality by which all conditioning and conditioned phenomena are related in various ways. Those twenty-four modes belong to the framework of the seventh and last work of the Abhidhamma Piṭaka, the *Paṭṭhāna*,[34] and in its introductory part they are listed and explained.[35] They are also

34. See *Conditional Relations (Paṭṭhāna)*, tr. by U Nārada (London: Pali Text Society, 1969).

35. Reproduced in *The Path of Purification* (*Visuddhimagga*), Ch. XVII, §66, and in *Guide through the Abhidhamma Piṭaka*, by Ñāṇatiloka Mahāthera (Kandy: Buddhist Publication Society).

necessary for understanding how the twelve links of dependent origination (*paṭicca-samuppāda*) are related.

We reproduce here excerpts of the explanation of the root-cause condition from a treatise by an eminent Burmese scholar-monk, Ledi Sayādaw:

What is the root-cause condition (*hetu-paccaya*)? Greed, hatred, delusion, and their respective opposites, non-greed (disinterestedness), non-hatred (amity), non-delusion (intelligence, wisdom)—these are the root-cause conditions.

What are the things that are conditioned by them? Those classes of mind and mental qualities[36] that co-exist along with greed, etc., or non-greed, etc., as well as the groups of material qualities which co-exist with the same—these are the things that are conditioned by way of root-cause condition (*hetu-paccayuppannā dhammā*). They are so called because they arise or come into existence by virtue of the root-cause condition.

Here by the phrase "the groups of material qualities which co-exist with the same" are meant the material qualities produced by *kamma* (*kammaja rūpa*) at the initial moment of the *hetu*-conditioned conception of a new being, as well as such material qualities as may be produced by the *hetu*-conditioned mind during the lifetime. Here, by the "moment of conception" is meant the nascent instant (*uppādakkhaṇa*) of the rebirth-conception, and by "the lifetime" is meant the period starting from the static instant (*ṭhitikkhaṇa*) of the rebirth, conception right on to the moment of the dying-thought.

In what sense is *hetu* to be understood? And in what sense, *paccaya*? *Hetu* is to be understood in the sense of root (*mūlaṭṭha*); and *paccaya* in the sense of assisting (*upakāraṭṭha*) in the arising, or the coming to be, of the conditionally arisen things (*paccayuppannā dhammā*).

The state of being a root (*mūlaṭṭha*) may be illustrated as follows.

Suppose a man is in love with a woman. Now, so long as he has not dispelled the lustful thought, all his acts, words and thoughts regarding this woman will be cooperating with lust (or greed), which at the same time has also under its control the

36. *Citta* and *cetasika*, consciousness and mental concomitants.

material qualities produced by the same thought (e.g., *kāya-vacī-viññatti*, the "bodily or verbal intimation" of his love). We see then that all these states of mental and material qualities have their root in lustful greed for that woman. Hence, by being a *hetu* (for it acts as a root) and by being a *paccaya* (for it assists in the arising of those states of mind and body), greed is a *hetu-paccaya*, a condition aiding by way of being a root-cause. The rest may be explained and understood in the same manner—i.e., the arising of greed by way of desire for desirable (inanimate) things; the arising of hatred by way of antipathy against hateful persons or things; and the arising of delusion by way of lack of knowledge (about persons, things and ideas not correctly perceived and understood).

Taking a tree as illustration—we see that the roots of a tree, having firmly established themselves in the ground and drawing up sap both from soil and water, carry that sap right up to the crown of the tree, and so the tree develops and grows for a long time. In the same way, greed having firmly established itself in desirable things and drawing up the essence of pleasure and enjoyment from them, conveys that essence to the concomitant mental elements, till they burst into immoral acts and words. The same is to be said of hatred, which by way of aversion draws up the essence of displeasure and discomfort; and also of delusion, which by way of lack of knowledge cherishes the growth of the essence of vain (and deceptive) thoughts at many an object.

Transporting the essence thus, the three elements, greed, hatred and delusion, operate upon the component parts, so that they become happy (so to speak) and joyful at the desirable objects, etc. The component parts also become so as they are operated upon, while the co-existent material qualities share the same effect.

Coming now to the bright side—suppose the man sees danger in sensual pleasure, and gives up that lustful thought for the woman. In doing so, disinterestedness (non-greed, *alobha*) as regards her arises in him. Before this, there took place impure acts, words and thoughts, having as their root delusion (and greed); but for the time being, these are no longer present, and in their stead there arise pure acts, words and thoughts, having their root in disinterestedness (non-greed). Moreover, renunciation, self-control, *jhāna*-exercise, or higher meditative thought, also come into being. Non-greed (*alobha*), therefore, is known as *hetu-paccaya*, it being a *hetu* because it acts as a root; while it is a *paccaya* because it assists in the arising of the concomitants. The same explanation applies to the remainder of non-greed, non-hate and non-delusion, which three are opposites of greed, etc.

Here, just as the root of the tree stimulates the whole stem and its parts, so it is with non-greed (disinterestedness). It dispels the desire for desirable things, and having promoted the growth of the essence of pleasure void of greed (*lobha-viveka-sukha-rasa*), it nurtures the concomitant elements with that essence till they become so happy (so to speak) and joyful that they even reach the height of *jhānic*-, path-, or fruition-happiness. Similarly, non-hatred (amity) and non-delusion (intelligence), respectively, dispel hatred and ignorance with regard to hateful and confused (or deceptive) things, and promote the growth of the essence of pleasure void of hate and delusion. Thus the operation of the three elements, non-greed, non-hatred and non-delusion, lasts for a long time, making their mental concomitants happy and joyful. The concomitant elements also become so as they are operated upon; while the co-existent groups of material qualities are affected in the same way.

(pp. 1–5)

... Let us say that greed springs into being within a man who desires to get money and grain. Under the influence of greed, he goes to a forest where he clears a piece of land and establishes fields, yards and gardens, and starts to work very hard. Eventually he obtains plenty of money and grain by reason of his strenuous labours. So he takes his gains, looks after his family and performs many virtuous deeds, from which he also will be entitled to reap rewards in his future existences. In this illustration, all the mental and material states coexisting with greed are called direct effects. Apart from these, all the outcomes, results and rewards, which are to be enjoyed later on in his future existences, are called indirect effects. Of these two kinds of effects, only the former is dealt with in the Paṭṭhāna. However, the latter kind finds its place in the Suttanta discourses. "If this exists, then that happens; or because of the occurrences of this, that also takes place"—such an exposition is called "expounding by way of Suttanta."

In fact, the three states, greed, hatred and delusion, are called root-conditions because they are roots whence springs the defilement of the whole animate world, of the whole inanimate world, and of the world of space. The three opposite states, non-greed, non-hatred and non-delusion, are also called root-conditions since they are the roots from which springs purification.

(pp. 117–118)

From: *Paṭṭhānuddesa Dīpanī: The Buddhist Philosophy of Relations, by the Venerable Ledi Sayādaw, tr. by the Venerable U Nyāna (Rangoon, 1935).*[37]

37. Wheel 331/333. Some of the English terms in that treatise have been replaced by those used in this book.

Life's Highest Blessings

The Mahā Maṅgala Sutta

Translation and Commentary
by
Dr. R. L. Soni

Revised by
Bhikkhu Khantipālo

WHEEL PUBLICATION NO. 254/255/256

Editor's Foreword

MAṄGALA: Popularly it means lucky sign, omen good or evil, auspicious or inauspicious, or a blessing. In all countries and times there have been superstitions about these things and this is as true of Western technological societies (the increasing dependence upon astrology), as it was of India in the Buddha's days. Though people now may not divine auspices from the shapes of cloth nibbled by rats, they have plenty of other signs of fortune and misfortune.

For some reason or other, signs of fortune are few now in English tradition and offhand the writer could think of only one: it is lucky to pick up pins. But unlucky signs and actions to ward off misfortune are many. For instance, a few years ago a sister in an English hospital insisted that flowers of other colours be mixed in with my mother's red and white carnations—"or we shall have a death in the ward." In Australia in the show biz world, to whistle in the dressing room before putting on an act will bring misfortune which can only be averted by leaving the room, turning round three times and swearing! Another generally unlucky sign is for a black cat to cross one's path. In Nepal, they consider an overturned shoe to be very inauspicious when one is setting out on a journey. And sailors the world over are well known for their attachment to good signs and dread of ill omens. Less specialized examples can be found in crossing one's fingers and in "touching wood" against disaster, and in the practice of throwing salt over the left shoulder (into the Devil's eye) whenever salt is spilt. (Did salt manufacturers have anything to do with this?)

Certainly a well-known Swedish match company did promote the idea of ill-luck following three smokers who light up on one match ("three on a match"). A bit nearer to commonsense is the superstition about not walking under ladders, but most of these beliefs are quite irrational, like the children's idea that a bad day will follow after stepping on cracks in the pavement when going to school.

Even nearer to the Buddhist idea of good omens (in Thailand) are dreaming of Bhikkhus (monks) or temples, or seeing a Bhikkhu when one comes out of the house first thing in the morning. How such things can be interpreted differently is well illustrated by some Chinese business people for whom the sight of a Bhikkhu—one who teaches the doctrine of *voidness*—at that time is a very bad omen! In Theravāda countries generally the word "*sumaṅgala*" (= good omen) is a popular name both among Bhikkhus and laymen.

But one could keep on and find innumerable examples of the popular idea of *maṅgala*. It was the Buddha's genius to show that it is the practice of Dhamma that is truly auspicious.

In Buddhist countries there are many works explaining the contents of the Maṅgala Sutta. Some are in Pāli but many are in the languages of the present Buddhist countries of Southeast Asia. They are popular books widely read by Buddhists there. Apart from this, lectures over the radio and sermons in temples and homes often take the form of a commentary upon this discourse or part of it.

English language lacks such a work, apart from the translation of the Pāli commentary to the Sutta by the Venerable Ñāṇamoli Thera in *Minor Readings and Illustrator* (Pali Text Society). The author's book, written before this was available, helps to fill an omission in English Buddhist literature.

As the reviser of this book, I have often referred to Ven. Ñāṇamoli's translation and sometimes inserted some material from that book into this one. Where it was felt necessary some passages by the author have been omitted or rewritten. It is my hope that he will be satisfied with these changes, which do not affect the plan of his work. John Dimmick, my good Buddhist friend for many years, has patiently disentangled and typed the revised copy.

The Mahā Maṅgala Sutta is so popular because of the wide range of its teaching within a few easily remembered verses. Also because of its clarity and straightforwardness, which are characteristic of the Dhamma as a whole.

Here are good omens for everyone, real blessings for everybody. You have only to practice!

Bhikkhu Khantipālo

Preface

Some two years back (1954) I shifted my library and manuscripts to Mandalay from my pre-war station, where the things had remained for over ten years separated from me, first because of the war and then because of the insecurity and insurgency in the country. Though several books were found infested with bookworms, yet it was a delightful experience to get back the main part of the library intact. The joy however was dampened by a profound shock, as the contents of a large and precious box were found damaged beyond recognition by white ants: precious, because apart from some valuable and rare books, the box contained several major manuscripts on which I had worked devotedly for over nine years. The files were a heap of wet mud with thousands of white ants wriggling in it.

It seemed these destructive creatures had found access to the box during the long journey in the goods-train. My shock can be better imagined than described! What had been safe from invaders, bombs, bullets, weather and storms was lost through the white ants on the final journey. Truly, it was an object lesson in *anicca*, the impermanence of all compounded things.

Disheartened, but not quite despondent, I began immediately to extricate and save everything possible. Hundreds of mutilated and withering sheets were thus reclaimed. Among these were some which had my researches on the phenomenon of rebirth and the psychology of consciousness, and also my writing and verses on the Mahā Maṅgala Sutta. With happy memories of the Sutta thus revived, I set to work shortly to rewrite this book. Two pleasant results followed: firstly, the shock was soothed away by new inspiration; and secondly, this book was the result. It is hoped that this work will serve a useful purpose, but it will remain a moot point as to who should earn the gratitude for producing it, the author or the white ants!

The Mahā Maṅgala Sutta is a rewarding text for the wholesome shaping of complex human civilization. In this work an attempt is made to offer some studies of this important discourse of the Buddha, which provides a plan, true at all times, for the material and spiritual well-being of individuals in a democratic society.

The discourse provides lessons of direct practical application, capable of immediate and fruitful use by people in all walks of life, irrespective of differences of sex or status, race or religion.

These precepts should have wide publicity so that they may be widely used, particularly at this juncture in human history when people are coming closer together, so that nations need a silken cord to unite them harmoniously into a family of cooperating and trusting members. Only such a transformation can save them from impending and utter disaster, which must be expected because of their terrible hatreds, greed and misunderstandings.

Conditioning of the individual towards wholesome conduct is really necessary. Such a change of attitudes leads to definite improvement not only in domestic and social affairs but also in national and international ones. For the introduction and promotion of such friendliness, the auspicious words of the Buddha reaching us from across the ages provide an excellent guide.

The present work introduces this worthy guide and this book is sent out in the faith and hope that it will help lead some people in the world towards better human relationships. It is a happy coincidence that it is starting its auspicious journey from the city that was once the capital of the good King Mindon and which even today is the centre of Buddhist learning in Burma.

Dr. R. L. Soni

Chapter I
Introduction

I. The Glorious Sutta

Superstitions and selfish desires weave a pattern of mind which interprets objective and subjective happenings in life as forebodings of personal weal and woe. Thus, if on waking up in the morning, or on the start of a trip, or in the course of a long journey, or at the beginning of an enterprise, or during a sacred ceremony, one meets with what is taken to be a sign of good fortune, such as a flower in bloom, a smiling face, good news or even something at first sight offensive but potentially considered good, some people feel assured of success in the subsequent course of events. An auto-suggestion like this might be of some use but to place complete reliance on it, neglecting the action necessary for fulfilment and success, would be too much of wishful thinking, bound to result in frustration or failure. So much importance is attached by some people to such omens of what is supposed to be auspicious that a sort of pseudoscience has grown up playing an undesirable role in the lives of those people by choking their initiative, by sustaining their fears, by suppressing self-confidence and by the promotion of irrational attitudes in them. In the time of the Buddha such a belief was as much in evidence as today, and as he was opposed to anything that fettered the healthy growth of the human mind he raised his voice against such superstitions. He denounced "luck" or "fortune" or "auspiciousness" and proclaimed instead human behaviour, associations and activities as the real origins of "fortune" or "misfortune." Thus the emphasis was shifted from unhealthy fears and fettering superstitions to individual responsibility, rational thinking, social obligations and self-confidence. This had far-reaching effects in improving both human relationships and the efficiency of the human mind.

In Indian society in the Buddha's time (as in our own), people were addicted to superstitions about omens of good and bad luck besides being divided on their nature and implications; so it was natural that someone should inquire into the views of the Great Teacher, the Buddha, on the subject. His words of wisdom had already been an immense success not only with ordinary people but also with those in positions of power and those with great learning. A special messenger was therefore sent to meet the Buddha while he was staying at the Jetavana monastery in the garden of Anāthapiṇḍika at Sāvatthī to inquire after his views on omens.

The views expressed by the Lord in the Mahā Maṅgala Sutta are a masterpiece of practical wisdom. This Sutta was recited at the First Buddhist Council by Venerable Ānanda, the attendant of the Buddha who had memorized so many of the Buddha's discourses.

The Discourse is a charter in outline of family responsibility, social obligations, moral purification and spiritual cultivation. Within the compass of a dozen stanzas are included profound counsels and golden rules, which admirably point out the way life's journey should go if it is to reach the haven of perfect harmony, love, peace and security. Beginning with emphasis on the need for a suitable environment, the Discourse lays appropriate stress on personal discipline, righteous conduct and adequate discharge of duties towards one's near and dear ones. Then the higher virtues of humility, gratitude, patience and chastity are introduced. And step by step are reached serenity, perception of truth and Enlightenment.

A well-drawn chart like this correctly indicates the true course of progress on the stormy sea of life. Not only is the course correctly shown but also the rocks and other perils always to be found on such a journey are clearly pointed out.

The wisdom of the Mahā Maṅgala Sutta is emphasized by its spiritual appeal, which is firmly planted on this earth, while providing (or rather helping to grow) wings to soar high into the ethereal regions and beyond. The Buddha, as usual in his teachings, does not forget the needs and difficulties of the everyday world. Here lies its greatest appeal to the ordinary man, who, however much he may be fascinated by the ideal of renunciation and full-time spiritual practice, is still attached to the world through contact with family, friends and relations and the inevitable duties and obligations that this entails.

It is true to say that the appeal of the Sutta is universal. A child in school may benefit from it as may a scholar in the university. It is as much applicable to the humblest citizen as to those in power. Though proclaimed by the Buddha, it is just as valuable to non-Buddhists, valuable in fact for all peoples at all times.

Above all the Sutta is a wonderful stimulus for reform. It indicates the simple and direct way the Buddha adopted to wean people from superstitions and irrational attitudes so that they could grow and mature towards an enlightened outlook. This gradual method is unique to the Buddha. He made people see "luck," "omens" and "auspiciousness" in quite a new light, rejecting superstition and encouraging reliance upon one's own good actions. In consequence signs and omens gave way to his emphasis upon social obligations and duties founded on individual good conduct and leading to a society lighted by understanding and individual hearts enlightened by penetration of the truth.

II. Location in the Scriptures

The Mahā Maṅgala Sutta is included in that ancient anthology of the Pāli Canon called "A Collection of Discourses" (Sutta-Nipāta). This work contains a great variety of discourses, some upon basic subjects suitable for lay people, while others which have great depth are addressed to those who practise Dhamma all the time. The Sutta-Nipāta is the fifth item of the Minor Collection (Khuddaka-Nikāya) and is divided into five sections. The Mahā Maṅgala Sutta is the fourth Sutta of the second of these, called the Lesser Section. The contents of this Sutta also appear in the first item of the Minor Collection, known as the Minor Readings (Khuddaka-pāṭha), called there simply "Maṅgala Sutta."

It is interesting to note that the tenth item of the same collection, the *Jātaka* (birth stories), which has 547 chapters, each relating a previous life of the Buddha, has as the titles of the 87th and 453rd Jātakas, the Maṅgala Jātaka and the Mahā Maṅgala Jātaka respectively. These stories, though their contents are different, are interesting supplements to the Sutta because the same spirit runs through all these texts.

The following table clearly indicates the exact location in the scriptures of the Maṅgala Sutta, the Mahā Maṅgala Sutta, the Maṅgala Jātaka and the Mahā Maṅgala Jātaka.

The Buddhist Canon
TI-PITAKA
(Three Baskets)

VINAYA PITAKA (The Basket of Discipline)

SUTTA PITAKA (The Basket of Discourses) Comprising 5 Nikāyas of which the fifth is

ABHIDHAMMA PITAKA (The Basket of Further Dhamma)

KHUDDAKA NIKĀYA
Comprising 15 Books

First Book — KHUDDHAKA-PĀTHA Comprising nine Minor Readings of which the fifth is — THE MAṄGALA-SUTTA

Fifth Book — SUTTA-NIPĀTA Comprising five sections of which the second is — CŪLA VAGGA Comprising 14 items of which the fourth is — THE MAHĀ MAṄGALA SUTTA

Tenth Book — JĀTAKA Comprising 547 stories of the past lives of the Buddha, of which the — 87th is the Maṅgala Jātaka; 453rd is Mahā Maṅgala Jātaka

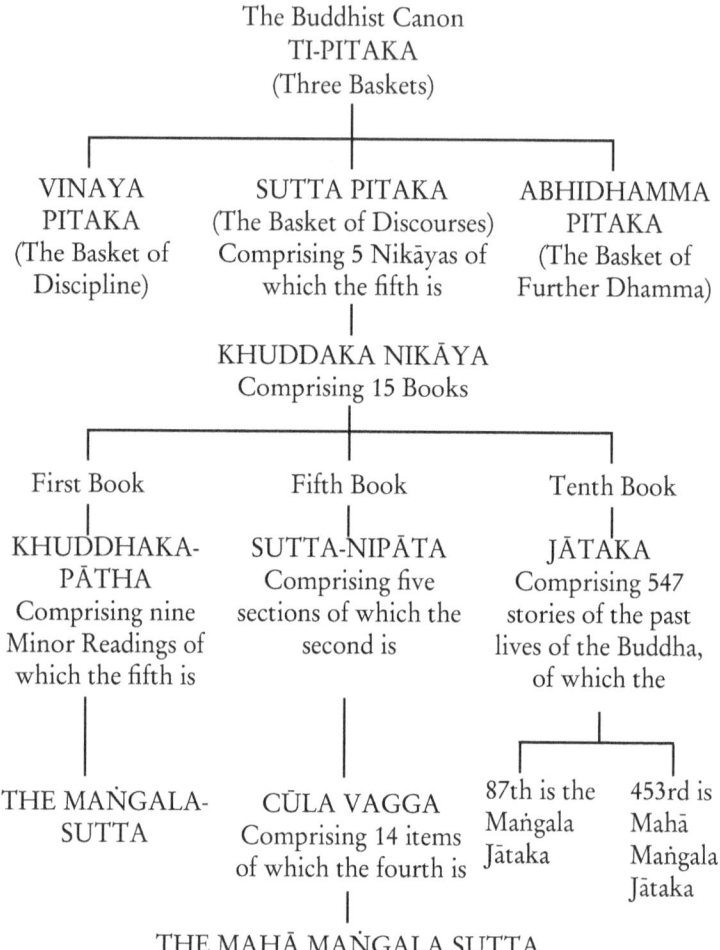

III. The Contents of These Texts

The story of the Maṅgala Jātaka concerns a brahmin said to be an expert in predictions drawn from cloth. Obsessed with the superstition that any cloth, however new or costly, once bitten by a rat was highly inauspicious (*amaṅgala*), he had a valuable garment of his thrown away into a cemetery on discovering a rat-bite on it. Hearing that the Buddha had picked up the discarded cloth, consternation seized the brahmin, as he expected ill-luck to strike down the Blessed One and those with him. He hastened to the Buddha to avert the danger before it was too late. But once in the Buddha's presence he was weaned out of his superstition and he attained insight into the Dhamma. The Buddha told him of his addiction to the same superstition in an earlier life.

The Buddha taught Mahā Maṅgala Jātaka about one of his previous births when he was leading the life of a hermit near Benares. He then expounded eight groups of blessings, viz. unqualified benevolence, humility, social service, liberality, domestic felicity, uprightness compelling universal respect, proper understanding of *kamma*-functioning and mental peace.

The above stories throw considerable light not only on the attitude of the Buddha towards superstitions, but also on the emphasis he laid on growing into an enlightened outlook and virtuous life. In the Maṅgala and the Mahā Maṅgala Suttas, the latter aspect is further amplified.

We have chosen the Mahā Maṅgala Sutta as the text of the present work. It has an introduction in prose but its main body is the twelve stanzas. Each stanza has the same number of lines, and all the stanzas are in the same meter and have the same refrain. The teachings contained in these verses, since they are in agreement with other parts of the Suttas, are obviously words from the Buddha's lips. The recitation of this composition in the First Council[1] was the work of the Venerable Ānanda, hence the words with which it opens "Thus have I heard."

IV. The Title

The title Mahā Maṅgala Sutta has three parts, namely, *mahā*, *maṅgala* and *sutta*. *Mahā* means "great"; used as a prefix it enlarges and emphasizes the meaning of the word or expression to which it is attached. Thus *mahādhana* (great wealth), *mahākaruṇā* (great compassion), *mahāpatha* (high road), *mahāpurisa* (great

1. This was held in the first year of the Buddhist Era, three months after the Final Nibbāna of the Great Master. No unenlightened persons sat in the Convocation, which consisted of 500 Arahants, who recited, classified and arranged the Teachings in seven months. Venerable Ānanda recited the Suttas, including of course the Mahā Maṅgala Sutta.

being), *mahārāja* (great king or emperor). Other examples are *mahābodhi*, *mahāvihāra*, etc.

The prefix *mahā* added to the title of a book or chapter adds weight and importance to the contents. The use of the prefix in this Sutta is an indication of its precious worth besides suggesting the recognition of this worth by the Arahants who compiled the Suttas in the First Council. The component *maṅgala* means an "omen," good luck, an auspice, etc. The word also signifies "auspicious ceremony," e.g. *vivāha-maṅgalaṃ* (marriage ceremony), *nāma-karaṇa-maṅgala* (name-giving ceremony). Such uses of the word are still common in India and reflect the popular and more or less superstitious ideas that the Buddha tried to supplant.

The Pāli commentators have derived the term *maṅgala* from *maṃ* (woeful condition) and *ga-la* (driving away and cutting off); therefore it means "that which is obstructive to woe". In practice it has the positive significance "conducive to weal."

Maṅgala, though at times used in a spiritual sense, usually has worldly associations. It generally stands for conditions making for satisfaction, happiness and prosperity. Thus it is the most yearned-for thing in worldly happiness and domestic welfare. No wonder any sign or omen, any *maṅgala* believed to point the way to such happiness is eagerly seized upon. When it is so much of a blessing, people will eagerly seek and look for it in physical omens and material signs which they think lead to it.

Because of the differences in outlook among various people, conflicting interpretations of the omens considered auspicious are naturally found. It was to settle such differences that the Buddha was approached. But rather than condemning some viewpoints or commending certain other interpretations, he looked at the subject from a different angle and from a higher horizon, with the result that the term *maṅgala* assumed a nobler significance.

Coming to the last component of the title, originally by the term *Sutta* was meant a string or a thread. In fact the word is still used in this sense. Just as beads can be strung together by a thread into a rosary or flowers into a garland, successive arguments can be strung together into a logically brilliant whole, and sections of a story or a sermon can be threaded together to present a good way to practice. The symbolic use of the word "*sutta*" to mean a discourse is this "threading together."

In English, too, the word "thread" has been the symbol of continuity as suggested by the phrase "a thread of thought." As progressive continuity is obvious in a series of logically connected ideas and events in a narrative, it is symbolized by a thread or a *sutta*. Evidently a knot in the thread represents "a concentrated deep idea" inviting focused attention for its unravelling. Such reflections result in flashes of wisdom and inspiration.

It was in this sense that the thinkers and sages in ancient India used the term "*sutta*"; also it was in this form that they expressed their thoughts.

The Discourse on the Highest Blessings is truly a "*sutta*," a threaded collection of gems of the highest blessings in life, blessings varied in nature and scope according to the needs of the individual in different stages on life's journey. The Sutta really is a sublime garland of blessings full of fragrance, radiant with benevolence, shining with truth and aglow with practical utility.

V. Burmese Enthusiasm

The Mahā Maṅgala Sutta by itself, or as part of the Sutta-Nipāta or of the Khuddakapāṭha or as a part of some compilations, is available in several editions in the Sinhalese, Thai and Burmese scripts, with or without translations and commentaries in those languages.

The Sutta has a special significance in the national life of Burma. It is certainly Burma's most valuable heritage of proven truth. The Sutta is one of the first lessons a child in Burma learns by heart. Memorizing it eagerly, he recites and untiringly repeats its stanzas naturally with gusto till their constituents seem to vibrate his entire being. And what is more marvellous is that the effect is lifelong. Even in rash youth and old age, the chanting of the Sutta coming from the precincts of a monastery or classroom recalls memories of childhood and the need for self-cultivation to direct one's steps towards those actions which lead to peace in one's own heart and happiness for others. Today throughout the length and breadth of the country children and adults are schooled in the Maṅgala Sutta.

There are dozens of admirable books and booklets on the Maṅgala Sutta available in Burmese. Most of these are recent works and very well written in a way to convey the practical message straight to the heart. Of the older works, *Maṅgalatthadīpani*,[2] a voluminous book of over 760 pages written by Maṅgalabon-gyaw Sayādaw at the court of Amarapura in 1854. This is not only an impressive piece of classical literature but also an abundant storehouse of well-told stories illustrating moral, practical and spiritual values in the Sutta. The method is commendable because of its proven value making the listeners and readers understand vividly the practical import of the Sutta's teachings. It is good to see that even the latest works freely draw upon this old method. Thus modern Burmese authors, while imparting a fresh touch to their writings, are wise in not losing hold of the treasure-store of the past. In the present work, unfortunately, the illustrative stories cannot find a place, because they would greatly increase its length.

VI. The Present Work

There have been many translations of this Sutta, some with the Pāli, some without, and it is not possible or necessary to list them here. That there are so many is an eloquent testimony to the popularity of the Sutta. In spite of this great appreciation, the author does not know any works in English exclusively devoted to the Sutta apart from one publication[3] and some leaflets. Considering the value, importance and popularity of this precious Sutta, the need for more and detailed works is obvious. Therefore, it seems there is no need for an apology in offering this book to the reader.

The plan of the present work is simple: the Mahā Maṅgala Sutta is presented first in original Pāli together with a word-by-word English rendering of it and a more literal translation. Then follow notes and comments explaining the contents. However, all the issues do not require exhaustive treatment. While it has been found necessary to deal thoroughly with certain subjects of

2. This must be a similar work to the Pāli language book of the same name which is widely studied in Thailand. It was written by Phra Sirimaṅgalācariya Thera of Chiengmai (northern Siam) and completed in 1528.

3. *Maṅgalasutta Vaṇṇanā* by Venerable K. Gunaratana Thera, published in Penang, 1952.

special Buddhist interest or of a complicated nature, others easily intelligible and needing no comments are barely mentioned. In the last chapter the Blessings are classified.

It was the author's desire to give a living Burmese touch to this work by assigning a chapter to a captivating contemporary popular song in Burmese on the Sutta but the difficulties encountered in rendering this into English proved insurmountable; so the attempt had to be given up.

In the preparation of this book the valuable assistance received from the Venerable Nyanatiloka's *Buddhist Dictionary*[4] is gratefully acknowledged. The author is also thankful to U Ba Thin and other friends who read the Burmese text to him.

4. Buddhist Publication Society, Kandy.

Chapter II
Mahā Maṅgala Sutta

I. The Pāli Text

Evaṃ me sutaṃ. Ekaṃ samayaṃ Bhagavā Sāvatthiyaṃ viharati Jetavane Anāthapiṇḍikassa ārāme. Atha kho aññatarā devatā abhikkantāya rattiyā abhikkantavaṇṇā kevalakappaṃ Jetavanaṃ obhāsetvā yena Bhagavā tena' upasaṅkami upasaṅkamitvā Bhagavantaṃ abhivādetvā ekamantaṃ aṭṭhāsi. Ekamantaṃ ṭhitā kho sā devatā Bhagavantaṃ gāthāya ajjhabhāsi:

I

Bahū devā manussā ca, maṅgalāni acintayuṃ
ākaṅkhamānā sotthānaṃ, brūhi maṅgalam-uttamaṃ.

II

Asevanā ca bālānaṃ, paṇḍitānañ ca sevanā
pūjā ca pūjanīyānaṃ, etam maṅgalam-uttamaṃ.

III

Patirūpadesavāso ca, pubbe ca kata-puññatā
attasammāpaṇidhi ca, etam maṅgalam-uttamaṃ.

IV

Bahusaccañ ca sippañ ca, vinayo ca susikkhito
subhāsitā ca yā vācā, etam maṅgalam-uttamaṃ.

V

Mātā-pitu upaṭṭhānaṃ, putta-dārassa saṅgaho
anākulā ca kammantā, etam maṅgalam-uttamaṃ.

VI

Dānañ ca dhammacariyā ca, ñātakānañ ca saṅgaho
anavajjāni kammāni, etam maṅgalam-uttamaṃ.

VII

Āratī viratī pāpā, majjapānā ca saññamo
appamādo ca dhammesu, etam maṅgalam-uttamaṃ.

VIII

Gāravo ca nivāto ca, santuṭṭhī ca kataññutā
kālena dhammasavanaṃ, etam maṅgalam-uttamaṃ.

IX

Khantī ca sovacassatā, samaṇānañ ca dassanaṃ
kālena dhammasākacchā, etam maṅgalam-uttamaṃ.

X

Tapo ca brahmacariyañ-ca, ariyasaccāna-dassanaṃ
nibbāna-sacchikiriyā ca etam maṅgalam-uttamaṃ.

XI

Phuṭṭhassa lokadhammehi, cittaṃ yassa na kampati
asokaṃ virajaṃ khemaṃ, etam maṅgalam-uttamaṃ.

XII

Etādisāni katvāna, sabbattham-aparājitā
sabbattha sotthiṃ gacchanti, taṃ tesaṃ maṅgalam-uttamaṃ.

(*Mahāmaṅgalasutaṃ niṭṭhitaṃ*)

II. Word by Word Rendering

Evaṃ (*thus*) *me* (*I*) *sutaṃ* (*heard*):

Ekaṃ (one) *samayaṃ* (time) *Bhagavā* (the Blessed One, the Buddha) *Sāvatthiyaṃ* (near Sāvatthī) *viharati* (was staying) *Jetavane* (in the Jeta Grove) *Anāthapiṇḍikassa ārāme* (in Anāthapiṇḍika's monastery). *Atha kho* (certainly then) *aññatarā* (a certain) *devatā* (deity, a *deva*) *abhikkantāya* (towards, far advanced) *rattiyā* (night) *abhikkantavaṇṇā* (of surpassing brilliance and beauty) *kevalakappaṃ* (the entire) *Jetavanaṃ* (Jeta Grove) *obhāsetvā* (having illumined) *yena Bhagavā* (where the Blessed One was) *tena upasaṅkami* (approached that place) *upasaṅkamitvā* (having reached) *Bhagavantaṃ abhivādetvā* (having offered profound salutations to the Blessed One) *ekamantaṃ* (aside) *aṭṭhāsi* (stood). *Ekamantaṃ ṭhitā kho* (having stood aside) *sā devatā* (the deity) *Bhagavantaṃ* (to the Blessed One) *gāthāya* (in verse) *ajjhabhāsi* (addressed respectfully).

I

Bahū (many) *devā* (deities) *manussā ca* (and human beings) *maṅgalāni* (over blessings) *acintayuṃ* (have pondered), *ākaṅkhamānā* (hoping for) *sotthānaṃ* (safety) *brūhi* (please expound) *maṅgalam-uttamaṃ* (the Highest Blessing).

II

Asevanā (not to associate with) *ca bālānaṃ* (the foolish people) *paṇḍitānañ ca* (and the wise) *sevanā* (to associate with) *pūjā ca* (homage) *pūjanīyānaṃ* (those worthy of homage) *etam* (this) *maṅgalam-uttamaṃ* (the Highest Blessing).

III

Paṭirūpa (congenial) *desa* (locality) *vāso* (for residence) *ca* (and) *pubbe ca* (in the past) *kata-puññatā* (having made merit) *atta* (one's self) *sammā* (rightly) *paṇidhi ca* (directed) *etam maṅgalam-uttamaṃ* (this, the Highest Blessing).

IV

Bahu (ample) *saccañ* (learning) *ca sippañ* (and proficiency in crafts) *ca* (and) *vinayo ca* (moral discipline) *susikkhito* (well trained) *subhāsitā ca* (and well spoken) *yā vācā* (words) *etam maṅgalam-uttamaṃ* (this, the Highest Blessing).

V

Mātā-pitu (mother and father) *upaṭṭhānaṃ* (to support) *putta-dārassa* (children and wife) *saṅgaho* (to cherish) *anākulā ca* (and unconflicting) *kammantā* (types of work) *etam maṅgalam-uttamaṃ* (this, the Highest Blessing).

VI

Dānañ (giving) *ca dhammacariyā* (living by Dhamma) *ca* (and) *ñātakānañ* (relatives) *ca saṅgaho* (supporting) *anavajjāni* (blameless) *kammāni* (actions) *etam maṅgalam-uttamaṃ* (this, the Highest Blessing).

VII

Āratī (avoidance) *viratī* (abstinence) *pāpā* (from evil) *majjapānā ca* (intoxicating drinks) *saññamo* (to refrain from) *appamādo ca* (and diligence in) *dhammesu* (acts of virtue) *etam maṅgalam-uttamaṃ* (this, the Highest Blessing).

VIII

Gāravo (reverence) *ca* (and) *nivāto* (humility) *ca* (and) *santuṭṭhī* (contentment) *ca kataññutā* (and gratitude) *kālena* (timely) *dhammasavanaṃ* (hearing Dhamma) *etam maṅgalam-uttamaṃ* (this, the Highest Blessing).

IX

Khantī (patience) *ca sovacassatā* (and amenability to correction) *samaṇānañ ca* (of monk) *dassanaṃ* (seeing) *kālena* (timely) *dhammasākacchā* (discussions on the Dhamma) *etam maṅgalam-uttamaṃ* (this, the Highest Blessing).

X

Tapo (energetic restraint) *ca brahmacariyāñ-ca* (and holy and chaste life) *ariyassaccāna*-(and the Noble Truths) *dassanaṃ* (seeing) *nibbāna-sacchikiriyā ca* (and realization of Nibbāna) *etam maṅgalam-uttamaṃ* (this, the Highest Blessing).

XI

Phuṭṭhassa (touched by) *lokadhammehi* (worldly conditions) *cittaṃ yassa* (whose mind) *na kampati* (is not shaken) *asokaṃ* (free from sorrow) *virajaṃ* (free from passion) *khemaṃ* (secure) *etam maṅgalam-uttamaṃ* (this, the Highest Blessing).

XII

Etādisāni (these things) *katvāna* (having fulfilled) *sabbattham-* (everywhere) *aparājitā* (unvanquished) *sabbattha* (everywhere) *sotthiṃ* (in happiness and safety) *gacchanti* (they go) *taṃ* (that) *tesaṃ* (to them) *maṅgalam-uttamaṃ* (the Highest Blessing).

Mahā Maṅgala Sutta (The Discourse on Great Blessings) *niṭṭhitaṃ* (is ended).

III. Translation

Thus have I heard:

Once while the Blessed One was staying in the vicinity of Sāvatthī, in the Jeta Grove, in Anāthapiṇḍika's monastery, a certain deity, whose surpassing brilliance and beauty illumined the entire Jeta Grove, late one night came to the presence of the Blessed One; having come to him and offered profound salutations he stood on one side and spoke to him reverently in the following verse:

I

Many deities and human beings
Have pondered what are blessings,
Which they hope will bring them safety.
Declare to them, Sir, the Highest Blessing.

(To this the Blessed One replied:)

II

With fools no company keeping,
With the wise ever consorting,
To the worthy homage paying:
This, the Highest Blessing.

III

Congenial place to dwell,
In the past merits making,
One's self directed well:
This, the Highest Blessing.

IV

Ample learning, in crafts ability,
With a well-trained disciplining,
Well-spoken words, civility:
This, the Highest Blessing.

V

Mother, father well supporting,
Wife and children duly cherishing,
Types of work unconflicting:
This, the Highest Blessing.

VI

Acts of giving, righteous living,
Relatives and kin supporting,
Actions blameless then pursuing:
This, the Highest Blessing.

VII

Avoiding evil and abstaining,
From besotting drinks refraining,
Diligence in Dhamma doing:
This, the Highest Blessing.

VIII

Right reverence and humility,
Contentment and a grateful bearing,
Hearing Dhamma when it's timely:
This, the Highest Blessing.

IX

Patience, meekness when corrected,
Seeing monks and then discussing
The Dhamma when it's timely:
This, the Highest Blessing.

X

Self-restraint and holy life,
Seeing the Noble Truths,
Realization of Nibbāna:
This, the Highest Blessing.

XI

Though touched by worldly circumstances,
Never his mind is wavering,
Sorrowless, stainless and secure:
This, the Highest Blessing.

XII

Since by acting in this way,
They are everywhere unvanquished,
And everywhere they go in safety:
Theirs, the Highest Blessings.

Here ends the Discourse on Great Blessings.

Chapter III
Notes and Comments

I. The Title

Mahā Maṅgala Sutta:
Discourse on the Highest Blessings, the real omens, or the most auspicious and "lucky" actions.

II. Introduction

(A) *Evaṃ me sutaṃ*

The Suttas of the Buddhist scriptures begin with these words. The history behind this short sentence is as follows. Some three months after the final Nibbāna of the Buddha, when King Ajātasattu had been on the throne already for about eight years, the First Great Council was held under royal patronage at the Sattapaṇṇi Cave in Rājagaha, the capital, where five hundred Arahants assembled to recite, classify and group together the Teachings of the Master. Venerable Mahā Kassapa presided, while the Venerables Upāli and Ānanda rehearsed the Vinaya (monastic discipline) and the Suttas or discourses respectively. The Council finished its work after seven months, during which time they arranged the entire Teachings of the Master, that is, the collections of the Vinaya rules and the Suttas.

To the Venerable Ānanda, as he was most learned in the Master's discourses, fell the arduous task of rehearsing the Suttas in the Great Council. He prefixed each discourse with the expression "*Evaṃ me suttaṃ*" ("Thus have I heard"), thus personally testifying to the authenticity of the Suttas. At that time religious teachings generally were committed to memory, so the Buddha's Teachings too were presented at first in this way. Venerable Ānanda's words, "Thus have I heard," were prefixed to the memorized version, which thereafter was passed down from teacher to pupil by oral tradition until it was committed to writing for the first time at

Aluvihārā in the central province of Sri Lanka (about 80 BCE in the reign and under the patronage of King Vaṭṭagāmaṇi Abhaya.

The Council was held at the capital of Anurādhapura with its conclusion, the writing down of the Suttas, Vinaya and Abhidhamma, at Aluvihāra. The Council was necessary for safeguarding the texts from loss through invasions, famines and the whims of kings; also from serious alterations and interpolations by unscrupulous people. There is a legend that the Ti-piṭaka was inscribed on gold sheets which were said to have been deposited in the rocks at Aluvihāra. Considering the amount of gold which would be needed, this seems very unlikely, though some condensed passages may have been inscribed in this way and enshrined.

As the Venerable Ānanda was a stream-winner[5] who had seen Dhamma himself, as well as being a devoted attendant of the Buddha, his words "Thus have I heard" prefixed to the Mahā Maṅgala Sutta, as to most other Suttas, invest these texts with the seal of authenticity.

(B) *Bhagavā*

As one of the epithets of the Buddha, it occurs frequently in the scriptures meaning "having good luck" i.e. auspicious, fortunate. It is generally translated as "the Blessed One" or "the Exalted One," though the full meaning of "One who apportions" (the Dhamma) with the knowledge of what is exactly suitable to them, cannot be conveyed in English. The usual formula of homage also has this epithet at the beginning: "*Namo tassa Bhagavato Arahato Sammāsambuddhassa*" meaning "Homage to the Blessed One, the Liberated One, the Fully Enlightened One." There are many other titles by which the Buddha is known such as *Tilokanātha* (Lord of the Three Worlds), *Dhammarāja* (the Lord of Truth), *Tathāgata* (lit. Thus Gone; but more fully meaning, "Gone" in the same way of Enlightenment and Nibbāna as Buddhas in the past), *Sugata* (the Happy One), *Sakyamuni* (the Sākyan Sage), and *Sākyasīha* (the Sākyan Lion) and so on. The term "Buddha" itself is not a name but means "the Enlightened One," "the Awakened One," which

5. This refers to the time when he listened to the Buddha's discourses. He attained Arahantship immediately before the commencement of the First Council (BPS Ed.).

signifies the zenith of perfection, supreme and final release from all types of existence or being, and the actual attainment of Nibbāna during life. (See also Stanza X on Nibbāna.)

(C) *Sāvatthi, Jetavana, Anāthapiṇḍika*

Sāvatthī (Sk. Srāvastī) was an ancient city which is identified with the village of Sahet-mahet in the present-day Indian state of Uttar Pradesh. It was the capital of the powerful kingdom of Kosala in the sixth century BCE. The great merchant and benefactor Anāthapiṇḍika, whose real name was Sudatta, bought Prince Jeta's pleasure grove in this city for a fabulous price (said to be as much as eighteen crores of gold coins) and built a monastery which he presented to the Buddha. The monastery was called Anāthapiṇḍika Ārāma and the grove was known as Jetavana, Prince Jeta's Grove. Here the Buddha stayed for twenty-four rainy seasons and gave many important discourses. The Mahā Maṅgala Sutta is one of them.

(D) *Devatā*

In Buddhist teachings there are six realms of celestial beings (*devaloka*) superior to the human world, which together comprise the "happy states" in the world of sensual desire or *kāmaloka.* These beings are of greater or lesser splendour and brilliance and they live very long lives enjoying the happy fruits of their past good *kamma*. On the expiry of this, however, they gravitate to a rebirth in accordance with their residual merit, for the *devas* make little new good *kamma* and can be compared to rich people living on their capital, which will run out sooner or later. And their new rebirth is not necessarily a better one; it may well be worse and even below the human state.

Though short-lived and having a coarse body, man is in a way superior to these celestials, as he can increase his merits by further wholesome actions and can even attain the highest goal, Nibbāna. That is why even celestial beings look to the Buddha for guidance and to Noble Ones for assistance.

At the time when the Buddha was teaching in India, it is said that not only human beings were divided about what was an omen, what was lucky or auspicious and what were really blessings, but also celestials were confused on the subject. As no one could decide this matter, an assembly of celestials deputed one of their number to visit the Buddha to get his views to clarify their doubts.

There are many stories of heavenly messengers visiting the Buddha. They usually visited him late at night, as the accounts say, "when the night was far spent," or just before dawn. Sometimes they visited him in human form and at other times they went in celestial form. Sometimes the designation "*devatā*" is even used for forest-dwelling spirits who also visited the Buddha. In this particular case it was a radiant being from a celestial abode whose presence filled the entire grove with splendour, turning the darkest hour of night into more than the brilliance of day. Materialists may consider such a being to be imagination but there are people with personal experience of such forms of existence.

These heavens have other states superior to them, two more spheres, namely, the world of subtle form (*rūpaloka*) and the formless world (*arūpaloka*). The former have sixteen realms while in the latter the inhabitants are super-celestial and even longer lived, their life span running into thousands of aeons.

Still, they are also subject to change. These celestial and super-celestial regions together with the human realms and the four subhuman planes or the evil states (*duggati*), in all totalling thrty-one planes of existence, comprise the range of phenomenal existence termed *saṃsāra*, literally the "wandering on".[6] The inhabitants of these planes, whether human or subhuman, celestial or super-celestial, are all alike in this: their existences depend on the different types of good and bad *kamma* made by them. They are alike too in that all are subject to the same law of impermanence (*anicca*), suffering (*dukkha*) and not-self (*anattā*), the difference being in the quality of their lives, with more or less of happiness and suffering, opportunities for development or lack of them. These are the fruits of *kamma* made in past and present lives. All these beings, high and low, are bound (by themselves) to the incessantly moving wheel of *saṃsāra*. If there were no way out, each individual would go on forever because of intoxication with greed (*lobha*), hatred (*dosa*) and delusion (*moha*) and so suffering here, suffering there

6. See Ledi Sayādaw, *The Noble Eightfold Path and Its Factors Explained*, Wheel Publication No. 245/247, for a diagram illustrating this.

and suffering everywhere—it would have no end. The way beyond what is marked by impermanence, suffering and non-self was pointed out by the Buddha, who, after his supreme awakening to truth, showed the path which leads to the final release of Nibbāna.

Birth as a human being is best according to the Buddha's teachings, for in spite of his frailties, man has adequate personal and environmental conditions for scaling spiritual heights, while he may have seen enough suffering to goad him on. Thus each human being has the potential to become an Arahant or a Buddha; though not everyone, of course, has golden chances and magnificent opportunities, still all are capable of raising themselves to some extent, and some to heights far above the range of even the highest gods. It depends on how each person avails oneself of the opportunities. One should always make the greatest effort to turn one's footsteps towards a good heavenly birth or towards Nibbāna, the highest goal; otherwise evil *kamma* may rivet chains which drag one down to sufferings or even into fires of the hells. The Buddha shows the way: the pilgrim has to walk that way himself.

The Buddha is called the "Light of the Three Worlds" and any of their inhabitants, even the gods, may approach him for everyday guidance or spiritual instruction. Usually people go to the gods (or to one of them, God) for guidance, but it is the various gods who came to the Buddha with their problems. In this way we can understand the significance of the god's visit mentioned in the Mahā Maṅgala Sutta.

III. The Body of the Sutta

Stanza I: *Many deities and human beings ...*

Here a question is asked to which the subsequent eleven stanzas provide the answer. The question is put by a *deva*, the accredited spokesman of the *deva*-world. The *deva* presents to the Buddha not only the contentions about "blessings" prevalent in the heavens but also those in the human world, thus covering the seven happy planes (*sugati*) of the sensual world (*kāmaloka*), and perhaps more.

The points mentioned or implied are:

1. That the inhabitants of the *deva* and human worlds desired happiness and safety, which were connected,

they thought, with what they considered "auspicious" or "lucky."
2. That many of them had been deeply pondering for a long time what were real blessings, omens or auspices.
3. That their reflection was rooted in a strong desire for personal welfare, safety and subjective happiness.
4. That in spite of their sincere and persistent efforts, they could not agree regarding the real nature of *maṅgalam-uttamaṃ*, the Highest Blessings.
5. That only the Buddha, the embodiment of Supreme Wisdom, could throw proper light on the subject.
6. That, therefore, the *deva* approached the Buddha with the question troubling the human and *deva* worlds.
7. That the Blessed One was earnestly implored to clearly expound the truth on the subject, for the welfare of gods and men.

From the above, two distinct issues emerge:

1. That happiness in the human and *deva* worlds leaves much to be desired.
2. That the inhabitants of these planes have an intense desire to attain perfection of happiness.

In the world of sensual desire, happiness is conditioned by subjective desire, efficiency of the senses and the existence of suitable objects. As all these are subject to incessant change, the consequent happiness of the senses is transient (cf. *sabbe kāmā aniccā*, "all sensual pleasure is impermanent") and therefore lacks lasting satisfaction. Sensual *gratification* is in fact a deception, though if it is understood, this may lead to the path of deliverance. This is the *escape* from sense-desires. But when gratification is not understood, it may intensify desire for sense pleasures, with dissatisfaction, regret or sorrow, which are the *danger* in them, following sooner or later. The Buddha has many times spoken about sense-desire, gratification, danger and escape.

With these clear facts, one must draw the following conclusions:

1. That in the human and *deva* worlds, beings desire to perfect their happiness.

2. That their happiness, when it is rooted in desire for sensual gratification, can never reach perfection.

So happiness in the world of sensual desire is, at best, only relative and therefore subject to constant change.

The Buddha immediately realized both the relative and the supramundane importance of this question concerning the acts of blessedness or true omens. He gave a reply in which both these aspects were thoroughly considered. By reinterpretation the Buddha boldly bypassed the superstitious meaning of the word "*maṅgala*," looking at auspiciousness from the practical viewpoint. Beginning his answer in a very down-to-earth way, he gradually described, in a steadily rising scale, blessings or omens leading higher and higher, finally to the supramundane state of Nibbāna.

Stanza II: *With fools no company keeping ...*

Sevanā and *asevanā* literally mean "service" and the "absence of service." Applied to the nouns "wise men" (*paṇḍita*) and "fools" (*bālā*), the meaning is "association" or "non-association"; thus we get "not associating with fools" and "associating with the wise." The underlying idea is that one must not follow after fools or take them as a standard for conduct or personal guidance, but follow the wise. One waxes or wanes in good qualities according to with whom one associates.

Paṇḍitā[7] means the wise, learned, experienced and those capable of giving advice which is practical and wholesome.

Bālā originally meant "children," and hence weak persons and then foolish and stupid people, the opposite of the wise, people with minds undeveloped, those whose behaviour is coarse and rough, troublemakers who tend to give advice which is unwholesome and evil. They lack discrimination and a sense of judgment, and are heedless of Dhamma, reckless in action and regardless of the consequences. These people are undesirable company. This interpretation of *bāla* does not include children who, are on the whole good and graceful.

7. For details see the Dhammapada verses of the chapters on Fools, *Bālavaggo*, and the Wise, *Paṇḍitavaggo*.

The emphasis is on keeping away from and not getting entangled with people who, though grown up in years, have none of the graces of children but all their failings and shortcomings; these are the people possessing the characteristics of "fools." Their company can only harm. They certainly are very unfortunate, but association with them is not auspicious and their mental and emotional constitution is such that they do not profit from beneficial guidance. Far from gaining anything themselves, they will rather drag even a good man into trouble and danger. The example usually given from the Suttas is that of the Buddha's cousin Devadatta dragging King Ajātasattu to hell by instigating him to kill his father who was a virtuous king.

The Suttas warn one against companionship with bad people in this way: because of bad company one gives ear to evil advice; because of such advice evil reflections occupy the mind; because of such reflections mental confusion prevails and the senses are uncontrolled; as a result of this, actions of body and speech are faulty and the five hindrances[8] gain strength holding one to sensual cravings and resulting in sufferings.

On the other hand, through companionship with the wise the sequence is: listening to good advice, rational faith, noble thoughts, clear thinking, self-control, good conduct, conquest of the hindrances, gaining of wisdom and the consequent liberation.

It should be said here that while it is essential for an ordinary person to keep away from bad company, one who is advanced in self-control, full of loving-kindness and compassion and thus immune to the evils of such association may live in the midst of such persons for the noble purpose of leading them to a better understanding while all the time on guard against evil influences. Though his body moves with them, his mind should be beyond their influence. If he is not certain of his own self-control, he should avoid the company of such people. He may associate with them only when he is sure that his good influence is flowing

8. These are five obstacles blinding mental vision, viz. lustful desire (*kāmacchanda*), ill-will (*vyāpāda*), lethargy and drowsiness (*thīna-middha*), agitation and worry (*uddhacca-kukkucca*) and sceptical doubt (*vicikicchā*). When these are present in the mind, discrimination, judgment and action become faulty.

to them, and not their evil influence to him. The advice of the Buddha is that there should not be any entanglement with fools, from which one can neither extricate oneself nor them.

Pūjā and *pūjanīyānaṃ* mean "homage" and "those worthy of homage." The examples are the Buddha, monks (*bhikkhus*), holy persons, parents, teachers—all of whom are of great assistance to us in life.

Some people do not like to show respect, or to express reverence, even when it is quite proper to do so in the presence of those who have greater and purer conduct in mind, speech and body, than they have. Such people suffer from pride, they estimate themselves too highly and do not want to admit that others could have achieved more than themselves. They are, so to speak, "standing in their own light" and they will not be able to see the right way to go. Their pride will only lead them to the strengthening of other defilements of mind, and so they go from bad to worse. They have shut the door in their own faces and can go no further. And how they quarrel with others!

Respectful persons are not like this. They are a pleasure to live and associate with, unlike people with much pride. They not only "fit" well into whatever society they are in, they also have the ability to learn more since they recognize that others know more than they do. So they have one of the factors necessary for any progress, whether in worldly prosperity or on the Path of Dhamma. We shall see later that humility is another "Blessing". This practice of honouring the honourable is the foundation for humility.

Stanza III: *Congenial place to dwell ...*

Patirūpa-desa-vāso means "residence in a suitable and pleasant locality". For life to be pleasant, the dwelling place must be comfortable, secure in construction, tidy and clean in appearance, properly maintained, and besides it is helpful if it is in a good neighbourhood and inhabited by agreeable people. The commentators amplify the meaning by explaining that a suitable locality should have in it people who practise the Noble Dhamma, the evidence of this being the existence of shrines, monks and monasteries and many good people engaged in meritorious deeds.

Residence in a place inhabited by quarrelsome and trouble-making citizens, where one is bossed about by a dictatorial and corrupt government, where the climate is inimical with frequent ravages by floods, famines, earthquakes and epidemics, where the air is charged with hatred and mutual suspicion, and where freedom of thought and action is reduced to a minimum; in brief, residence in a place having many factors and conditions obstructive to the practice of Dhamma and not conducive to physical, moral and spiritual well-being, is just the opposite of what is meant by a suitable environment.

When selection of a place for residence is considered, a Buddhist bears in mind the advantage of being near a source of Dhamma, besides, of course, more mundane advantages such as nearness to his work place.

Pubbe ca kata-puññatā: "merit made in the past." Obviously it is a blessing to have done meritorious deeds in the past. A Buddhist, unlike others who take existence as beginning with birth in this life, understands the range covered by the term "*pubbe*" (the past) to comprise a vast chain of existences, each life preceded by an earlier one in an unbroken and unlimited succession. The Buddha has said that the beginning of the round of birth and death is inconceivable, for beings are blinded by ignorance and impelled by their cravings to make more and more *kamma*, which means the experience of more and more lives.

Action is performed by one's body (*kāya-kamma*) or by speech (*vacī-kamma*) or by mind (*mano-kamma*). These actions are called *kamma* when will, intention or volition is involved in the performance of "action." If there were no "will" involved, there would be no results or fruits of *kamma*. Throughout life one goes on making *kamma* and experiencing the results: some *kamma* bears immediate results, some are delayed in result, whereas another fails to fruit because suitable conditions for this to occur are not found. At death the continuity of the potential results of *kamma* (*kamma-vipāka*) in the stream of mind—which includes feeling (*vedanā*), perception (*saññā*), mental formations (*saṅkhārā*) and consciousness (*viññāṇa*)—are the only real traces of the individual, his body (*rūpa*) having suffered disintegration. These potential results of *kamma* must ripen, and the only way that this can happen is through rebirth.

This means the attraction of the mental continuity to a suitable couple who are having sexual intercourse and where conception is possible. This applies among human beings and animals where reproduction involves sexual union. With other kinds of *kamma* governing the place of birth, existence begins spontaneously without parents, as among all the gods and among all types of subhuman birth with the exception of animals. Where one is born depends generally upon the quality of the past *kamma* which is ready to ripen, more specifically it depends upon the last thought in the mind of the dying person.

In the new existence, that individual will experience the fruits of some of the past *kamma*, while if born as a human being he will make more new *kamma* to add to the store of potential results. At the end of that new term of life what remains of the individual is again his mental continuity containing his potential results of *kamma*, and it is this which again determines and conditions his next existence. Thus the cycle goes on, death followed by birth, birth by death, and so on.

The final release from this ocean of "death-birth-death" comes only for a Buddha or Arahant whose body is worn out, who has broken the pattern of making *kamma* and has no potential result to experience. Such a person is freed from the rounds of suffering, incessant change and selfhood, to know and see for himself or herself the highest goal, Nibbāna.

As *kamma* is varied in nature, so are its results. Kamma may be unwholesome (*akusala-kamma*) or wholesome (*kusala-kamma*), the former being rooted in greed (*lobha*), hatred (*dosa*) or delusion (*moha*), while the latter has its roots in generosity (literally, greedlessness, *alobha*), loving-kindness (*adosa* or hatelessness) or wisdom (literally, undeludedness, *amoha*). Wholesome *kamma* made with these last three roots is also known as merit—those actions which cleanse and purify the mind of the doer.

Each person makes wholesome and unwholesome *kamma* as well as having a store of resultants from past *kamma*, some actual and bearing fruit while others are potential, so the ingredients vary with each person. "Whatever *kamma* a person performs, good or evil, he will be the heir to it," says the Buddha. Thus the influence of past lives of an individual on his present experience can be more or less strong. If he tormented other beings, he may suffer with a disease; if he was habitually angry, he inherits ugliness; while stinginess gives him the heritage of poverty, indolence of illiteracy;

envy in the past a low position in this one and so on. On the other hand, from wholesome actions one inherits health, beauty, wealth, wisdom, noble birth and so on. Truly it is a blessing to have done good deeds in the past! There is no inheritance better than that resulting from good *kamma*: to be an heir to such an inheritance means that one starts life with an excellent advantage. It is for this reason that the Buddha praised "the merit garnered in the past" and declared it a blessing in this life.

Attasammāpaṇidhi: "one's self rightly directed." This means one must decide on a proper objective in life and set oneself on the right path leading to it.

The emphasis is on "one's own self": one should try to direct oneself to the desired goal by the efforts one makes.[9] This encourages self-confidence and discourages dependence upon the grace of gods or men. Many people pass their lives in the wrong course, engaged in evil practices of the body, speech and mind. Such people, perhaps we are among them, should cherish right desires and open a new and wholesome direction for their lives. Others, who already consider themselves to have a wholesome way of living, should review their situation from time to time not only to avoid lapses but also to progress further in the right direction.

We can understand clearly what is meant by rightly directing oneself, in this comment: The un-virtuous person establishes himself in virtue (the five precepts for instance); the faithless person establishes himself in excellent faith; the avaricious person establishes himself in generosity. Along these lines everyone has something to do.

Stanza IV: *Ample learning, in crafts ability ...*

Bahusaccañ ca sippañ ca: "ample learning and proficiency in crafts."

Bahusaccaṃ is read by some as *bahussutaṃ*, which means "great learning through hearing." In the time of the Buddha, education was mostly through oral tradition, written knowledge not being very common. Consequently one was considered learned according

---

9. What about concern for others? This is just the initial stage of practice when one must be concerned with one's own good conduct. Later, having developed in Dhamma, one can manifest compassion for other people.

to what one had memorized after having heard learned people talk. This standard of erudition applied particularly to religious learning. Obviously a pupil needed certain abilities such as a good memory, keen desire to learn and to associate with the learned, also a capacity to understand their teachings. Thus *bahusaccaṃ* means "much learning through direct contact with the learned." This is a blessing whether the knowledge gained is used for Dhamma-practice or, restrained by moral conduct, for one's livelihood.

Bahu-sippaṃ means "proficiency in some art or handicraft," which implies "practical knowledge of some art, science or handicraft." We understand that the Buddha saw skill in some art or craft as a blessing too. Not only knowledge is praised by him but also manual work wherever this is not tainted by unwholesome actions. One's "craft" should therefore be in accordance with the precepts when it may be used either for hobby or livelihood. Among Bhikkhus too there are "crafts" which it is good to be skilled in—such as making robes—and such skills are a blessing for one's fellow monks.

Vinayo ca susikkhito: "well-learned discipline."

For one who leads the householder's life this means abstaining from the ten courses of unwholesome action.

The ten that should be abstained from so that one makes no evil *kamma* are:

1. *kamma* by way of body: killing living beings, taking what is not given, wrong conduct in sexual desires,
2. *kamma* by way of speech: false speech, malicious speech, harsh speech, gossip,
3. *kamma* by way of mind: covetousness, ill will and wrong views.

A layman who disciplines himself in these ten is rightly called an excellent person. People like this are sure to make further gains on the path whenever they make efforts. (See also "practice of Dhamma" under stanza VI.)

The moral discipline in the case of a monk is stricter than for a householder; he must train himself not to fall into the various classes of offences laid down by the Buddha.

Subhāsitā ca yā vācā: "well-spoken words, civility."

By this, one would usually understand speech which is devoid of the four defects, as given in the list under "well-trained discipline." And certainly what one speaks and how one speaks it are very important, considering all the words which pour out of our mouths every day. However, the commentary says that "well-spoken words" consist of words used while teaching Dhamma to other people. This must be true, for Dhamma is always for one's benefit though of course much depends on how it is taught. Dhamma words can never be ill-spoken words, since they

1. are true,
2. bring concord,
3. are compassionate,
4. and meaningful.

In this way they are a blessing both to the speaker and to the listener.

Stanza V: *Mother, father well supporting ...*

Mātā-pitu upaṭṭhānaṃ means adequately supporting, looking after properly, waiting on patiently and rendering proper service to mother and father.

People these days do not always look after their parents. In western lands they often prefer to get some institution to take care of them as they age. But they do not consider, perhaps, that because they have not given good support or even neglected their old parents, it is likely that they too, as they grow old, will have to suffer the same misfortune. Contrast this with the Buddha's teaching that children's debt to parents is so great that it can never be repaid by only material support. One should certainly give this but the support of Dhamma should also be given to them.

Are they stingy? Teach them generosity and its benefits. Perhaps their moral conduct is not good in some way? Then lead them to see the dangers of unwholesome conduct. Or maybe they lack understanding. Open the gates of Dhamma so that they understand good and evil, the causal arising of events and so on.

Only in this way can parents be repaid by their children. One's parents should be honoured—the Buddha has called them God (*Brahmā*) and it is surely better to pay homage to them with devoted service and loving-kindness, which will bring them joy in their declining years, than to worship any kind of god unknown to oneself personally. A good Buddhist thinks and acts in this way towards his parents: "I who was sustained by them, shall sustain them; I shall do their work for them; I shall keep up their family traditions; I shall make myself worthy of my inheritance; I shall make continual offerings for them when they have died." These are the Buddha's words to young Sigāla. Regarding the last, this means the well-known Buddhist practice of giving alms (to Bhikkhus and others) on death anniversaries and dedicating the merits to those who have died. In this way parents are supported even beyond this life. This is a blessing for those who are so kind and grateful, as they have the chance to make much good *kamma.*

Putta-dārassa saṅgaho: "cherishing one's wife and children."[10] Surely everyone knows that this should be done. But one hears also of many cases when they are neglected or abandoned by a husband gone elsewhere. When a man has such commitments, he has the duty to support the wife and help the children. The Buddha taught young Sigāla that a husband can help his wife in five ways: by cherishing her, by not looking down on her, by not being unfaithful to her, by giving her authority in her sphere of work and by making presents to her of such things as ornaments. Any way of helpfulness which is in accord with the Dhamma is a true blessing because all such actions are good *kamma*—wholesome and with happy results. If done in the right spirit, "cherishing wife and children" must bring harmony into the home, and just in this life to live at peace with others is a blessing, what of the good results in lives to come?

Anākulā ca kammantā means activities and livelihood which bring no conflicts and can be attended to peacefully without mental confusion. Not only should one's work bring no conflicts but one should avoid disturbing others.

The significance of the expression will be much better appreciated by understanding that *kamma* (in this context meaning work) should be a means to an end (*anta*). The adjective

10. In the days of the Buddha women were not as mobile socially as they are now, so he had no cause to say "cherishing one's husband and children" but this is obviously included here.

anākulā—"unconflicting"—shows how the work (*kamma*) should be done to reach the end (*anta*).

Life is a state of (*ākulā*) conflict brought about by the roots of the unwholesome, greed, hatred and delusion, which are the sources of so many (*kamma*) actions. The fruits arising from this action are various kinds of sufferings and limitations, further causes for conflict. The objective in life is not to further complicate conflicts but to act, work and attend to business in a way that leads to the lessening and eventual riddance of conflicts. The emphasis is on making wholesome *kamma* as a means of achieving noble and desirable objectives. It is not the quality of the objective alone that decides the worth of an activity, it is the objective taken together with the means to it and related activities, which decides final worth. Thus the "means" (*kamma*) have as much importance as the "ends." To sum up this blessing: what is important here is right livelihood—that one's work leads to no harm for oneself or other beings. This kind of work everyone will agree is a blessing.

Stanza VI: *Acts of giving, righteous living ...*

Dāna: charity, liberality, offering of gifts, etc.

The important thing here is not the act as it appears, but the intention behind it. Thus *dāna* may be graded as low, medium and superior according to whether the motive is selfish, unselfish or a mixture of these. The results vary accordingly both in quality and quantity.

The mental purity of the recipient and the amount of what is given, though undoubtedly important factors, are yet subsidiary to the intention motivating the offering.

Apart from the material *dāna* visibly given through the body, *dāna* may also be practised by speech and mind: a friendly smile, words of goodwill, a generous nature and a mind full of loving-kindness.

Giving also works in harmony with other good qualities and strengthens them. For instance, a generous person develops both renunciation in being able to give freely and compassion, concern to aid the plight of others. Giving is also related to moral conduct, that one gives gifts which do not conflict with the precepts. And this brings in another relationship with wisdom, for one should give wisely, not unwisely.

Finally, another division of types of giving often seen is into material offerings (such as lay people make to Bhikkhus and nuns and so make their lives possible), and the gift of Dhamma (often given by Bhikkhus and others who have learned and practised, to those who want to know). This *Dhamma-dāna* excels all other kinds of gift, since, unlike material gifts, it never wears out, instead becoming stronger with use, as well as being of benefit in future lives, besides the present one. A great blessing!

Dhammacariyā: practice of Dhamma.

"Living by the Dhamma" means making efforts to maintain and increase one's practice of the ten wholesome paths of *kamma*. Restraint from their evil counterparts has already been mentioned under "well-trained discipline." So here they are explained in a positive way.

Refraining from killing living beings implies the growth of *loving-kindness* and *compassion* in one's speech and bodily actions.
By not stealing (and so on) is meant the presence of *right livelihood*, a factor of the Noble Eightfold Path.
Right conduct in sex means that *contentment* with one's partner is strong in the mind.
One's speech is *truthful*.
It is also *harmonious* and brings people together in concord.
And it is *gentle* as well, so that one's words are loved by others.
Finally it is *meaningful*, not concerned with stupid trifles but has value for one's listeners.
Renunciation becomes stronger.
While *loving-kindness* is established in the emotions.

Finally one understands rightly and clearly about Dhamma and oneself.

In the context of the stanza the term Dhamma has the connotation of "righteousness." This is supported by a commentary which gives as a synonym, *samacariyā* (*sama*, here means "just").

Anavajjāni: "not forbidden," "not blameworthy," "not to be shunned or avoided," "without reproach."

Kammāni: actions, works.

Anavajjāni kammāni: blameless actions.

The expressions, "unconflicting types of work" and "blameless actions," are accepted as synonymous by some authors. They might be so at first glance but they differ in their emphasis.

Thus while the unconflicting types of work lay emphasis on the nature of the activities with which one is occupied, the expression "blameless actions" stresses the making of *kamma* which will not lead to obstacles and hindrances in the future. One could say that here the intention in the mind is stressed. The Pāli commentary bears this out when under this blessing it suggests a number of actions which are blameless, such as keeping the eight precepts on the *Uposatha* days, social services, planting gardens and groves (for public use), making bridges (again for the benefit of all).

Then there are the hospitable actions for which Buddhists are famous: the full jar of cool water to refresh thirsty travellers and the rest house giving shade which anyone may use. All such actions are praiseworthy, irrespective of one's belief—for where is kindliness not praised? It is a great blessing wherever many kindly people are found.

Stanza VII: *Avoiding evil and abstaining ...*

Ārati viratī pāpā: avoiding and abstaining from evil.

The words "*ārati*" and "*virati*" occur together in several places in the scriptures. Taken together they mean "leaving off," "abstinence," "keeping away from," "avoiding," etc. Though the two terms have similarity of meaning they are not the same, as we shall see. Both signify effort at detachment from something unwholesome in the range of sensual pleasure, that is, the evil mentioned in the stanza. It is the difference in scope between the two terms that makes them into two distinct blessings in the Sutta. Thus the expression "avoiding and abstaining from evil," means *avoiding evil* and *abstaining from evil.*

The commentary explains avoiding evil to mean "mental non-delight" in it, a shrinking away from evil thoughts that have arisen so that they cease, having run out of fuel to burn. Only when this avoidance is not present in the mind can the fires of greed, aversion and delusion be fuelled up with the persistent flames of evil thoughts.

But abstaining from evil means "abstinence by way of bodily and verbal actions." Where mental avoidance of evil is present there will also be abstinence from it through body and speech but the presence of the latter does not guarantee the former. Why this is so is explained by the commentary when it says that abstinence may be the result of following custom or tradition. For if people do not steal, let us say, thinking "It would disgrace the family" then they have present only "abstinence as custom." A better reason for abstinence is found in the person who remembers the precepts, thinking, "Oh, I shall break that training rule." This is called "abstinence as undertaking." Best of all is "abstinence as severance" found in the Noble (*Ariya*) disciple who can abstain quite naturally and without struggle because the power of evil has been weakened in his heart.

The scriptures also teach three kinds of avoiding and abstaining, namely, from wrong speech, wrong (bodily) action and wrong livelihood. This means that both of these blessings are concerned with *sīla* or morality.

Concerning this word "evil" (*pāpa*), what does it mean? Why do we say that this or that action is wrong speech, wrong (bodily) action or wrong livelihood? All the actions listed under these headings bring trouble and suffering to oneself and to others. They lead to blame from other people and for the doer of them they cause many obstacles and difficulties in the future. Here they are:

1. Wrong speech means false speech, malicious speech, harsh speech and gossip. Wrong bodily actions are killing living beings, taking what is not given, wrong conduct in sexual desires.
2. Wrong livelihood is one that harms others, e.g., trading in arms, slaves, intoxicants and professions involving killing, cheating, astrology or other prognosticating trickery.

Majjapānā ca saññamo: "refraining from intoxicating drinks." *Majja*: intoxicating; *pānā*: drinks. *Majja*: this is related to our English word "mad" and there is a play on intoxication and maddening which English cannot reproduce. However, everyone the world over knows the effects of alcohol and other intoxicants. Though drinks are mentioned here, anything which leads to more delusion of the mind, whether swallowed, injected or smoked should be included. A Buddhist wants a clear mind that can understand easily what is going on in his own mind and body, as well as other actions. But these besotting substances just lead to more and more foolishness. Thoroughly drunk, a person knows nothing but must suffer when he wakes. Partly drunk a person becomes capable of actions which he would be ashamed to do while sober. And carelessness from intoxication leads to the death or maiming of how many people these days? So those who are intoxicated are rightly blamed by wise men. The commentary remarks that these people are censured in this very life, get themselves an unhappy future life and when finally they return to the human state after long subhuman existences, they are born mad. This seems just enough for they madden themselves with intoxicants now, so the fruits of such *kamma* bring madness, a whole life without understanding. Taking all this into account an earnest follower of the Buddha should abstain completely from all intoxicants.

Appamādo ca dhammesu: "diligence in Dhamma doing"; "*a*" (a negative prefix, not) *-pamāda* (negligence and heedlessness). *Pamāda*, like *majja* in the last blessing, is also related linguistically to madness. This is the opposite of what the Buddha taught! He constantly urged people to cultivate *appamāda* or diligence. The word in Pāli has the flavour of three good qualities: effort, mindfulness and wisdom. These three go along together in anyone who tries to develop the Dhamma in himself and such a person is *appamatta*, diligent or heedful. Now here the Buddha is admonishing us to be diligent in cultivating Dhamma—all aspects of it—in ourselves.

This means we should try to protect whatever good practices we have already, and make the effort also to develop further in *dhamma*-qualities or practices. If we find any of the following in our hearts then we are slipping:

1. carelessness
2. inattentiveness
3. heedlessness
4. hanging back
5. unzealousness
6. uninterestedness
7. non-repetition (of Dhamma learned by heart)

8. non-development
9. non-cultivation
10. non-resolution
11. non-application
12. negligence

concerning the development of wholesome dhammas (*Vibhaṅga* 350). Surely diligence is a blessing!

Stanza VIII: *Right Reverence and Humility ...*

Gāravo: reverence. This includes the proper veneration of the Buddha, Dhamma and Sangha, and respect for parents and teachers, wise people, good persons and elders—in fact, a general high regard for everyone. Even the Buddha after his Enlightenment surveyed the world to try to find a teacher to revere. When he realized that no teacher surpassed his own attainments he then proclaimed in verse that he would live revering the Dhamma through which Enlightenment had been discovered.

And the Arahant-disciples too had reverence for the Buddha as their guide, for the Dhamma, for other senior Bhikkhus and for the way of training.

The further one has gone along the path of Dhamma the more reverence one has for it—and for others who also practice correctly. It is not that reverence grows less as one practises! This is a way of estimating one's own position, for if a lot of pride and conceit can be seen then one has not got very far!

How does one show respect or reverence? The Buddha says that one gives such a person a good seat, stands up to receive them, makes way for them and for religious teachers, one places one's hands together and bows at their feet. This is a blessing resulting in good future births and harmony in the present life.

Nivāto: humility. Yet another factor which stresses the importance of having no pride. The fact that we encounter a number of "blessings" which deal with non-pride should make us realize how important humility is for the successful practice of Dhamma. The person who knows it all, who always replies "I know," who has his own theories about Dhamma, or anyone else's theories for that matter, does not have humility. Because of this he can never train under a good teacher. The Commentary gives the right attitude to have: to be lowly "like a foot-wiping cloth," "like a bull with horns cut off" or "like a snake with fangs extracted." People like this get on with Dhamma. Of course, this does not mean that one is obsequiously 'humble'—just another disguise for pride and a revolting one at that. But the wise person tries to make displays of self less and less evident. He does not advertise himself; he is not exuberant in body or speech but instead is restrained. It is interesting to note that this humility in Pāli is literally "not-wind" which ties up well with such English expressions of conceit and pride as "puffery," "vapouring," or more colloquially "hot air" and "gas."

Santuṭṭhī: contentment. This implies acceptance of Conditions and situations as they arise, with equanimity and without grumbling.

This is a quality which Bhikkhus must have, as the commentary emphasizes when it does not mention lay people at all here. This is a much needed quality in those parts of the world and among those families where there is affluence. Contentment spells peace of mind for the person who has it; craving more and more spells out the opposite. What should one be content with? With enough clothes, enough food, enough living room and enough medicines. But then what is enough and what is excess? "Enough" gives one little trouble to keep and maintain but more than that brings anxiety and worry. This blessing should also not be misunderstood as counsel not to make an effort in life. Bhikkhus do not have to possess many things for happiness in their life but lay people need much more. Lay people must make effort to obtain what is necessary for a happy life without poverty and starvation. Everyone has to decide for oneself whether possessions will bring more happiness or more trouble. Being able to know this clearly is an aspect of wisdom.

Kataññutā: gratitude. Literally, this is "knowing what has been done," that is, remembering what others have done for oneself. The Buddha has said: "Two sorts of people are hard to find in the world: one who first does (something kind or helpful), and one who is grateful and recognizes (that kindness)." Without this quality a person forgets parents, relatives, friends, teachers and those who teach him Dhamma; he turns his back on them just when they could be helped by him or when they are in need of aid.

A selfish person seems to try to isolate himself from the world's web. "I alone am important," he says, and forgets all the benefit derived from others. On the other hand the grateful person makes for harmony and peace. How many good things have we obtained through others in this life and how many are we grateful for and then express our gratitude in speech and action?

Kālena dhammasavanaṃ: "timely hearing of Dhamma," means that the occasion for hearing the teachings of the Buddha should be well-timed. Hearing of Dhamma should be opportune.

Obviously, the hearing of Dhamma will be more profitable if regularly attended to at times when one has healthy body and mind: when one is exhausted, except perhaps during disease or suffering, this may lead to sleepiness, and so it is not suitable.

Some of the excellent general occasions for the hearing of the teachings are:

1. Sacred days such as the Full Moon days, or during Buddhist festivals.
2. When disease and suffering make one thoughtful enough to want to understand the truth of suffering (*dukkha*), and ready enough to find a way out of the sufferings.
3. When the mind is specially inclined towards the teachings, as when one does concentrated meditation practice for some time.
4. When evil thoughts have invaded the mind but have not yet fully taken possession of it.
5. A special meaning of "*savana*" (hearing) these days is to know Dhamma from book-study. In the Buddha's time knowledge was gained only by hearing but now it is more by way of books. This should also find a place here.
6. At the time of death, when concentration of mind can condition a happy rebirth or may even help attain one of the Paths and Fruits.

Regarding the suitable time of the day, no definite rules can be laid down, for what suits one may not suit another. It is proper to take into consideration the following general points:

1. There should not be any undue tiredness of body or mind, for this distracts attention and makes one sleepy.

2. There should be sufficient freedom from personal business or domestic worries.
3. The mind should be in a receptive state.
4. The mind also should be free from the influences of all kinds of drugs and intoxicants.

Timely hearing of the Dhamma is a great blessing since because of it the five hindrances can be abandoned even while one sits there, and the ten fetters too, so that even the three kinds of taints may be exhausted and Arahantship won through listening attentively. Even if such attainments do not occur, then one comes to know Dhamma which one had not heard before, while what one had heard is learned in detail. With such a store of Dhamma one can apply it to one's life for one's own benefit and the happiness of others. A great blessing!

Stanza IX: *Patience, Meekness When Corrected ...*

Khantī: This is an important virtue, in fact one of the highest. It can be translated as patience but it includes the virtues of forbearance, forgiveness and tolerance. It finds expression as a serene attitude towards stresses in oneself and outside, which enables a person to accept with equanimity the flow of events. Because of this the impressions entering the mind from the sense doors cannot upset the peace reigning there; so one goes on serenely with the work in hand. Though all sorts of upsetting situations occur and send their disturbing messages to the mind, it does not become heated. In fact with even a little of this virtue the mind becomes cool, clean and calm, like a refreshing pool of crystal clear water, quite unlike the minds of most people, which can rightly be compared to a pot of boiling soup or a cup of water with swirls of colour in it.

A person who practises patience has a "cool heart," the mark of a person who has applied the Dhamma to his life. "Cool-heartedness," not worried, flustered or impatient, marks the good Buddhist, while "hot-heartedness" shows how little of Dhamma a person has in his heart.

Khantī is one of the *pāramitās* (perfections) which one who aspires to Enlightenment must perfect to a far greater degree than just not being impatient or impetuous. This we know from that famous story of the *Bodhisatta's* life when he was the

Preacher of Patience, a monk living harmlessly in the forest who was slaughtered by a maddened king, about which it is said in that story:

> *In olden times there was a monk,*
> *Of patience he was paragon;*
> *He kept his patience even when*
> *The king of Kāsi murdered him.*

Even if our patience is not tried by such extreme events, still we have to encounter heat and cold, hunger and thirst, various insects and so on which attack this body, and the sharp words of others which seem to attack the ego; then there are occasions for being patient about time, and how many times for being patient with the frailties of other people? But the basis of all patience is to be patient with oneself.

Patience is thus the foundation of *mettā* (loving-kindness). It is reckoned as a great power; and the strength of those who have patience is often praised in Buddhist writings.

Sovacassatā: the meaning given in the Commentaries is "one who can easily be addressed, spoken to or advised" and it further means "a person who can be corrected." Also implied are the qualities of tolerance of criticism directed at oneself and courtesy and gratitude in accepting advice.

The Commentary says that a person who is meek when corrected has the chance to learn Dhamma, which is the opposite of the person who is "difficult to speak to." The latter "indulge in prevarication, silence or think up virtues and vices." Prevarication is only a fancy word for lying, the method used by some people when they are admonished. Another way is sullen silence, while the third is blaming the adviser by charging him with faults or else praising one's own virtue. People like this are difficult to train; others find them hard to get on with. One should examine oneself to find out whether or not one has the blessing of being meek when corrected.

Obviously a gentle person will only need to be told to do a thing gently: he is like a well-bred horse, needing just a soft touch, unlike an obstinate beast, which only responds to harsh treatment. He is a thoroughbred with the attributes of broadmindedness of outlook, instant acceptance of good advice and habitual courtesy in manners and speech.

Samaṇānañ ca dassanaṃ: "seeing monks or holy men." *Samaṇa* (lit., one who has made oneself peaceful), a monk, a holy man. The Buddha was often addressed as Samaṇa, by those who were not his followers.

In the ordinary sense *dassanaṃ* means "seeing" with the physical eye. But generally the expression signifies more than mere "seeing," even when used in the restricted sense of seeing in the ordinary way. The underlying sense is conveyed when the act of visual "seeing" has as its objectives holy persons of purity and real worth. "Seeing" is generally performed with the desire to pay respects to them. This is also the sense of the modern Hindi word *darshan*. For a Buddhist, however, it is not enough just to gaze with devotion and perform acts of worship. So the expression means much more than mere "meeting" or "seeing." It involves mind, speech and body in a harmonious synthesis:

1. A desire to meet holy persons, particularly the monks and nuns following the teachings of the Buddha.
2. Making genuine efforts to visit them at their monasteries or making use of any opportunity available to pay one's respects to them such as when they are on their rounds for almsfood or during their visits to friends and relatives, or when one is able to receive them reverently at one's house.
3. Deriving inspiration from their company.

There is no better company than holy persons, whose very presence spreads a purifying aura and inspires a constructive approach to one's problems. Such company is an antidote to evil ways of life besides leading one to discover for oneself spiritual treasures in due course.

In the deeper sense *dassanaṃ* means "seeing" with the mental eye, e.g., *ñāṇadassana* (insight through knowledge) and *dhamma-dassana* (rightly understanding the Doctrine). So in the deepest sense *dassana* means perception of the Noble Truths. All those deeper meanings can come about through simply "seeing the monks."

Kālena dhammasākacchā: "timely discussion on the Dhamma."

As Dhamma is a profound subject it needs sincere effort to understand it properly and grasp it for practical use in life. This can be made easier through discussions with others who have a thorough knowledge of the theory and practice of Dhamma.

Discussions should be well-timed. The right times for discussions with intelligent, wise and experienced people should not be missed, even though it means personal inconvenience. Still, one should remember that discussions would not be opportune if the convenience of the other person is neglected.

It is particularly timely to discuss the Dhamma when one's mind is troubled either by defilements of the mind such as uncertainty, or by exterior troubles in the family, at work or in any kind of relationship.

Stanza X: *Self-Restraint and Holy Life ...*

Tapo literally means "heat." Its brahmanical meaning was "ascetic practices," which the Buddha showed were useless for the attainment of deliverance. Though he denounced the torment of one's own body, the Buddha used this word to mean self-control, as with the restraint of one's sense faculties. When these are restrained then such unwholesome mental states as covetousness and grief have no chance to appear. But "tapo" was used in another sense by the Buddha to mean vigorous efforts, the sort which a Bhikkhu has to make if he is to win Enlightenment. It is the kind of effort which *burns up* the defilements.

Brahmacariyaṃ: holy life. The general Buddhist meaning is "the best life," but in some places it means "the Buddha's Dispensation" (*sāsana*) while elsewhere it is "the monk's ideal life" (*samaṇa-dhamma*). Here it can include these two besides the more common meaning of "leading a holy life" which implies abstaining from sex. With *brahmacariya* may also be included the practice of the Four Sublime States (*brahma-vihāra*), viz. *mettā* (loving-kindness), *karuṇā* (compassion), *muditā* (altruistic joy) and *upekkhā* (equanimity).

The word *brahmacariyā*, while including all aspects of Dhamma-practice in its scope, emphasizes moral purity. Through the study and practice of Dhamma one attains self-control; and an important part of this is sex control, which energy empowers the clear meditative mind as well as providing the drive for beneficial social activities.

Sensual desire generally is a cause of many lives and much suffering. As sexual desire is a concentrated form of sensuality, and so is the cause of much trouble, the Buddha has shown how it can be checked first by precepts (*sīla*), and then through meditation. For the lay followers, sex is limited to that allowed in the third of the five precepts, while for Bhikkhus complete sexual abstinence is necessary. Bhikkhus are bound to practise it strictly and even lay followers may undertake the precept of sexual abstinence if they wish. Worldly life, though not much help for this practice, does not make it impossible. Buddhists observe this vow on the Uposatha days, and some who are endowed with strong self-control and a firm determination to advance in meditation, practise it all the time while engaged in the general round of worldly duties.

Ariyasaccāna dassanaṃ: "seeing the Noble Truths," i.e., the Four Noble Truths, which constitute the central pillar of the Buddha's Dhamma and of which all other Buddhist doctrines are a preparation or elaboration. The Four Noble Truths are the briefest factual description of experience during life. They constitute the unique and vital discovery made by the Buddha which was announced by him in his very first discourse.

The truths are:

That all forms of existence are subject to suffering (this is the Truth of Suffering: *dukkha-sacca*).[11]

That craving (*taṇhā*) is the cause of suffering (this is the Truth of the Cause of Suffering: *dukkha-samudaya-sacca*).

That the removal of the cause results in the absence of the effect (this is the Truth of the Cessation of Suffering: *dukkha-nirodha-sacca*).

That the path is the means to attain the cessation of suffering (this is the Truth of the Path, the Noble Eightfold Path, for the cessation of suffering: *magga-sacca*).

The eight steps of the Noble Eightfold Path are:

1. *sammā-diṭṭhi*: right view
2. *sammā-saṅkappa*: right intention

11. One should remember that the English word "suffering" does not include all *dukkha*. All experience is impermanent, unreliable or insecure and therefore *dukkha*. Pleasant experience too is *dukkha* but it cannot be called suffering.

3. *sammā-vācā*: right speech
4. *sammā-kammanta*: right action
5. *sammā-ājīva*: right livelihood
6. *sammā-vāyāma*: right (mental) effort
7. *sammā-sati*: right mindfulness
8. *sammā-samādhi*: right concentration.[12]

These eight steps are usually grouped into the following three divisions:

A. *sīla* (morality): 3, 4, and 5.
B. *samādhi* (mental concentration): 6, 7 and 8.
C. *paññā* (deep wisdom): 1 and 2.

Knowledge of these truths may be intellectual or by way of realization. The former variety of knowledge, as it is intellectual or hearsay evidence, only helps understanding the formulation of these truths, which still remain to be realized. The knowledge gained in this way remains limited as relative truth.

The knowledge based on direct perception is that of realization: it is the "knowledge penetrated by truth" (*paṭivedha-ñāṇa*). The former type of knowledge is termed "mundane" (*lokiya*) and the latter "supramundane" (*lokuttara*).

As "mundane knowledge," the Four Noble Truths are generally perceived as separate events; nevertheless their understanding helps to dispel certain prejudices and wrong beliefs. In the supramundane stage all four truths are simultaneously realized: whoever realizes suffering, also realizes its origin, its cessation and the path to its cessation. Though at first one has an intellectual appreciation of them—for certainly this is also a blessing—here direct perception is meant, the former usually leading to the latter.

The expression means the perception of the Four Noble Truths at work in life. This insight results in the realization of the facts of (1) suffering (*dukkha*), (2) its roots in the cravings of *lobha*, *dosa* and *moha* (greed, hatred and delusion), (3) its extinction through the exhaustion of the cravings and (4) the technique of the conquest. Once direct insight arises, one arrives at the doorway to the Final Goal.

---

12. For a systematic description of the path see Ledi Sayādaw, *The Noble Eightfold Path and Its Factors Explained*, BPS Wheel Publication No. 245/247.

Nibbāna-sacchikiriyā: "the realization of Nibbāna." Nibbāna, the Final Goal, is a blessed state of freedom from desire, of freedom from greed, hatred and delusion, of perfect safety from the vicissitudes of existence, of bliss that is resplendent, of knowledge that is supreme, in brief, a state that is perfection itself.

In life, one is plagued by desires; in Nibbāna, all desires are extinguished and all clinging is nullified. In life, one lives in a forest of conflicting views and theories: in Nibbāna all these vanish under the direct perception of truth, just as the dew vanishes with the direct touch of the sun's rays.

The state of Nibbāna, which is supramundane (*lokuttara*), is beyond the power of language to describe, for words can only convey *relatively* true concepts. Therefore, it is beyond the power of anyone, even the Supreme Buddha, to describe or define Nibbāna except by using negation and occasionally more positive imagery. Hence, the Buddha has not described Nibbāna at any length although he uses similes sometimes for effect.

The attainment of Nibbāna is the most excellent achievement, needing a strong determination backed by strenuous endeavours in the right way. These endeavours must be patiently and perseveringly directed towards the eradication of the roots of evil bound up with life, namely, *lobha* (greed), *dosa* (hatred) and *moha* (delusion). These evils, rooted in ignorance (*avijjā*), generate strong fetters (*saṃyojana*) which tie beings to the painful circle of suffering, the wheel of existence, the round of birth, death and rebirth. The fetters are ten in number:

1. *sakkāyadiṭṭhi*: belief in the permanence of personality;
2. *vicikicchā*: irrational doubts;
3. *sīlabbataparāmāsa*: clinging to rituals and superstitions;
4. *kāma-rāga*: craving for sensual enjoyment;
5. *vyāpāda*: ill-will;
6. *rūpa-rāga*: craving for existence in fine-material worlds;
7. *arūpa-rāga*: craving for existence in worlds without material form;
8. *māna*: conceit;
9. *uddhacca*: restlessness;
10. *avijjā*: ignorance.

Those possessed of all the ten fetters are termed ordinary people (*puthujjana*). We are those ordinary people who are in the stormy ocean of existence (*saṃsāra*), feverishly twitching to the tune of sensual cravings while tightly bound to the wheel of suffering. We are prisoners in chains, chains riveted by our cravings.

The dissolution of these "fetters" is the highest aim of the Buddha's teaching. Though the effort needed for this is very great, the resulting fruit is sweet beyond compare. Once the right course is found, further progress is assured. The right method is mental culture through reflection, meditation and concentration. The resulting insight (*vipassanā*) is the solvent of all fetters, dissolving them away.

The dissolution of the "first three fetters" makes one a *sotāpanna* (stream-winner). This means success in shifting from the stormy ocean of life (*saṃsāra*) to the cool and steady "stream" that unmistakably leads to Nibbāna, the release. This is the first stage of Nobility. With the attainment of it, one is known as an Ariya, a Noble One. In the next stage, the next two fetters are weakened and the Noble One becomes a *sakadāgāmī* (once-returner to this world). The destruction of the next two fetters makes the Noble One an *anāgāmi* (non-returner). Freedom from all ten fetters makes one an Arahant, a Perfect One, a Fully Liberated One. He has attained the highest, that is, Nibbāna, and after death there is no more rebirth for him.

The Buddha is an Arahant as he has destroyed all the fetters. He is more than that too, for he reached the goal by a longer and more strenuous path with the object of amply profiting the world through his supreme wisdom and compassion.

The Buddha and the Arahants, unlike ordinary people, make no more mental-formations or *kamma*. They stand with rock-like firmness, unshaken by the winds and storms all around. They are beyond the clutches of any temptations: they are delivered of all evils, are perfectly pure and holy and full of supreme understanding. They have achieved the Goal, Nibbāna. They live only for the period necessary to expend their kammic momentum left from the past. At the end of that, as no more *kamma* fruits (*kamma-vipāka*) remain, they attain *Parinibbāna*, no more to return to rebirth anywhere.

There are obviously two aspects of Nibbāna:

1. *Sa-upādi-sesa-nibbāna*, Nibbāna with the groups of personality still remaining, such as the Buddha when he taught for 45 years, or an Arahant living.
2. *An-upādi-sesa-nibbāna*, Nibbāna with no more psycho-physical elements existing, i.e., the Parinibbāna of the Buddha or an Arahant.

One often hears a strange question: Who or what attains Nibbāna after the final death? The question is meaningless as there are neither any *kamma*-resultants nor any of the five groups (*pañcakkhandhā*) of the psychophysical being left; so the question does not arise as to who or what "enters" Nibbāna. To explain this more fully one should know about one's "self" and what this means.

The Buddha's analysis of personality reveals five groups (*khandha*) as making up a human being: *rūpakkhandha* (physical body), *vedanākkhandha* (feelings), *saññākkhandha* (perceptions), *saṅkhārakkhandha* (mental formations and their fruits) and *viññāṇakkhandha* (consciousness). A common classification is the grouping of these five into two sections: *nāma* (mind, i.e., the psychological part of personality) comprising the last four, and *rūpa* (body, i.e., the physical aspect of personality), the first group. All these are characterized by the three qualities common to all living beings (impermanence, suffering and not-self). And as there is nothing in the human person outside these five, a human being is in reality without a permanent ego-entity, self or soul. He is like a bubble of water, or a cart on the road, things which give the impression of being entities because of the combination of certain factors, but which have no permanent substance to endure forever.

There are two aspects of truth (*sacca*), namely,

1. the conventional truth (*vohāra-sacca* or *sammuti-sacca*) and
2. the ultimate truth (*paramattha-sacca*). The former means "things as they appear" and the latter, "things as they really are."

The Buddha, in his discourses, while addressing ordinary people or while expounding the common-sense viewpoint, generally spoke of conventional truth. Thus in this Sutta the term *attā*, self (see stanza III), is used only as a conventional mode of speech, meaning "the human being as he appears." In the ultimate sense the personality is a flux, ever-changing and never the same even for two consecutive fractions of a moment. This is the doctrine of *anattā*. It is a unique Buddhist discovery—in fact the most revolutionary discovery ever made in the field of human personality. Without a proper grasp of its import, Buddhism will be understood only superficially.

The conventional recognition of a self as a convenient mode of speech, however, should not lead people astray into belief in the existence of a "higher self." There is no "higher self" or soul in the ultimate sense, for no "self" of any kind, higher or lower, here or hereafter, can be found. That is why the Buddha laid emphasis on "selflessness" (*anattā*) and classed it as one of the three fundamental characteristics of all living beings, including human personality.

The proper study for a man is himself, for once the emptiness of self is understood, all the rest becomes easy to grasp. As tersely explained in the *Visuddhimagga*, according to ultimate truth:

There is suffering but no sufferer,
There are deeds, but no doer,
There is Nibbāna but none to enter it,
There is the Path, but no traveller on it.

Yet with this direct view of truth, in which personality finds no foothold at all, the Buddha did not ignore the truth of the conventional self. He gave it the recognition it merited, and used it as a base for directing the individual ultimately to the realization of the truth of "non-personality" (*anattā*). This is where the expression *attasammāpaṇidhi* "one's self rightly directed" (stanza III) eventually leads. Thus, evil tendencies and practices (really existing because of the love for or lust about "self") give way to the wholesome tendencies and practices, once the delusion of self is penetrated.

From the very start, one should know that the "self" is accepted merely as a convenient or conventional designation and that its apparent reality can certainly be understood as a delusion, once its non-existence in the ultimate sense is realized. The very fact of starting the life's journey in this way becomes the "act of directing or setting oneself in the right course by oneself." Though there may be external help available, the emphasis is on the "right direction" and self-reliance. All available wholesome assistance should be used but not too much dependence should be shown to any aid apart from that springing from within one's self. So Nibbāna is not attained by any person (= self) in the highest sense.

Nibbāna-sacchikiriyā: the expression means the very realization of Nibbāna or at least an actual glimpse of it, which can be had by no less a person than a *sotāpanna* (the winner of the stream leading to Nibbāna).

It may here be pointed out that the expression "the realization of Nibbāna" implies that by one's own efforts one reaches the goal. Through determination and perseverance in the right direction the goal is reached, and not through grace: it is not a "Gift from the Heavens," but the fruit of one's supreme endeavours. In brief, the goal is one's own earnings: verily Nibbāna is well earned. Blessed is the person who earns it.

Stanza XI: *Though Touched by Worldly Circumstances ...*

Phuṭṭhassa lokadhammehi, cittaṃ yassa na kampati: "a mind which does not waver when touched by worldly conditions." Worldly conditions, inseparable from life, are eight in number: *lābha* (gain), *alābhā* (loss), *ayaso* (disgrace), *yasa* (fame), *nindā* (blame), *pasaṃsā* (praise), *sukha* (happiness, pleasure) and *dukkha* (pain). While ordinary people grasp the pleasant halves of these pairs and reject the unpleasant (which means they use greed and hatred), Noble Ones, especially Arahants, are not shaken by either of the halves. We, as ordinary people, should try to develop more equanimity towards gains and loss, and so on.

Asokaṃ (sorrowless), *virājaṃ* (unstained by passion) and *khemaṃ* (secure from sensuality) are the attributes of an Arahant. These describe the mental state of a Fully Liberated One. The mind of such a person is unique—free from disturbances, purified of passion and finished with sensuality, it is calm and serene, without the storms of desires and the waves of worries. The worldly conditions (*lokadhamma*) do not sway him; he stands firmly, witnessing but untouched by the changeful and sorrowful drama of life going on all around.

Stanza XII: *Since by Acting in This Way ...*

This stanza concludes the Sutta.

The fulfilment of these blessings is shown by

invincibility everywhere
perfect happiness and security.

This is the most sublime of all attainments, the Everest of human achievements, Nibbāna in this life.

Chapter IV
The Highroad of Blessings

I. *The Thirty-eight Blessings*

Stanza I

The Buddha was asked:
What are the highest Blessings in life?
The Blessed One replied:
The Supreme Blessings are:

Stanza II

1. *Asevanā ca bālānaṃ*: Not associating with fools.
2. *Paṇḍitānañ ca sevanā*: Associating with the wise.
3. *Pūjā ca pūjanīyānaṃ*: Reverencing those worthy of respect.

Stanza III

4. *Paṭirūpadesavāso*: Residence in a suitable locality.
5. *Pubbe ca kata-puññatā*: Having made merit in the past.
6. *Attasammāpaṇidhi*: One's mind properly directed.

Stanza IV

7. *Bahusaccañ*: Profound learning.
8. *Bahusippañ*: Proficiency in one's work.
9. *Vinayo ca susikkhito*: Well-trained moral discipline.
10. *Subhāsitā ca yā vācā*: Gracious kindly speech.

Stanza V

11. *Mātā-pitu upaṭṭhānaṃ*: Giving support to parents.
12. *Putta-dārassa saṅgaho*: Cherishing wife and children.
13. *Anākulā ca kammantā*: Business pursuits, peaceful and free from conflicts.

Stanza VI

14. *Dānañ*: Acts of giving.
15. *Dhammacariyā*: Conduct according to Dhamma.
16. *Ñātakānañ ca saṅgaho*: Helping one's relatives.
17. *Anavajjāni kammāni*: Blameless actions.

Stanza VII

18. *Ārati pāpā*: Shunning evil.
19. *Virati pāpā*: Abstaining from evil.
20. *Majjapānā ca saññamo*: Refraining from intoxicants.
21. *Appamādo ca dhammesu*: Diligence in practice of what is Dhamma.

Stanza VIII

22. *Gāravo*: Reverence.
23. *Nivāto*: Humility.
24. *Santuṭṭhi*: Contentment.
25. *Kataññutā*: Gratefulness.
26. *Kālena dhammasavanaṃ*: Timely hearing of the Dhamma.

Stanza IX

27. *Khantī*: Patience.
28. *Sovacassatā*: Meekness (amenability) when corrected.
29. *Samaṇānañ ca dassanaṃ*: Meeting (seeing) monks.
30. *Kālena dhammasākacchā*: Discussing the Dhamma at the proper time.

Stanza X

31. *Tapo*: Energetic self-restraint.
32. *Brahmacariyaṃ*: Holy and chaste life.
33. *Ariyasaccāna dassanaṃ*: Insight into the Noble Truths.
34. *Nibbāna sacchikiriyā*: Realization of Nibbāna.

Stanza XI

35. *Phuṭṭhassa lokadhammehi cittaṃ yassa na kampati*: A mind unshaken by the ups and downs of life.
36. *Asokaṃ*: Freedom from sorrow.

37. *Virājaṃ*: Freedom from defilements of passion.
38. *Khemaṃ*: Perfect security.

Stanza XII

Etādisāni katvāna, sabbattham-aparājitā sabbattha sotthiṃ gacchanti: Those who have acted in this way cannot be defeated and always live in safety.

II. General Review

The thirty-eight blessings detailed in the Mahā Maṅgala Sutta are not arranged in random order. Their arrangement is strictly logical and their sequence is natural and progressive.

Up to this point we have dealt with the various issues individually because an analytic study was necessary for the proper understanding of the subject.

Now, with the perspective of the entire Sutta, we are in a position to consider the subject as a whole. This enlarged view, while giving us a chance to appreciate the cultural integrity of the Sutta, also gives an understanding of the synthesis of its thirty-eight constituents. These constituents are so arranged that they not only follow one another in proper sequence, but they also group themselves into categories which are themselves in the progressive order of development in Dhamma.

Before we pass on to a systematic classification of these blessings, it will be refreshing to read the following comments on the Sutta, adapted from Shway Yoe,[13] who is quoting the Christian Bishop Bigandet:

"Within a narrow compass, the Buddha has condensed an abridgment of almost all moral virtues. The first portion of these precepts contains injunctions to shun all that may prove an impediment to the practice of good works. The second part inculcates the necessity of regulating one's mind and intention for a regular discharge of the duties incumbent on each man in his separate station. Then follows a recommendation to bestow assistance on parents, relatives and all men in general. Next to

13. Shway Yoe, *The Burman: His Life and Notions*. London: Macmillan & Co., 1896, p. 571.

that we find recommended the virtues of humility, resignation,[14] gratitude and patience. After this, the Teacher insists on the necessity of studying the Law, visiting the religious, conversing on religious subjects. When this is done, one is recommended to study with great attention the four great Truths, and keep the mind's eye ever fixed on the happy state of Nibbāna, which, though as yet distant, ought never to be lost sight of. Thus prepared, one must be bent upon acquiring the qualifications befitting the true sage who would remain firm, fearless and unmoved, even in the midst of the ruins of the crumbling universe; the Buddhist sage ever remains calm, composed and unshaken among all the vicissitudes of life. There is again clearly pointed out the final end to be arrived at, viz. that of perfect mental stability. This state is the foreshadowing of Nibbāna."

III. A Synthetic View

The ingredients of the Mahā Maṅgala Sutta, because of their moral excellence and practical appeal, are capable of many classifications. Thus, the thirty-eight blessings can be presented in a variety of combinations. The author, after thinking deeply over the possible groupings, has arrived at a pattern worked out by himself. This classification is based on practical considerations and is expected to be generally useful.

Before we present our own classification, it is proposed to offer another, the essential feature of which is the division of the Sutta into the three classical sections, namely, *sīla* (moral culture), *samādhi* (mental culture) and *paññā* (wisdom). The credit for developing this admirable classification goes to *Maṅgala* U Ba Than, the very honorific prefix to whose name is significant of the excellent work done by him in Burma in popularizing the teaching and the practice of the *Maṅgala* Sutta.[15] He groups the first twenty-one *maṅgalas* under *sīla* and divides them into five

14. But "resignation" is not in the Sutta, nor a virtue recommended by the Buddha. See Stanzas VIII–IX.

15. The information given here is from conversations over a week between the author and Maṅgala U Ba Than at the former's residence during the summer of 1954.

groups. These ensure the basic training of the individual as well as assisting with the discharge of his obligations in the social sphere. The next nine *maṅgalas* are classed under *samādhi* as aspects of mental culture. The last eight *maṅgalas* come under *paññā* and are either the practice towards or the fruit of wisdom and insight.

Steady and regular practice of the twenty-one *maṅgalas* grouped under *sīla* brings the utmost happiness, prosperity and satisfaction possible in the human state. These admirable achievements are not only adequately stabilized and ensured against possible setbacks, but are also further enhanced by the practice of the nine *maṅgalas* grouped under *samādhi*. The last eight *maṅgalas* grouped under *paññā* assist the progressive realization of the highest wisdom.

The above classification is schematically represented below:[16]

I. *Sīla*: moral culture (21 *maṅgalas*)	1. Fundamental rules: M_1 M_2 M_3 M_4 M_5 M_6
A. The preparation	2. Essential training of the senses, body, mind & speech: M_7 M_8 M_9 M_{10}
B. Compulsory obligations	3. The foundation of the domestic order: M_{11} M_{12} M_{13}
	4. Social welfare: M_{14} M_{15} M_{16} M_{17}
C. Vigilance	5. Protection against evil: M_{18} M_{19} M_{20} M_{21}
II. *Samādhi*: mental culture (9 *maṅgalas*)	M_{22} M_{23} M_{24} M_{25} M_{26} M_{27} M_{28} M_{29} M_{30}
III. *Paññā*: wisdom culture (8 *maṅgalas*)	M_{31} M_{32} M_{33} M_{34} M_{35} M_{36} M_{37} M_{38}

IV. Our Classification

The Mahā Maṅgala Sutta, a well-charted course of personal culture and progress, is an excellent guide for reaching even the highest goal. It is a four-sectioned ladder which helps one to climb step by step to the zenith of noble achievements.

16. "M" stands for "*maṅgala*" and the number following it represents the number among the 38 blessings as listed in Section I of this chapter.

The ideal of life is deliverance from fears and insecurities. This is achieved through steady, strenuous effort, and righteous wayfaring in the world. Such a great venture as this obviously needs adequate preparation and thorough training. The Mahā Maṅgala Sutta indicates not only the course of the preparatory training but also safely guides the individual through the journey of life and ultimately leads him to the secure haven of Nibbāna.

The first five *maṅgalas* (1–5) provide material for the foundation of life's building. The sixth (6) gives the necessary plan for the construction work, while the next four (7–10) complete the structure. In this way the building is made ready to house the other *maṅgalas*. This constitutes the phase of preparation.

The next phase is concerned with how the building already prepared is occupied. The first seven *maṅgalas* (11–17) of this deal with the proper discharge of domestic duties and social obligations. The next three (18–20) are a matter of personal conduct, and the one (21) following these aims at conserving the progress hitherto achieved through the practice of all the twenty *maṅgalas* mentioned so far. The next five *maṅgalas* (22–26) are the cultivation of the higher virtues which are absolutely essential for venturing into the cultivation of the Dhamma's highest aspects. Thus through the operation of the last sixteen *maṅgalas* the residence of life, prepared by the first ten, becomes a workshop producing the goods of worldly obligations and the cultivation of benevolent feelings. This is the phase of "wayfaring in the world which transforms the building into a temple of life."

The next stage is spiritual growth. This invites the occupation of the temple by the most refined and exalted *maṅgalas*. The cultivation of two *maṅgalas* (27–28) leads to ability in the practice of the spiritual life and the next two (29–30) make contact with those leading a religious life. Then four more *maṅgalas* (31–34) open the gates of realization of the Dhamma. And the last four *maṅgalas* (35–38) constitute the Great Awakening, which transforms the temple into a lighthouse for humanity. This is the ultimate benefit of Dhamma-practice, the signs of which are the invincibility of such a person and Supreme Bliss.

Schematically listed the above phases are:

I. The Preparation:

1. Laying the Right Foundation through
    a. Suitable associations: M_1 M_2 M_3
    b. A good place to live: M_4
    c. Past merits: M_5
2. Right Planning: M_6
3. Right Training: M_7 M_8 M_9 M_{10}

II. Wayfaring in the World:

17. Basic Responsibilities: M_{11} M_{12} M_{13}
18. Social Obligations: M_{14} M_{15} M_{16} M_{17}
19. Self-Protection: M_{18} M_{19} M_{20}
20. Conservation of Personal Progress: M_{21}
21. Cultivation of Higher Qualities: M_{22} M_{23} M_{24} M_{25} M_{26}

III. Spiritual Growth:

1. Spiritual Eligibility: M_{27} M_{28}
2. Contact with Religious Life: M_{29} M_{30}
3. On the Path: M_{31} M_{32} M_{33} M_{34}
4. The Fruit: M_{35} M_{36} M_{37} M_{38}

IV. The Conclusion of Life: The Summum Bonum:

26. Perfect invincibility of the person
27. Durable happiness.

A comparison of the above classification with that of Maṅgala U Ba Than shows several points of contact. The major agreement is in the phase of preparation, which in both cases is taken up by the first ten *maṅgalas*. Also the terminal sections in both cases are identical.

An examination of our classification makes it evident that section one of the Sutta is concerned with preparation for the second section, which in turn is a preparation for section number three. The fourth section is the final result.

Each of these sections has several stages. The last stage of the first section qualifies the person to enter the second section of the worldly journey, and the last stage of the second section brings the pilgrim right to the threshold of the third section. The final stage of the third section spells the supreme realization of the highest aim that people can aspire to. The fourth phase is the goal itself.

The traveller through the above sections is really a pilgrim who takes up the journey of life with a definite plan covering bodily, verbal and mental activities. His object is to make of life a happy and moral means to a glorious end. The Mahā Maṅgala Sutta provides the map which takes the pilgrim safely through life's journey to the final destination so that he gains deliverance from *dukkha* and the delusions of existence.

The eleven stanzas, comprising the reply to the issue raised in the first stanza, are apportioned to the four sections as follows:

1. The Preparation: First three stanzas.
2. Wayfaring in the World: Next four stanzas.
3. The Religious Life: Next three stanzas.
4. The Highest Goal: Last stanza.

The position of Wayfaring in the World between the stages of Preparation and that of the Religious Life, while it does not mean that marriage is essential for all people at some period in life, does lay emphasis on the cultivation of moral principles and in the discharge of social and familial obligations. According to the Buddha and in contrast with the four stages of Hindu life, marriage is not a compulsory institution, though it provides sometimes a fruitful field for the cultivation of certain virtues and so appears here as an intermediate phase which can be utilized as a training ground for entrance upon the third phase of spiritual values. Thus marriage is an optional part of the second section of life. As a means to a desirable end it is commendable, but if accepted as an end in itself, it clogs the wheels of progress and becomes a sort of a labyrinth beset with passions and crowded with peculiar obstacles, which do not easily allow the pilgrim a chance to find the path leading to awakening. Therefore, those who can practice the necessary *maṅgalas* of this stage without entering into matrimonial bondage, as monks and nuns, for instance, are free to do so, the emphasis being on the cultivation of the associated virtues and the adequate discharge of certain obligations expected of the pilgrim. However, in case marriage is excluded from the program, the question of obligations due to wife and children obviously does not arise, as the pilgrim is quite free from this burden.

Chapter V
Conclusion

Usually human beings are heavily burdened, fettered with the weighty chains riveted by themselves, the chains of fears and superstitions, dogmas and rituals. Egoistic tendencies worked by the forces of greed, hatred and delusion bring about this bondage. Bound by these self-created chains, human beings suffer repeated difficulties, hardships and miseries, which rob people of self-confidence and courage. The result is belief in prayers and priests, rites and rituals, sacrifices and sacraments, speculations and the supernatural, all prompting slavish dependence on extraneous agencies and forces, imaginary or real. Thus the mind of man is entombed by the prison walls of his own making.

The Buddha was moved by great compassion at the sight of the pitiable condition of humanity drowning in its own blind beliefs. He sounded the clarion call of freedom and showed the right way of breaking through the self-made crust of superstitions smothering individual initiative, confidence and courage. His Mahā Maṅgala Sutta is a masterly antidote to all blind beliefs and superstitions.

When approached to declare the "*maṅgalāni*" or "auspicious signs," he enumerated instead the "acts of blessedness," thus bringing about a psychological revolution in the beliefs of many people.

Every section of the Sutta is a storehouse full of practical wisdom. Precious ideas and valuable counsel are packed in every line in condensed form so that their expansion is really necessary. Just as letters were micro-photographed during the war to reduce freight in air shipment and then "blown up" before delivery, so the thoughts and ideas behind the factors of the Mahā Maṅgala Sutta have to be expanded for easy study and understanding.

It should, however, be pointed out that, though the essentials of the enlarged picture will not change at different times and places, yet certain factors, such as the colour of the picture and the texture of the materials used, may differ. That is why the practical exposition of the Sutta is sure to vary under different circumstances, without altering the central values.

In the eleven stanzas of the Sutta is given counsel which can make anyone an ideal citizen. There are instructions which prepare people excellently well for a fruitful journey through life. Further counsel progressively matures the individual till he successfully passes from the worldly state to the sphere of higher virtues and certain spiritual experiences. These in due course lead to perfect liberation. Thus the phases of preparation, worldly life, religious life and spiritual consummation follow one another in logical sequence. In this way all the due obligations are adequately discharged. The ultimate fruits are flawless happiness and perfect security.

It is undoubtedly true that the Sutta is an excellent moral foundation for children. But that is just a beginning. The Sutta also is a cultural, moral and spiritual compass for guiding the ship of life through the stormy ocean of existence to the safe final haven of the Further Shore. At every step in life, at every stage and under all circumstances, the Sutta has practical advice to offer, advice which if followed may be expected to lead to the effective solution of many complicated problems. The Sutta provides unfailing guidance not only to a child at school or to youngsters in their teens but also to grown-ups, no matter what age and what their status or work, race or nation, creed or education. Homes, schools, universities, law courts, hospitals, factories, monasteries, government and business offices, laboratories and all the other places of human activity can derive substantial benefit from the teachings of the Mahā Maṅgala Sutta. A poor and humble person may gain from the practice of these golden precepts even more than a wealthy man. A prime minister may benefit as much as any humble citizen, a new *sāmaṇera* (novice) as much as a senior Bhikkhu, a labourer in the field as much as a king on his throne, a school teacher, a compounder or a petition-writer as much as a professor or a doctor or a pleader. The Sutta is a general prescription most excellent for the difficulties of everyone, for alleviating moral decay and for mending the spiritual fractures of all men and women of all times and places, of all races and religions. Such is its grandeur! Such is the glory of this short discourse which may rightly be designated a universal panacea.

In the practical application of the teachings of the Sutta is the effective solution of all problems whether personal or domestic, private or public, national or international. The benefit, however, is in accordance with the degree of practice, which if habitual leads to a mental state in which it is natural to distinguish between the *maṅgala* and the *amaṅgala*[17] practices, and to flow only with the former according with one's practice.

Though the Sutta is a part of the Buddhist canon, its contents breathe such a harmonious air that they are the property of the whole human race. In its sublime teaching the distinctions of creed, race and nationality vanish and the rigid frontiers of religion melt away, making the peoples of the human race seem as members of one undivided family. Bound together by common problems and by the urge to find their solutions, mankind is certain to benefit from the wisdom enshrined in the Sutta.

The teachings of the Sutta are an excellent instrument for conditioning humanity in the direction of intellectual clarity and emotional purity towards efficiency in work and amity in human relationship. The world today sorely needs such advice. Shaken by the two worst wars in history and tormented by the possibility of a third one, worse than any before, most of the world's peoples today are naturally thirsting for peace. To quench this thirst, apart from suitable economic readjustments, intellectual honesty and emotional strength are essential. They are of paramount importance; in fact, much more important than the deluded trust in the strength of armies and the hollow hope in the potency of atomic and hydrogen bombs and other devilish weapons. It is our experience that wars, far from solving the problems causing them, create more unsolvable problems in their wake. To go to war heedlessly is madness and a suicidal policy. Besides the fact of coming to blows is evidently an admission of the moral and intellectual bankruptcy among those nations which fight.

The trouble with the world today is more a matter of its individual human inhabitants than the state of the objective world. The causes of these troubles are greed, hatred and delusion. These fires within manifest as conflicts without, unleashing manifold sufferings.

There can be no peace without moral and intellectual concord among mankind. There can be no real love in human relationships

17. I.e., inauspicious, evil and not commendable.

so long as the fires of hate, dishonesty, anger and greed fiercely burn in the human heart. Like war, peace has to be won. The Mahā Maṅgala Sutta of the Buddha shows the way to do it. It shows the way of genuine victory through non-violence and real love. Rather than conquering thousands and millions in battle, the Buddha teaches the conquest of self through self-culture and self-control. This is a victory well worth winning! It leads to peace—its substance is unshakable happiness and its fruit, perfect security.

Effective victory over self illumines every sphere of life: personal, family, social, national and international; also physical, mental, moral and spiritual. Thus the Mahā Maṅgala Sutta deals with the harmonious development of the whole man in his total environment.

There are thirty-eight *maṅgalaṃ* or acts of blessedness, each of which is designated the "best" or the "highest." In view of the fact that these acts include such different spheres as worldly pursuits, family life, religious practices and spiritual ideals, it may reasonably be asked as to why all of these are each called the best, as *maṅgalam-uttamaṃ*.

The Sutta deals with personal life as a whole. But, as life has different stages, different precepts condition each stage towards a wholesome state. Step by step the evolution of the individual proceeds, each step having some acts or blessings as unique to itself. As the individual progresses, his attention increases and his outlook is focused on different ends. On looking back he may well feel like a mature person looking at the toys of his childhood. Certainly, what was highest or best then is not so for him now. And it is true too that what he regards as the highest or the best will be rejected by a child. At the different stages of life different counsels are needed, the best for each phase of the journey. Just as man going off to market with a bag of charcoal on his back, on finding wool discards the charcoal, on finding silver discards wool, on finding gold discards silver, on finding diamonds discards gold and on finding the secret of enduring happiness discards everything else, so too we successively shift the level of our outlook, focusing our consciousness to ideals higher and higher till the highest is reached.

The Mahā Maṅgala Sutta gives the best counsel for each stage of life; it is thus that worldly felicity and spiritual bliss cease to be conflicting ideals. Every ideal that is good is "best" in its own place. That is why each of the thirty-eight Blessings is the "highest" and the "best."

So great is the importance of the Mahā Maṅgala Sutta that if one had to face a situation where it was necessary to surrender all the teachings of the Buddha except a single discourse, one would do well to hold on to the Mahā Maṅgala Sutta. Having this as a possession it would be possible, even quite easy, to reconstruct the entire teachings of the Buddha. This opinion is ventured to emphasize vividly the practical value of the sublime Sutta, which provides an all-round and unfailing guidance for worldly promotion and spiritual salvation. The understanding and proper practice of the Sutta would help the world more towards prosperity, moral excellence, harmony, peace, happiness and spiritual glory, than a hundred international conferences.

Because man has become cleverer than wiser, he has to face endless trouble today. Unless his cleverness is properly balanced by wisdom, there is every danger of his being wiped out of existence, not unlike the fate suffered by a monkey recklessly playing with a flaming cigarette lighter surrounded by open drums of gasoline. Certainly there is enough of the monkey still in man. The Mahā Maṅgala Sutta holds out the promise of evolving man towards true humanity. It makes of him a complete personality, physically healthy, vocationally efficient, intellectually brilliant, socially benevolent, culturally talented, morally wholesome, materially resplendent and spiritually unexcelled.

The Mahā Maṅgala Sutta is truly the

HOPE OF THE WORLD

May all be well and happy!

The Contemporary Relevance of Buddhist Philosophy

By

K. N. Jayatilleke

B.A. (Ceylon), M.A. (Cantab.), Ph.D. (London)

Professor & Head, Department of Philosophy

University of Sri Lanka

WHEEL PUBLICATION NO. 258

The Contemporary Relevance of Buddhist Philosophy

Let me first congratulate the Government of Ceylon and the Indian Philosophical Congress for the foresight they have displayed in creating this lectureship and thus perpetuating the close cultural ties which bind our two countries. Let me also thank the Congress for the honour of inviting me to give the Buddha Jayanti lecture this year.

I chose to speak on the above topic for at least two reasons, although in doing so I am well aware that I may provoke adverse comment and criticism from orthodox philosophers, who may have expected me to deal with some specific problem or topic of Buddhist philosophy. One of the reasons for not doing so is that the philosophy of the Buddha, perhaps owing to the vastness of the literary sources, seems to have suffered as a result of scholars failing to see the wood for the trees. The present paper, therefore, attempts a comprehensive outline and a synoptic view of different aspects of the philosophy of the Buddha insofar as this may be gleaned from what is explicit and implicit in the statements ascribed to the Buddha as well as from the legitimate later development of his thought.

The second main reason for speaking on this topic is that, in my opinion, the philosophy of the Buddha, as presented, is particularly relevant to the contemporary scene. How and why it is relevant may become evident from the sequel. Sceptics may question whether the views of any philosopher of the ancient or medieval world can at all be relevant for the modern world. The sceptics would be right to the extent to which thinkers are bound and limited by the questions and concepts they have grappled with in their respective social and historical milieus and which have little significance outside them. But it may be that the questions raised have a universality and the answers suggested a depth of insight that confers on them a validity which extends beyond the time at which they were promulgated. It is, therefore, wiser to proceed cautiously and empirically without any presumptions or preconceptions.

Our contemporary world, as we know, is one dominated by science and technology. Despite the contributions to scientific knowledge in ancient and medieval India and China, the predominant developments took place in the West in the last few centuries or decades. While medieval Western philosophy was an attempt to reconcile the conflicting claims of faith and reason culminating in the work of Aquinas, the modern period from Descartes onwards was mainly an attempt to reconcile science with what could be considered rational in the religion and ethics of Christianity. With the contemporary period, starting with the reactions against Hegel and post-Hegelian idealisms, we find the full impact of secular science.

The two great philosophical movements, which stem from this, bear the imprint of this impact. The growth and productivity of science as compared with the sterility of metaphysics as well as the developments in logic, mathematics and linguistic studies resulted in Logical Positivism and the Analytic movement, which became the dominant trend in philosophy in the English-speaking world. Following the model of factually meaningful propositions in science, Logical Positivism openly rejected the propositions of metaphysics, religion and ethics as strictly nonsensical, though not lacking in emotive or poetic meaning. Later Analytic philosophy adopted a less polemical and more neutral attitude in its study of the meaning of such propositions. However, the onslaughts of Positivism and Analysis virtually ended the era of speculative metaphysics (as opposed to descriptive metaphysics)[1] or rational theology, even though the more conservative forms of analysis were prepared to tolerate metaphysical propositions grounded in experience as giving insights into the structure of reality.

The other development reacting against Hegelian metaphysics and idealism was the Marxist philosophy parading as "scientific socialism." Here again its secularism, derived from science, gave a radically new interpretation of religion as the opium of the masses, while traditional ethical values were also undermined. A new ethic is, however, not lacking; for quite apart from the ethical overtones and the general appeal to ethical values in the writings of Marxism-Leninism, the attainment of a classless

1. See P. F. Strawson, *Individuals*, University Paperbacks, Reprint, 1969, London, pp. 9 ff.

society in which most social evils are supposed to be eliminated, is considered a good in itself, while whatever is helpful in the process of establishing such a society is deemed to be instrumentally good.

These philosophies originating in the Western world have had their repercussions in other parts of the world as well, following the tide of science and technology. American Pragmatism is itself a product of the temper and techniques of science, though it is receding in the face of the Analytic movement. In China, Marxism-Leninism has become the official, philosophy of the state though it is blended somewhat with the ethical values of Mahayana Buddhism.[2] In Japan, despite the modernity, tradition persists in the new religions of Japan, Zen Buddhism and the Soka Gakkai (Value-Creation) movement stressing the need for moral commitment and group discipline in the light of the philosophy and prophetic writings of the Buddhist saint Nichiren, who predicted that in the future "the union of the state law and the Buddhist Truth shall be established ... and the moral law (*kaiho*) will be achieved in the actual life of mankind.[3] In the Southeast Asian countries, including Ceylon, Buddhist philosophy is coming into its own with the modernisation process. In countries with an Islamic tradition, Islamic philosophy is represented with modifications and a modern emphasis and so is Vedanta in India. The impact of modernism on Christian theology may be seen from the Death of God movement.

Existentialism, which developed in the European continent, reflects not so much the mood of science as the negative reaction of technology on the human person. It too is empirical to the extent of avoiding abstract metaphysical speculation and confining itself to personal experience, especially in the realm of values, with its stress on the importance of choice, responsibility and authentic existence.

It is in this contemporary background that we have to evaluate the philosophy of the Buddha. In order to avoid prolixity I would confine my observations to noting briefly certain salient resemblances and differences in respect of Analytic philosophy, Existentialism and Marxism, since my main intention is to indicate

---

2. See T. Ling, *Buddha, Marx and God*, St. Martin's Press, New York, 1956.
3. *The Buddhist Tradition in India, China and Japan*, ed. Wm. Theodore de Bary, The Modern Library, New York, p. 354.

a new approach to philosophy which the Buddha tends to suggest in the modern context.

The philosophy of the Buddha comprehends a theory of knowledge, a theory of reality, an ethical system, a social and political philosophy as well as suggestions for a philosophy of law and international relations. A careful examination of the essentials of these aspects of its philosophy show that they are interrelated and interconnected.

I have tried to give an account of its theory of knowledge in one of my works.[4] Here I would only make a brief reference to some of the essentials.

One of the characteristic features of the philosophy of the Buddha, which distinguishes it from Upaniṣadic philosophy and the non-Vedic schools, is its causal conception of the universe. The Buddha states: "What is causation? On account of birth arises decay and death. Whether Tathāgatas arise or not, this order exists, namely, the fixed nature of phenomena, the regular pattern of phenomena. This the Tathāgata discovers and comprehends; having discovered and comprehended it, he points it out, teaches it, lays it down, establishes, reveals, analyses, clarifies it and says, Look!" (S II 25). Its importance is seen from the fact that an understanding of the Dhamma is not possible without comprehending the causal theory: "He who sees the nature of causation sees the Dhamma and he who sees the Dhamma sees the nature of causation" (M I 191). The two principles of causal determination are formally stated. There is a causal correlation between two sets of events A and B: "if whenever A happens, B happens and whenever A does not happen, B does not happen" (or "whenever B does not happen, A does not happen"). These formulae are stated both in an abstract as well as in a concrete form as applying to the world of dynamic reality. Causation is an objective feature of the world and not a category imposed by the mind: "Causation has the characteristics of objectivity, empirical necessity, invariability and conditionality" (S II 26).

A further analysis of the causal situation reveals the presence of different forms of relationships (*paccaya*) such as mutual

4. *Early Buddhist Theory of Knowledge*, George, Allen & Unwin, London, 1963.

dependence or reciprocity (*aññamañña-paccaya*), unilateral dependence (*nissaya-paccaya*), dominance (*adhipati-paccaya*), etc., which is denoted by the concept of conditionality (*idappaccayatā*). The concept of a causal law or correlation (*dhammatā*) is further developed in the post-Canonical texts, which speak of physical regularities or laws (*utu-niyāma*), biological laws (*bija-niyāma*), psychological laws (*citta-niyāma*) as well as karmic or spiritual laws (*kamma-*, *dhamma-niyāma*). The Buddhist causal theory is distinguished from the Activity view of Saktivāda and other theories suggestive of entailment (e.g. *Satkāryavāda*). Apart from divesting itself of such metaphysical elements, the Buddhist theory of causation is presented as avoiding the two extremes of determinism (*niyati*), whether it be theistic (*issara-kāraṇa-vada*) or natural (*svabhāva-vāda*), on the one hand, and of tychism or total indeterminism (*adhicca-samuppāda*) on the other. All explanations of phenomena are, therefore, to be in terms of causal correlations understood in the light of conditioned genesis (*paṭicca-samuppāda*).

Along with this causal conception of phenomena is emphasised the importance of an impartial and objective outlook in understanding the nature of things as they are. We have to avoid prejudice for (*chanda*) or against (*dosa*) and not allow ourselves to be influenced by fear (*bhaya*) or erroneous beliefs (*moha*). We should not depend on the argument from authority, nor on defective forms of reasoning in arriving at factual truth. The Buddha instructed the Kālāmas "not to accept anything on the grounds of revelation (*anussava*), tradition (*paramparā*) or report (*itikira*), or because it is in conformity with the scriptures (*piṭaka-sampadā*), or because it is a product of mere reasoning (*takka-hetu*) or because of a superficial assessment of facts (*ākāra-parivitakka*), or because it is true from a standpoint (*naya-hetu*), or because it conforms with one's preconceived notions (*diṭṭhi-nijjhāna-khanti*) or because it is authoritative (*bhavyarūpatā*), or because of the prestige of one's teacher (*samaṇo no garu*)" (A I 189); truth has to be verifiable (*ehipassika*) in the light of one's own experience as well as the experiences of competent observers. Revelation is unsatisfactory because a claim to revelation is in itself no criterion of truth and alleged revelations are found to contain falsehoods, contradictions and tautologies. Likewise, pure reasoning (*takka*) is no guide to factual truth since the reasoning may be valid (*sutakkitaṃ*) or invalid (*duttakkitaṃ*) and even if valid, may turn out to be true (*tathā*) or false (*aññathā*).

Statements are classified as true or false, useful or useless, pleasant or unpleasant, giving eight possibilities in all. Truth corresponds with fact (*yathābhutaṃ*). Consistency is a necessary but not a sufficient criterion of factual truth since theories which are mutually contradictory may be internally consistent though they may not correspond with fact. The Buddha's statements are claimed to be true and useful, whether they be pleasant or unpleasant. Since statements could be either useful or useless, Buddhism does not subscribe to a pragmatic theory of truth, although the Buddha's statements are claimed to be pragmatic because they are confined to them. It is also possible to have "partial truths" (*pacceka-sacca*) since the correspondence with fact could admit of degrees. There is also a distinction partly post-Canonical into relative or conventional truths (*sammuti-sacca*) and absolute truths (*paramattha-sacca*). This is because things as they are, are sometimes different from things as they appear.

Besides, language has a static structure, although we have to use it to describe a dynamic world. Once we see reality for what it is and the limitations of language, we can still employ the conventional terminology without being misled by the erroneous implications of language and the assumptions we make because of our distorted view of reality. Though language is a necessary tool of thought and communication, we have to guard against the linguistic sources of error in describing and understanding the nature of reality. Referring to the limitations of ordinary language, the Buddha says, "They are expressions, turns of speech, designations in common use in the world which the Buddha makes use of without being led astray by them" (D I 202).

While discarding authority and pure reason, the means of knowledge acknowledged by the Buddha are perception and inference. Perception is, however, used with a wider connotation to include both sensory as well as extrasensory forms of perception such as telepathy, clairvoyance and the recall of prior lives. Early Buddhism, therefore, adopts an empiricist theory of knowledge which is also evident in its treatment of the problems of soul and substance, causation, perception, meaning and metaphysics.

At the same time, since experience is conditioned and limited, the truths that we arrive at may often be partial and limited and in need of revision and modification. The Buddha says in the Brahmajāla Sutta that the religious teachers and philosophers who were Eternalists (*sassata-vāda*), Semi-eternalists (*ekaccā-sassatikā*) such as the Theists (*issara-nimmāna-vāda*) who asserted that God was eternal while his creation was not, Cosmologists (*antānantika*) who posited various theories about the extent of the universe, Sceptics (*amarāvikkhepikā*), Indeterminists (*adhiccasamuppannikā*), Primordialists (*pubbanta-kappika*) who speculated about pre-existence and first-causes, Eschatologists (*uddhamāghātanikā*) who speculated about survival and final causes, Materialists (*ucchedavāda*) who claimed the annihilation of the personality at death and various Existentialist Moral Philosophers (*diṭṭhadhamma-nibbānavāda*) who posited their various philosophies did so "on the basis of conditioned and limited personal experiences" (*chahi phassāyatanaṃ phussa phussa paṭisaṃvedenti*, D I 45).

It is significant that early Buddhism distinguishes propositions as meaningful (*sappāṭihāriya*) and meaningless. A proposition whose mode of verification we cannot specify is held to be lacking in meaning (*appāṭihīrakataṃ bhāsitaṃ sampajjati*[5]). Likewise, certain questions (Did the flame of the fire that went out go West? Is the daughter of that barren woman fair?) are to be set aside (*ṭhapanīya*) as meaningless[6] since they arise out of the misunderstanding of the nature of concepts contained in them.

5. See K. N. Jayatilleke, op. cit., pp. 322 ff.

6. Ibid., pp. 288 ff.; cp. *Mind*, Vol. LXXV, N.S., No. 299, July, 1966, p. 454: "Perhaps the most interesting feature of early Buddhism was the recognition that certain questions cannot be answered, not because of lack of information, etc., but because of the nature of the questions themselves. Certain metaphysical problems were classified by the Buddha together with the question 'Where does the flame go when it goes out?' Some commentators, both Eastern and Western, have misunderstood this point, and have attributed the Buddha's silence to a pragmatic concern that people should not waste their time on speculation. But Professor Jayatilleke conclusively argues for a Wittgensteinian interpretation (indeed, Wittgenstein used the same example: was this a coincidence?)"

It is this Buddhist theory of knowledge which makes a comparison with Logical Positivism and contemporary Analytic philosophy significant. These modern philosophers approach philosophy with the preconceptions of science and a respect for the scientific outlook, even though they consider it their task or examine these preconceptions and assumptions. They would agree with Buddhism that a priori knowledge or pure reasoning, however useful it may be, cannot give us factual knowledge of nature, which has to be based on observation. They would also agree that some problems of metaphysics and even certain metaphysical systems arise out of a misunderstanding of the nature of concepts or linguistic usage and that the dissolution of these problems requires an accurate analysis of the sources of conceptual error and linguistic confusion.

Buddhism disagrees with the Positivist in holding that not all traditional problems of metaphysics can be so dissolved. If we take the problem as to whether there is an afterlife or not (in other words, whether we survive death or not), then certainly some of the sources of confusion here are in the linguistic origin and concern the use of the word "survive," while others revolve around the problem of personal identities (we cannot be said to survive unless we are somehow the same person). But if personal identity is not closely tied up without bodies as to make it senseless to speak of identity without our present body (as in today's law courts) there is a sense in which the question is empirical and meaningful, and evidence could not tend to confirm or disconfirm the truth of a statement claiming survival after death (or not), then certainly some of the sources of confusion here are linguistic in origin and concern the use of the word "survive," while others revolve round the problem of personal identity (we cannot be said to survive unless we are in some sense the same person). But if "personal identity" is not so closely tied up with our bodies as to make it senseless to speak of identity without our present bodies (as in the law courts), there is a sense in which the question is empirical and meaningful and evidence could tend to confirm or disconfirm the truth of a statement claiming survival after death.

Buddhism would also not discard some of the traditional metaphysical theories as meaningless for it depends on what interpretation is to be given to the concepts contained in them.

For example, a Personal Theist who asserts that, "There is a God who is omniscient, omnipotent and infinitely good," is not necessarily making a factually meaningless or vacuous assertion even if we cannot locate such a God. It would be meaningless only if the concept of "good" as used here bears little relation with the normal use of the word to such an extent that we do not know how "good" here differs from "evil." For if the proposition admits of an implication and its truth (i.e. of the implication) is ascertainable, it would follow that if the implication is false, the original proposition would be false, but if it is true, then there would be a certain degree of probability in its truth.

Another salient difference is that unlike modern Positivism or Analysis, Buddhism presents a conception of "man and his destiny in the universe," which it claims is in principle verifiable, although the mode of verification may differ in some respects from the methods of the natural sciences.

This brings us to the Buddhist theory of reality, which I would rather not call its "metaphysics" because of the verificationist claim.

Many people are interested in studying philosophy not with the idea of learning about the nuances and niceties of the English language (or any other language) but with an ardent desire to know something about the fundamental questions of life or the nature and destiny of man in the universe. They are not interested in cultivating the art of philosophical discourse as a fad or fashion but in examining what answers are possible to these questions. It may be that to some of these questions no answer is possible and that to others the answers may be very disappointing but, at least, it is the duty of the philosopher to examine both the possibility and probability of the proffered solutions to these questions. According to Kant the central issues of philosophy revolved round the question as to whether there was "God, freedom and immortality." Kant himself found that their reality could not be proved by pure reason but that practical reason demands that it is in our interests to act on the basis of faith in their reality.

Several philosophers today consider it their task to examine in minute detail the nature of the theories put forward by thinkers in the past in the light of their writings and relevant literature. Many also examine the meaning of what they have said and try to restate their theories. But the intellectual exercise seems to stop there and few, indeed, seem inclined to examine the truth or falsity of theories after presenting them in a modern context and where they are relevant in the light of modern evidence. There may be several reasons for this. Some philosophies are so outmoded that no restatement of them would make them significant for modern man.

Others do not lend themselves to such examination. Yet there are at least a few theories which deserve to be examined for their relevance and veracity and the philosophy of the Buddha seems to be one of them. I am, therefore, presenting the elements of the early Buddhist theory of reality not with the idea of establishing its truth but because such a task should fall within the purview of a modern student of philosophy for the reasons stated.

The Buddhist theory of reality is distinguished from other leading theories about the nature and destiny of man in the universe by the Buddha himself. The six leading thinkers in the time of the Buddha seem to represent standard types of philosophical thought met with in the history of human speculation.

Makkhalī Gosāla was a Theist (*issara-kāraṇa-vādi*) and according to him the world was created by a divine fiat and continues to unfold itself like a ball of thread that unwinds itself when flung on the ground. Beings under the impact of evolutionary forces over which they have no control gradually evolve under varying conditions of existence until they eventually attain final salvation. In the other extreme was Ajita Kesakambali, the Materialist, according to whom fools and the wise alike are annihilated at death and there was no such thing as a "good life," which religious men talked about. Opposed to both these views was Sañjaya Bellaṭṭhiputta, the Sceptic or Positivist who held that beliefs about an afterlife, moral responsibility and transcendent existence were beyond verification and, therefore, one could not with reason hold any firm opinion about them. The other three leading thinkers also represent certain specific types of thought. Pūraṇa Kassapa was a Natural Determinist holding that everything was strictly determined by natural forces, and, as a corollary to his determinism, he was, like scientists who held a deterministic view of nature, an Amoralist, who believed that there was nothing good or evil as such. Pakudha Kaccāyana was, like Empedocles or Aristotle, a Categorialist who tried to explain and comprehend man and the universe by classifying reality into discrete categories. Lastly, Nigaṇṭha Nātaputta, the historical founder of Jainism, was a Relativist (*anekantavādi*) in his theory of knowledge, holding that there was some truth in every point of view and an Eclectic in his metaphysics, who tried to combine all these different, even contradictory standpoints.

Reasons are adduced for discarding these theories: For instance, there are two arguments in the Canonical texts against Personal Theism. One may be called the Puppet argument: "If God designs the life of the entire world—the glory and the misery, the good and the evil acts—man is but an instrument of his will (*niddesa-kāri*) and God alone is responsible" (JV 238). The other is the argument from evil. If God is the omnipotent and omniscient creator, then certain evils are inexplicable: "If God is the lord of the whole universe and the creator of the multitude of beings, then why has he ordained misfortune in the world instead of making the world happy?" (JVI 208). The validity of these arguments is not generally questioned even today. An Analytic philosopher, who has recently made a careful and comprehensive study of the concept of God, avers that both these arguments are valid. Personal Theism implies a rigged universe in which everything including our thoughts and actions is preordained.[7] The several attempts to explain evil are also unsatisfactory.[8]

I have mentioned these various philosophical theories with which Buddhism is contrasted to indicate that such philosophies are recurrent types, while the soundness or validity of arguments do not, likewise, vary with time, although we may take time to discover their soundness or validity. Truth is relevant to any age which respects the pursuit of truth.

Early Buddhism is realistic in that it held matter (*rūpa*) to be non-mental (*acetasikaṃ*) and independent of thought (*citta-vippayutta*). Such matter was classified into three categories. First, there is the category of material attributes which are visible (*sanidassana*) and can be apprehended by the senses (*sappaṭigha*) such as colours and shapes. Secondly, there is matter which is

7. Antony Flew, *God and Philosophy*, Hutchinson & Co., Ltd., 1966, p. 44.

8. Ibid., p. 54.

not visible (*anidassana*) but is apprehensible by the other senses. Thirdly, there is matter which is neither visible to the naked eye nor apprehensible by the senses but whose existence can be inferred or observed by paranormal vision. There is no direct reference to an atomic theory in Canonical Buddhism but the conception of a dynamic atom in a state of flux was conceived in some of the later Buddhist schools of thought. On the other hand the idealist school (*vijñānavāda*) of Buddhism, which conceived of the natural world as a product of mind (*sarvaṃ buddhimayaṃ jagat*), seemed to have strayed from the standpoint of early Buddhism.

The early Buddhist analysis of mind deserves to be carefully studied by modern psychologists. We get here the earliest naturalistic conceptions of the mind or mental phenomena. Here again, one has to record a history of neglect. A modern psychologist, who recently made a study of this material, has remarked that the oldest Pali writings are of great interest to the psychologist not only because their analysis of mind is in many ways comparable to his own but because their teaching has been used for practical purposes with enviable success. He deplores the lack of any serious study of this material.[9] Of particular interest is its analysis of mental phenomena and its theory of motivation. Mental phenomena are analysed into impressions, images, ideas and concepts (*saññā*), the hedonic tone or feeling element which accompanies them (*vedanā*), the conative acts (*saṅkhārā*), which find expression as trains of thought (*manosaṅkhārā*), speech activity (*vacīsaṅkhārā*), and bodily behaviour (*kāyasaṅkhārā*), as well as the cognitive and quasi-cognitive acts (*viññāṇa*). The view that "the consciousness of a person ran along and fared on without change of identity" (*viññāṇaṃ sandhāvati saṃsarati anaññaṃ*) is

9. See, Rune Johansson, *The Psychology of Nirvana*, George Allen & Unwin, Ltd., London, 1969; cp. "The original Buddhism was a psychologically sophisticated doctrine with a very rich and differentiated psychological terminology ... The psychology of Nikāya Buddhism has not yet been adequately analysed and described. An early attempt by Mrs. Rhys Davids (9) is superficial and biased. The work of Jayatilleke, referred to previously (4), is reliable but touches psychological matters only occasionally. An interesting treatment of some special questions of psychological interest is found in an article by him (5) ..." (p. 65).

held to be an erroneous view since consciousness was causally conditioned under the impact of the environment, the state of the body and the effects of prior experiences.

This accumulation of mental phenomena under the impact of conditioning is conceived of as a "stream of consciousness" (*viññāṇa-sota*), part of which, it is said, has reference to this world (*idhaloke patiṭṭhitaṃ*), while the other part is located in the world beyond (*paraloke patiṭṭhitaṃ*) in the living person without a sharp division into two parts (*ubhayato abbhocchinnaṃ*). This means that man's stream of consciousness has a conscious and unconscious component. There are other references to unconscious mental processes, as when it is stated that conative acts of mind may operate while we are aware of them (*sampajāna*) or unaware of them (*asampajāna*). Similarly, intentions and desires may be either conscious or subconscious and latent (*āsayānusaya*). Conscious mental activity functions with a physical basis; there is a reference to "the physical basis of perceptual and conceptual activity" (*yaṃ rūpaṃ nissaya mano-dhātu ca manoviññāṇa-dhātu ca vattati,* Paṭṭhāna).

While this account of the content of the mind may be fruitfully compared with modern analyses of mental phenomena, there is an interesting theory of motivation which has certain striking resemblances with Freudian theory.

According to this theory man is motivated to act under the impetus of his needs, desires and beliefs. On the one hand there is greed (*rāga*), hatred (*dosa*) and ignorance (*moha*), and on the other selflessness (*cāga*), compassion (*karuṇā*) and understanding (*paññā*): Greed constitutes the desire to gratify one's senses and sex (*kāma-rāga, kāma-taṇhā*) and the desire to satisfy our egoistic drives or impulses (*bhava-rāga, bhava-taṇhā*), such as the desire for possessions, for power, for fame, for personal immortality, etc. Hatred constitutes our aggressive tendencies (*paṭigha*) or the desire for destruction (*vibhava-taṇhā*), i.e., the desire to get rid of or eliminate what causes dissatisfaction. Both greed and hatred are fed by ignorance (i.e., our erroneous beliefs, illusions and rationalisations) and vice-versa. Indulgence in these desires gives temporary satisfaction and constitutes the pleasure and happiness which most people enjoy. But according to Buddhist psychology there is a law of diminishing returns, which operates in our attempt to find satisfaction through gratification. This process eventually makes us slaves of our desires as in the case of alcoholics, misers, sex-addicts, power hungry individuals, etc.

Our endeavour should be to gradually change the basis of our motivation from greed, hatred and ignorance to selflessness, compassion and understanding. This, it is suggested, could be done by a process of sublimation consisting in developing the desire to be selfless, compassionate and wise, the desire to eliminate greed, hatred and ignorance and as an aid to the elimination of erroneous beliefs or ignorance, to adopt right beliefs or the right philosophy of life (*sammādiṭṭhi*) on the basis of rational faith (*ākāravatī saddhā*) to bridge the gap between ignorance and understanding.

However, men are of different psychological types owing to their divergent conditioning in the *saṃsāric* and evolutionary process and different meditational methods adapted to their temperament are recommended for them to effect the transition and transform the basis of their motivation.

Buddhist psychology does not share with Freud his psychic determinism and his consequent pessimism about the possibility of transforming human nature, but the Buddhist theory of motivation outlined above shows a marked similarity with that of Freud's. The similarity, as we may observe, even extends to the classification of desires and the use of terminology.[10] In a later phase of Freud's thought there was a division of drives into *eros* (lust) or the life instinct and *thanatos* or the death instinct.[11] At this stage eros comprehended both libido, the sex instinct, as well as the egoistic instincts. In Buddhism we find *rāga* (*eros*) subdivided into sex (*kāma-rāga*) and ego-instincts (*bhava-rāga*). *Vibhavataṇhā* is the desire for destruction or annihilation since *vibhava* and *vināsa* are synonyms, in the Pali texts (cp. ... *ucchedavādā sato sattassa ucchedaṃ vināsaṃ vibhavaṃ paññāpenti*, i.e. annihilationists

10. A pupil of mine, Dr. M. W. P. de Silva of the University of Ceylon, obtained his Ph.D. from the University of Hawaii on a thesis on "Buddha and Freud." He found similarity in the analysis of mind and a difference in the methods adopted for the mastery of the unconscious. He did not examine the problem of influence.

11. See Clara Thompson, M. D., *Psychoanalysis: Evolution and Development*, Grove Press, Inc., New York, 1957, pp. 50 ff.

posit the annihilation, destruction and extermination of an existent being, D I 34). This is what Freud calls the death instinct, sometimes (mistakenly) referring to it as the Nirvana principle. In view of the close similarity of concepts the question as to whether Freud was influenced by Buddhism should be carefully examined especially since Freud had made a thorough study of Schopenhauer, who claimed to be a Buddhist deeply influenced by Buddhist and Upaniṣadic literature.

All conditioned phenomena are in a state of perpetual flux (*anicca*). It follows from this that sentient beings with a desire for security would find this state of affairs unsatisfactory (*dukkha*) and also find no permanent entity or substance (*anattā*) in it.

The central doctrines concerning man's destiny in the universe are mentioned as the objects of the liberating "threefold wisdom" (*tisso vijjā*). Despite the lack of a persistent entity called "the person," there is a continuity (*santati*) of processes which constitutes becoming (*bhava*), causing the birth, decay, death and re-becoming of individuals. The early Buddhist theory of survival is another area of study in which scholarly investigation is lacking. Many scholars have naively assumed that the Buddha uncritically took the prevailing doctrine of rebirth for granted despite the claims to the contrary in the Buddhist texts. A careful study of the data would show that the Buddha put forward his own doctrine of survival or re-becoming (*punabbhava*) after examining several alternative theories regarding the question of survival such as those of the Sceptics, Materialists, Single-afterlife theorists and several Rebirth theorists when he was convinced of it on the basis of his own alleged clairvoyant capacity to recall his own past lives as well as the past lives of others. Buddhist re-becoming may involve both an afterlife as a discarnate spirit or rebirth on earth.

Here again, it is the task of philosophers to examine the meaningfulness of assertions concerning an afterlife. If the concept of a "discarnate spirit" or "rebirth" does, not make sense, the question of the truth of these theories do not arise.

Although no Indian philosopher (to the best of my knowledge) has even examined this question, it is worth noting that as far as the doctrine of 'rebirth' goes, some of the leading exponents of the British empiricist tradition in philosophy such as John Locke, David Hume and A. J. Ayer have all pronounced in favour of the meaningfulness, at least, of a claim to "rebirth." John Locke in his *Essay Concerning Human Understanding* examines "rebirth" claims and argues that identity of memory and consciousness is the criterion for personal identity, independent of the body. He concludes: "This may show us wherein personal identity consists: not in the identity of substance, but, as I have said, in the identity of consciousness, wherein if Socrates and the present mayor of Queenborough agree, they are the same person: if the Socrates waking and sleeping does not partake of the same consciousness, Socrates waking and sleeping is not the same person" (II. XXVII. 19). David Hume in his *Essays on Suicide* comes to the conclusion that "the Metempsychosis is therefore the only system of this kind (that is, the only conception of immortality) that philosophy can hearken to."[12] The contemporary Analytic philosopher A. J. Ayer grants "the logical possibility of reincarnation."[13]

If "rebirth" is meaningful, the next question would be whether it is true. This is a matter which can be decided only on the basis of the relevant empirical evidence. A leading philosopher, Professor C. J. Ducasse, thinks that the data from age-regression experiments, while not establishing the theory of rebirth, tend to give it some degree of probability.[14] A professor of psychiatry who has examined several authentic spontaneous cases of recall of alleged prior lives mainly on the part of children from different parts of the world thinks, after trying to account for the evidence in terms of several alternate normal and paranormal hypotheses, that the theory of "rebirth" is "the most plausible hypothesis for understanding cases of this series."[15]

It is logically possible that "rebirth" could be true without the law of karma being true. It means that its truth has to be independently attested. The Buddhist doctrine of karma merely states that there

12. *Essays and Treatises on Various Subjects*, Boston, 1881, p. 228.

13. *The Concept of a Person*, Macmillan and Co., Ltd., London, 1963, p. 127; cp. A. J. Ayer, *The Problem of Knowledge*, Penguin Books; reprint 1957, Edinburgh, pp. 184–185, 193–194.

14. *The Belief in a Life after Death*, Illinois, 1961, pp. 241–299.

15. Ian Stevenson, M.D., *The Evidence from Survival for Claimed Memories of Former Incarnations*, Essex, 1961, p. 34; cp. Ian Stevenson, *Twenty Cases Suggestive of Reincarnation*, New York, 1966 (pp. x plus 362).

is an observable correlation between moral acts and their personal consequences, such that morally good and evil acts tend to result in specific pleasant and unpleasant consequences, as the case may be, to the individual. According to the texts, the Buddha claimed to verify the truth of this theory by his extra-sensory powers of clairvoyant observation. This raises several questions, the question as to whether the Buddha ever made such a claim and, if so, whether there is evidence for the validity of clairvoyance, etc. In this respect one may compare and study the historically attested case of Edgar Cayce of Virginia Beach, U.S.A., who just over two decades back claimed the exercise of these faculties and whose records are still available for inspection and scrutiny.[16]

To explain rebirth and karma, some Upaniṣads resorted to the conception of a perdurable soul, which was the agent of actions and the recipient of reactions. But Buddhism, which discarded the concept of the soul tries to explain all this in terms of its theory of the conditioned genesis of the individual.

According to this theory, there is a cycle of conditioning which promotes the growth and development of the individual. The stages of conditioning (which have often been misinterpreted by scholars as an evolutionary series going back to a first cause) are as follows: "Ignorance, i.e., our beliefs, true or false, about the nature and destiny of man in the universe, conditions our volitional activities" (*avijjā-paccayā saṅkhārā*). "The volitional activities condition the nature and tone of our consciousness" (*saṅkhārā-paccayā viññāṇaṃ*); we may note here that this is one of the central themes of the modern Existentialist. "The nature of our consciousness conditions the new personality in the subsequent life" (*viññāṇa paccayā nāmarūpaṃ*). "Conditioned by the nature of our personality is our external world" (*nāmarūpa-paccayā saḷāyatana*). "This external world (physical, social and ideological) conditions our impressions" (*saḷāyatana-paccayā phasso*). "The impressions condition our hedonic tone or the pleasant, unpleasant or neutral feelings we have" (*phassa-paccayā vedanā*). "These feelings condition the functioning of our desires, the pleasant sensations arousing or reinforcing the desires for sexual and sensuous gratification (*kāma-taṇhā*) and the desire

16. See Gina Cerminara, M.A., Ph.D. *Many Mansions*, William Sloan Associates, Inc., New York, 12th ed., 1964.

for egoistic pursuits (*bhava-taṇhā*) while the unpleasant sensations arouse the desire for elimination or destruction" (*vibhava-taṇhā*; *vedanā-paccayā taṇhā*). "These desires condition our entanglements with objects or persons (*kāmupādāna*), philosophical, religious or political theories (*diṭṭhupādāna*); habits, customs, rites or rituals (*sīlabbatūpādānaṃ*) as well as our beliefs in soul and substance" (*attavādupādāna*; *taṇhā-paccayā upādānaṃ*). "The kinds of things around which we have formed entanglements condition our future becoming" (*upādāna-paccayā bhavo*). "This becoming conditions our birth" (*bhava-paccayā jāti*). "Birth results in decay and death" (*jāti-paccayā jarāmaraṇaṃ*). This is the wheel of becoming (*bhava-cakka*) that we are caught up in, but the emergence from this condition is also pictured as a process of conditioning: "Suffering is instrumental in arousing faith in moral and spiritual values, such faith results in gladness and composure of mind, giving rise to insight regarding reality and eventual salvation" (*dukkhūpanisā saddhā* ... S II 31). However, in the last resort it is the understanding of the nature of our conditioning which liberates us and makes it possible for us to attain the Unconditioned.

As we can see, we are conditioned by the environment, by our heredity (*bija-niyama*) owing to the fact that our new personality is made up of the fusion of the dynamic Unconscious coming down from a previous life as well as what is derived from our parents, our psychological past going back to prior lives, and the desires and beliefs which motivate our behaviour. Yet although we are *conditioned* we are *not determined* by these factors since we have an element of freedom from constraint, which makes it possible for us within limits to control and direct our future course of *saṃsāric* evolution.

According to the Buddhist theory, we have been conditioned from time immemorial, in the course of which our forms of existence have changed from one setting to another in the vast cosmos. The smallest unit in the world of space (*okāsa-loka*) is defined as "a thousandfold minor world-system" (*sahassī-cūḷanikā-lokadhātu*). This is described as follows: "As far as these suns and moons revolve, shining and shedding their light in space, so far extends the thousands-fold world-system. In it are thousands of suns, thousands of moons ... thousands of Jambudīpas, thousands of Aparagoyānas, thousands of Uttarakurūs and thousands of

Pubbavidehas" (A I 227; V 59). The next unit is the middling world-system (*majjhamika-lokadhātu*) made up of two, three, four, up to a hundred or a thousand of such minor world-systems. Each such world-system is formed of clusters of minor world-systems. The major world-system (*mahā-lokadhātu*) is formed of thousands of such middling world-systems. If we translate these conceptions into those of modern astronomy, the minor world-system, which is the unit of the cosmos, would be a galaxy. A galaxy contains thousands upon thousands of suns and moons and planets, some of which, in the opinion of modern astronomers, are likely to be inhabited. A middling world-system would be a cluster of such galaxies, and the metagalaxy or the cosmos, as we know it, would consist of clusters of such clusters. This metagalaxy goes through two immense periods of time, a period of opening out (*vivaṭṭamāna-kappa*) and a period of closing in, culminating "in the destruction of the cosmos" (*saṃvaṭṭamāna-kappa*). In modern terminology, this is comparable to the oscillating model of a universe, which periodically expands and contracts.

So the conception of man and his destiny in the universe, as described in the Buddhist texts, is not one which does not fit in with the conceptions of man and the universe in our present space age, however fantastic it would seem.

There is, however, one defect in the Buddhist texts when we compare the picture of man and his destiny in the universe with the modern conception of things.

Although the Buddhist account fits in with the new psychology and the new cosmology, there is hardly any mention of the new biology. The texts fail to mention that man, at least on earth, is at the apex of biological evolution, having reached his present state by a process of slow evolutionary change from the primitive forms of life. To try and explain this away would be to indulge in apologetics, which I have no desire to do. All that can be said in favour of the philosophy of the Buddha in this respect is that, although a concept of biological evolution is not found, life is pictured as a struggle for existence in which one species of life feeds on another "the stronger overpowering the weaker" (*dubbala-mārika*).[17]

17. Professor C.D. Broad says, "Now I do not think that there need be any great difficulty in fitting religion in general or certain of the great historical

The above Buddhist theory of reality is an attempt to answer the question "What do we know?" According to Buddhist conceptions this has to be justified in the light of its theory of knowledge, which in turn was an attempt to answer the question "How do we know?" Our next question would be "What do we do?" in a personal or collective sense. The former part of this question takes us to the Buddhist theory of ethics and the latter to its social and political philosophy.

Ethical propositions would have no significance in a strictly deterministic or indeterministic universe. In the former, because there would be no freedom for people to choose between alternative courses of action and in the latter because one's decisions and voluntary actions would not contribute to or be correlated with one's betterment or degeneration, as the case may be.

In Buddhism, the propositions of ethics are significant but this is dependent on the truth of certain factual propositions. Kant argued that "ought implies can" but this need not necessarily be so since our use of ought-propositions may be mistaken. What he should have said was that ought-statements are significant only if at least some can-statements are true. In greater detail, there can be no ethics without a concept of moral responsibility. But there cannot be moral responsibility unless (i) some of our actions are free (though conditioned) and not constrained, (ii) morally good and evil actions are followed by pleasant and unpleasant consequences, as the case may be and (iii) there is human survival after death to make this possible with justice. Now the question as to whether these conditions are fulfilled or not is a purely factual question. If there was no free will and human actions were strictly determined, there would be no sense in our talking about moral responsibility for our actions. According to Buddhism, nature is such that all these conditions are fulfilled and, therefore, moral responsibility is a fact. The universe is such that the moral and spiritual life is both possible and desirable.

Buddhism considers human perfection or the attainment of arahantship as a good in itself and likewise the material and spiritual

---

religions, such as Buddhism, into this changed biological framework" (*Religion, Philosophy, and Psychical Research*, Routledge and Kegan Paul, Ltd., London, 1953, p. 241; Chapter on "Relations of Science and Religion").

welfare of mankind. Whatever is good as a means in bringing about these good ends is instrumentally good and these means are called right actions, defined as actions which promote one's welfare as well as the welfare of others. It therefore propounds the doctrine of ethical universalism as opposed to ethical egoism or ethical altruism. The goal of perfection and happiness (the hedonist ideal) is also therapeutic in that only a perfect person, it is said, has a perfectly healthy mind, which enjoys supreme happiness. Hence the necessity for cleansing the mind, which consists in changing the basis of our motivation from greed, hatred and ignorance to selfless service, compassion and understanding.

The Buddhist theory of reality and ethics is summed up in the Four Noble Truths.

The account of personal experience and of man's condition as portrayed in the writings of some of the Existentialists in some respects closely resembles the Buddhist analysis of man's predicament. The attention drawn to the experience of dread, anxiety, melancholy and despair on the part of the human person may be compared with the Buddhist version of man's confrontation with the insecurity and unsatisfactoriness of existence. Existentialists also focus attention on the individual and stress the importance of choice and responsibility for the achievement of authentic existence and selfhood. So does Buddhism draw attention to the need for man to emerge from his unhappy condition. But while choice is completely free for the Existentialist, choice is conditioned though not strictly determined from the Buddhist point of view. Choice makes for authentic living but for some Existentialists morality does not come into the picture and what is important is that one does what one wishes to do without being subject to the inhibitions and constraints of society. In such a situation both Hitler and Gandhi would equally well exemplify instances of authentic living.

It is true that Kierkegaard indirectly suggests the superiority of the ethical to the purely aesthetic life of romantic hedonism and abstract intellectualism, which lacks commitment and also of the religious to the ethical stage of life, arguing that each is transfigured in the other, which is superior. This resembles in some respects the Buddhist way of moral and spiritual progress past the stage of the aesthetic (the life of the gratification of the basic desires) to the ethical (*sīla*), the meditational (*samādhi*) and the intuitive (*paññā*), but neither the psychology nor the *raison d'être* of such development is as clearly formulated as in Buddhism.

The social and political philosophy of Buddhism is equally relevant and enlightening. Again, the Buddha was the first thinker in history to teach the doctrine of equality.[18] Man was one species and the division into social classes and castes was not a permanent or inevitable division of society, although this was given divine sanction at the time. Historical and economic factors brought about, as the Buddha relates in the Aggañña Sutta, the division of people into occupational classes, which later became castes. All men are capable of moral and spiritual development and should be afforded the opportunity for this. The doctrine of equality does not imply that all men are physically and psychologically alike, but that there is a sufficient degree of homogeneity amongst men in terms of their capacities and potentialities as to warrant their being treated equally and with human dignity (*samānattatā*).

Society, according to the Buddha, like every other process in nature was liable to change from time to time.

The factors that determined this change were economic and ideological, for men were led to action by their desires and beliefs. It was the duty of the state to uphold justice and promote the material and spiritual welfare of its subjects. There is a social contract theory of society and government. Ultimate power, whether it be legislative, executive or judiciary, is vested with the people but delegated to the king or body of people elected to govern. If the contract of upholding law and order and promoting the material and spiritual interests of the people is seriously violated, the people have a right to revolt and overthrow such a tyrannical government (see *Padamānavakusala Jātaka*).

Sovereignty is subject to the necessity to conform to the rule of righteousness. The rule of power has to be dependent on the rule of righteousness. Punishment has to be reformatory and only secondarily deterrent and never retributive. In international

---

18. For the arguments in detail see G. P. Malalasekera and K. N. Jayatilleke, *Buddhism and the Race Question*, UNESCO Race Series, Paris, 1958. For an abridged version, see The Wheel No. 200–201.

relations[19] the necessity for subjecting sovereignty to the rule of righteousness requires that no nation be a power unto itself, while in its dealings with other nations it should always have the good and happiness of mankind at heart. The ideal just society is both democratic and socialistic and ensures human rights as well as economic equity and full employment. It is likely to come into existence after a catastrophic world war, when the remnant who are likely to escape its dire destruction would set up a new order based on a change of heart and a change of system, guaranteeing both freedom and economic security for all

This social and political philosophy could be fruitfully compared and contrasted with the Marxist. Both are realistic in granting the impact of the material environment and economic relationships in the development of society. Both emphasise the changeable nature of the forms of society. In both we get a picture of the emergence of a new ideal form of society in the future. But the differences are equally important. In Buddhism, the ideological factor is at least equally relevant and effective in bringing about social change. Hence there is no economic determinism. Finally, according to the Buddhist social contract, the government is bound to promote both freedom and economic security and the ideal form of government is both democratic and socialistic.

In conclusion, we may observe that the philosophy of the Buddha is of great relevance to modern thought and the modern world. While it endorses the program of analytic philosophy in stressing the need for clarity and clarification (Buddhism itself was known as the philosophy of analysis—*vibhajjavāda*), it offers a positive account of man's nature and destiny in the universe, which is compatible with the temper and findings of science. Its ethic is basically humanistic, though it gives a basis for such an ethic, lacking in mere humanism. It gives a realistic account of social and political philosophy embodying values which are generally held in high regard in the modern world even if they are not evident in practice.

In giving an account of this philosophy it is not my primary intention to establish its truth but rather to indicate that it is

19. On this topic, see my Hague lectures: *Recueil des Cours*, Vol. II, 1967, pp. 443–566.

worthy of serious study and consideration by the best minds of the present age, in view of the nature of the answers it gives to certain fundamental questions asked today and at all times by men who reflected on the riddle of the universe. In my opinion, the philosophy of the Buddha presents a challenge to the modern mind, and it should be a primary function and duty of modern philosophers to examine its solutions to basic questions.

Nourishing the Roots

Essays on Buddhist Ethics

by

Bhikkhu Bodhi

WHEEL PUBLICATION NO. 259/260

Nourishing the Roots

The course of spiritual training taught by the Buddha is a double process of self-transformation and self-transcendence issuing in complete emancipation from suffering. The process of self-transformation involves the elimination of unwholesome mental dispositions and their replacement by pure dispositions conducing to the benefit of oneself and others; the process of self-transcendence focuses on the abandoning of egocentric notions by seeing with direct insight the essenceless nature of the bodily and mental processes we normally take to be "I" and "mine." When this double process is brought to its culmination, suffering is extinguished, for with the awakening of wisdom the basic root of suffering—craving backed by blinding ignorance—falls away never to rise again.

Because the unwholesome tendencies and selfish clinging spring from seeds buried deep in the bottom-most strata of the mind, to eradicate these sources of affliction and nurture the growth of the liberating vision of reality the Buddha presents his teaching in the form of a gradual training. Buddhist discipline involves gradual practice and gradual attainment. It does not burst into completeness at a stroke, but like a tree or any other living organism, it unfolds organically, as a sequence of stages in which each stage rests upon its predecessor as its indispensable foundation and gives rise to its successor as its natural consequence. The principal stages of this gradual training are three: the training in *sīla* or virtue, the training in *samādhi* or concentration, and the training in *paññā* or wisdom. If we follow through the comparison of the Buddhist discipline to a tree, faith (*saddha*) would be the seed, for it is faith that provides the initial impulse through which the training is taken up, and faith again that nourishes the training through every phase of its development. Virtue would be the roots, for it is virtue that gives grounding to our spiritual endeavours just as the roots give grounding to a tree. Concentration would be the trunk, the symbol of strength, non-vacillation, and stability. And wisdom would be the branches, which yield the flowers of enlightenment and the fruits of deliverance.

The vigour of the spiritual life, like the vigour of a tree, depends upon healthy roots. Just as a tree with weak and shallow roots cannot flourish but will grow up stunted, withered, and barren, so a spiritual life devoid of strong roots will also have a stunted growth incapable of bearing fruit. To attempt to scale the higher stages of the path it is essential at the outset to nourish the proper roots of the path; otherwise the result will be frustration, disillusionment, and perhaps even danger. The roots of the path are the constituents of *sīla,* the factors of moral virtue. These are the basis for meditation, the ground for all wisdom and higher achievement.

To say that *sīla* is the precondition for success, however, does not mean, as is too often believed in conservative Buddhist circles, that one cannot begin to meditate until one's *sīla* is perfect. Such a stipulation would make it almost impossible to start meditation, since it is the mindfulness, concentration, and wisdom of the meditative process that bring about the gradual purification of virtue. But to say that virtue is the basis of practice does mean that the capacity for achievement in meditation hinges upon the purity of our *sīla.* If our roots of virtue are weak, our meditation will likewise be weak. If our actions repeatedly clash with the basic principles of right conduct, our attempts to control the mind in the discipline of meditation will turn into a self-defeating enterprise, since the springs of our conduct will be the same defiled states of mind the meditation is intended to eliminate.

Only when we secure our cultivation upon the foundation of blameless principles of right action can the inward endeavour of meditation prosper and issue in success. With true principles of conduct as the base, the roots of virtue will give birth to the trunk of concentration, the concentrated mind shoot forth the branches of wisdom, and the branches of wisdom yield the flowers and fruits of enlightenment, culminating in total freedom from bondage. Therefore, just as a skilful gardener brings a sapling to growth by first tending to the roots, so the earnest seeker of enlightenment should begin his cultivation by tending to the roots of his practice—that is, to his *sīla* or moral virtue.

The Pali word *sīla* originally meant simply conduct. But in the context of the Buddhist spiritual training the term is used to signify only a specific kind of conduct, i.e., good conduct, and by an extension of meaning, the type of character for which such conduct stands, i.e., good character. Hence *sīla* means both moral conduct, a body of habits governed by moral principles, and moral virtue, the interior quality the regular observance of these principles is intended to produce.

Both shades of meaning are essential to understand the place of *sīla* in the spectrum of Buddhist discipline. *Sīla* in the former sense consists in the non-transgression through body or speech of the basic precepts regulating the moral life. It is moral discipline in deed and word, beginning as the inhibition of immoral impulses seeking an outlet through body and speech, and developing into the habitual conformation to the principles of righteous conduct. But the full range of *sīla* is not exhausted by mere outward behavioural control, for the term has in addition a deeper, more psychological significance. In this second sense *sīla* is moral purity, the inner purification of character which results from a life consistently moulded upon moral principles. This aspect of *sīla* places the stress on the subjective, motivational side of action. It looks not towards the outward act itself, but towards the rectitude of mind from which good conduct springs.

Upon inspection *sīla* thus reveals itself to be a two-dimensional quality: it contains an external dimension consisting in purification of conduct, and an internal dimension consisting in purification of character. However, in the Teaching of the Buddha, these two dimensions of experience, the internal and the external, are not torn apart and consigned to separate, self-sufficient domains. They are recognized, rather, to be two facets of a single whole, complementary poles of a unified field which mirror one another, implicate one another, and penetrate one another with their own respective potentialities of influence. Actions performed by body and speech are not, from the Buddhist standpoint, so many detachable appendages of a distinct spiritual essence, but concrete revelations of the states of mind which stand behind them as their activating source. And states of mind, in turn, do not remain closed up in a purely mental isolation, but spill forth according to the play of circumstances from the fountain of consciousness where they arise, through the channels of body, speech, and thought, out into the world of inter-personally significant events. From the action we can infer the state of mind, and from the state of mind we can predict the probable course of action. The relationship between the two is as integral as that between a musical score and its orchestrated performance on the concert stage.

Because of this mutual dependence of the two domains, moral conduct and purity of character lock up with one another in a subtle and complex interrelationship. The fulfilment of the purification of virtue requires that both aspects of *sīla* be realized: on the one side, behaviour of body and speech must be brought into accord with the moral ideal; on the other, the mental disposition must be cleansed of its corruptions until it is impeccably pure. The former without the latter is insufficient; the latter without the former is impossible. Between the two, the internal aspect is the more important from the standpoint of spiritual development, since bodily and verbal deeds acquire ethical significance primarily as expressions of a corresponding disposition of mind. In the sequence of spiritual training, however, it is moral discipline that comes first. For at the beginning of training, purification of character stands as an ideal which must be reached; it is not a reality with which one can start.

According to the Buddhist principle of conditionality, the actualization of any given state is only possible through the actualization of its appropriate conditions, and this applies as much to the achievement of the various stages of the training as to the bare phenomena of matter and mind. Since beginningless time the consciousness-continuum has been corrupted by the unwholesome roots of greed, hatred and delusion; it is these defilements which have functioned as the source for the greatest number of our thoughts, the ground for our habits, and the springs for our actions and general orientation towards other people and the world as a whole. To uproot these defiling afflictions at a single stroke and reach the peak of spiritual perfection by a mere act of will is a well-near impossible task. A realistic system of spiritual training must work with the raw material of human nature; it cannot rest content merely with postulated paragons of human excellence or demands for achievement without showing the method by which such demands can be realized.

The Buddha rests his Teaching upon the thesis that with the right method we have the capacity to change and transform ourselves. We are not doomed to be for ever burdened by the weight of accumulated tendencies, but through our own effort we can cast off all these tendencies and attain a condition of complete purity and freedom. When given the proper means in the context of right understanding, we can bring about radical alterations in the workings of consciousness and mould a new shape out of the seemingly immutable stuff of our own minds.

The first step on this path is the purification of character, and the efficient means for the restructuring of character the Buddha provides in the observance of *sīla* as a set of precepts regulating bodily and verbal conduct. *Sīla* as moral discipline, in other words, becomes the means for inducing *sīla* as moral virtue. The effectiveness of this measure stems from the reciprocal interlocking of the internal and external spheres of experience already referred to. Because the inner and outer domains are mutually implicated, the one can become the means for producing deep and lasting changes in the other. Just as a state of mind expresses itself outwardly in an action—in deed or speech—so too the avoidance and performance of certain actions can recoil upon the mind and alter the basic disposition of the mental life. If mental states dominated by greed and hatred can engender deeds of killing, stealing, lying, etc., then the abstinence on principle from killing, stealing, and lying can engender a mental disposition towards kindliness, contentment, honesty, and truthfulness. Thus, although *sīla* as moral purity may not be the starting point of spiritual training, conformity to righteous standards of conduct can make it an attainable end.

The medium which bridges the two dimensions of *sīla*, facilitating the translation of outward behaviour into inner purity, is volition or *cetanā*. Volition is a mental factor common to every occasion of experience, a universal concomitant of every act of consciousness. It is the factor which makes experience teleological, i.e., oriented to a goal, since its specific function is to direct its associated factors towards the attainment of a particular end. All action (*kamma*), the Buddha teaches, is in essence volition, for the act itself is from the ultimate standpoint a manifestation of volition through one of the three doors of action—body, speech, or mind: "It is volition, bhikkhus, that I call action. For having willed, one performs an action through body, speech, or mind."

Volition determines an action as being of a definite sort, and thence imparts to action its moral significance. But since volition is invariably present in every state of consciousness, it is in its own nature without ethical distinctiveness. Volition acquires its distinctive ethical quality from certain other mental factors known as roots (*mūla*), in association with which it always arises on occasions of active experience. Roots are of two morally determinate kinds: unwholesome (*akusala*) and wholesome (*kusala*). The unwholesome roots are greed, hatred, and delusion; the wholesome roots are non-greed, non-hatred, and non-delusion. These latter, though expressed negatively, signify not merely the absence of the defiling factors, but the presence of positive moral qualities as well; generosity, loving-kindness, and wisdom, respectively.

When volition is driven by the unwholesome roots of greed, hatred, and delusion, it breaks out through the doors of the body and speech in the form of evil deeds—as killing, stealing, and fornication, as lying, slander, harsh speech, and gossip. In this way the inner world of mental defilement darkens the outer world of spatio-temporal extension. But the defiled trend of volitional movement, though strong, is not irrevocable. Unwholesome volition can be supplanted by wholesome volition, and thence the entire disposition of the mental life made subject to a reversal at its foundation. This redirecting of volition is initiated by voluntarily undertaking the observance of principles of conduct belonging to a righteous order—by willing to abstain from evil and to practise the good. Then, when volition tending to break out as evil action is restrained and replaced by volition of the opposite kind, by the will to behave virtuously in word and deed, a process of reversal will have been started which, if followed through, can produce far-reaching alterations in the moral tone of character. For acts of volition do not spend their full force in their immediate exercise, but rebound upon the mental current which gave birth to them, re-orienting that current in the direction towards which they point as their own immanent tendency: the unwholesome volitions towards moral depravation, and the wholesome volitions towards moral purification. Each time, therefore, an unwholesome volition is supplanted by its wholesome opposite, the will to the good is strengthened.

A process of factor substitution, built upon the law that incompatible mental qualities cannot be simultaneously present on a single occasion of experience, then completes the transformation through the efficacy of the associated roots. Just as unwholesome volitions invariably arise in association with the unwholesome roots—with greed, hatred and delusion—so do wholesome volitions inevitably bring along with them as their concomitants the wholesome roots of non-greed, non-hatred, and non-delusion. Since opposite qualities cannot co-exist, the replacement of unwholesome volition by wholesome volition at the same time means the transposition of the unwholesome and the wholesome roots. Continually called into play by the surge of volition, the wholesome roots "perfume" the mental stream with the qualities for which they stand—with generosity, loving-kindness, and wisdom; and these, as they gather cumulative force, come to prominence as regular propensities of the personality, eclipsing the inclination towards the unwholesome. In this way the exercise of wholesome volitions on repeated and varied occasions effects a transformation of character from its initial moral susceptibility to a pitch of purity where even the temptation to evil remains at a safe remove.

Though volition or *cetanā* is the primary instrument of change, the will in itself is indeterminate and requires specific guidelines to direct its energy towards the actualization of the good. A mere "good will," from the Buddhist standpoint, is altogether inadequate, for despite the nobility of the intention, as long as the intelligence of the agent is clouded with the dust of delusion, the possibility always lies open that laudable motives might express themselves in foolish or even destructive courses of action. This has been the case often enough in the past, and still stands as the perennial bugbear of the ethical generalist. According to the Buddhist outlook, goodness of will must be translated into concrete courses of action. It must be regulated by specific principles of right conduct, principles which, though flexible in their application, possess normative validity independently of any historical culture or existing scheme of values, entirely by virtue of their relation to a universal law of moral retribution and their place in the timeless path of practice leading to deliverance from suffering and the *saṃsāric* round.

To guide the will in its aspiration for the good, the Buddha has prescribed in definite and lucid terms the factors of moral training which must be fulfilled to safeguard progress along the path to enlightenment. These factors are comprised in the three items which make up the aggregate of virtue in the Noble Eightfold Path: namely, right speech, right action, and right livelihood. Right speech is the avoidance of all harmful forms of speech—the abstinence from falsehood, slander, harsh speech, and idle chatter. The speech of the aspirant must be constantly truthful, conducive to harmony, gentle and meaningful. Right action applies a brake upon unwholesome bodily action, by prescribing abstinence from the destruction of life, from stealing, and from sexual misconduct; the latter means incelibacy in the case of monks, and adultery and other illicit relations in the case of householders. The behaviour of the aspirant must always be compassionate, honest, and pure. And right livelihood requires the avoidance of trades which inflict harm and suffering upon other living beings, such as dealing in meat, slaves, weapons, poisons, and intoxicants. Avoiding such harmful trades, the noble disciple earns his living by a peaceful and righteous occupation.

The training factors embedded in these components of the Noble Eightfold Path simultaneously inhibit the base, ignoble and destructive impulses of the human mind and promote the performance of whatever is noble and pure. Though worded negatively, in terms of the types of conduct they are intended to shut out, they are positive in effect, for when adopted as guidelines to action, they stimulate the growth of healthy mental attitudes which come to expression as beneficent courses of conduct. Intensively, these training rules reach into the recesses of the mind, blunt the force of unwholesome volition, and redirect the will to the attainment of the good. Extensively, they reach into the commotion of man's social existence, and arrest the tide of competition, exploitation, grasping, violence and war. In their psychological dimension they confer mental health, in their social dimension they promote peace, in their spiritual dimension they serve as the irreplaceable foundation for all higher progress along the path to emancipation. Regularly undertaken and put into practice, they check all mental states rooted in greed, hatred, and delusion; promote actions rooted in non-greed, non-hatred, and non-delusion, and lead to a life of charity, love, and wisdom.

From this it will be seen that from the Buddhist point of view formulated rules of conduct are not superfluous accessories to a good will, but necessary guidelines to right action. They are an essential part of the training, and when implemented by the force of volition, become a fundamental means to purification. Especially in the context of the practice of meditation, the training precepts prevent the eruption of defiled actions destructive to the purpose of the meditative discipline. By following carefully the prescribed rules of conduct, we can rest assured that we are avoiding at least the coarser expressions of greed, hatred, and delusion, and that we will not have to face the obstacle of guilt, anxiety, and restlessness that comes in the trail of regular moral transgressions.

If we return to our earlier comparison of the Buddhist discipline to a tree, and take virtue to be the roots, then the principles of right conduct become the soil in which the roots grow. Just as the soil contains the nutritive essences required for the tree to sprout and flourish, so do the precepts contain the nutriment of purity and virtue required for the growth of the spiritual life. The precepts embody the natural conduct of the arahat or perfected saint. For the arahat, his conduct flows outward as the spontaneous expression of his innate purity. By his very nature, all his deeds are flawless, free from blemish. He cannot follow any course of action motivated by desire, ill will, delusion, or fear—not through any forced conformity to rules, but by the very law of his being.

The worldling, however, is not immune from the possibility of immoral conduct. To the contrary, because the unwholesome roots remain firmly planted in the makeup of his mind, he is constantly prone to the temptation to moral transgression. He is liable to kill, steal, commit adultery, lie, drink, etc.; and in the absence of any sound moral code prohibiting such actions, he will often succumb to these liabilities. Hence the necessity of providing him with a set of ethical principles built upon the pillars of wisdom and compassion, by which he can regulate his actions and conform to the natural, spontaneous behaviour of the Liberated One.

A precept is, therefore, from the Buddhist perspective much more than a prohibition imposed upon conduct from without. Each precept is a tangible expression of a corresponding attitude of mind, a principle which clothes in the form of concrete action a beam of the light of inward purity. The precepts render visible the invisible state of purification. They make it accessible to us by refracting it through the media of body and speech into specific rules of conduct we can apply as guides to action when we find ourselves in the diverse situations they are designed to cover. By bringing our conduct into harmony with the precepts, we can nourish the root of our spiritual endeavours, our virtue. And when virtue is made secure, the succeeding stages of the path unfold spontaneously through the law of the spiritual life, culminating at the crest in the perfection of knowledge and the serene azure of deliverance. As the Master says:

For one who is virtuous, bhikkhus, endowed with virtue, no deliberate volition need be exerted: "Let freedom from remorse arise in me." This is the natural law, bhikkhus, that freedom from remorse arises in one who is virtuous, endowed with virtue.

For one who is free from remorse, no deliberate volition need be exerted: "Let gladness arise in me." This is the natural law, bhikkhus, that gladness arises in one free from remorse.

For one who is gladdened, no deliberate volition need be exerted: "Let rapture arise in me." This is the natural law, bhikkhus, that rapture arises in one who is gladdened.

For one filled with rapture, no deliberate volition need be exerted: "Let my body become tranquil." This is the natural law, bhikkhus, that for one filled with rapture the body becomes tranquil.

For one tranquil in body, no deliberate volition need be exerted: "May I experience bliss." This is the natural law, bhikkhus, that one tranquil in body experiences bliss.

For one who is blissful, no deliberate volition need be exerted: "Let my mind become concentrated." This is the natural law, bhikkhus, that for one who is blissful the mind becomes concentrated.

For one who is concentrated, no deliberate volition need be exerted: "May I know and see things as they really are." This is the natural law, bhikkhus, that one who is concentrated knows and sees things as they really are.

For one knowing and seeing things as they really are, no deliberate volition need be exerted: "May I become disenchanted and dispassionate." This is the natural law, bhikkhus, that one knowing and seeing things as they really are becomes disenchanted and dispassionate.

For one who has become disenchanted and dispassionate, no deliberate volition need be exerted: "May I realize the knowledge and vision of deliverance." This is the natural law, bhikkhus, that one who is disenchanted and dispassionate realizes the knowledge and vision of deliverance...

Thus, bhikkhus, one stage flows into the succeeding stage, one stage comes to fulfilment in the succeeding stage, for crossing over from the hither shore to the beyond.

Aṅguttara Nikāya, 10:2

Mind and the Animate Order

As we cast our gaze out upon the landscape of animate nature, it does not take long before our attention is struck by the tremendous diversity of forms the animate order displays. The folds of nature's lap, we find, teem with a multitude of living beings as staggering in their range of specific differentiation as in the sheer impression of their quantitative force. Before our eyes countless varieties of creatures—insects and reptiles, fish and birds, mammals domestic and wild—turn the earth with its seas and skies into a complex metropolis, throbbing with the pulse of sentient life. But realms of being beyond sight—vouched for by spiritual cosmology, folklore, and the reports of seers—are no less crowded, and no less diversified in their composition. According to this testimony, gods, Brahmās, angels, and demons populate boroughs of the city of life invisible to fleshly eyes, while other creatures, such as fairies, ghosts, and goblins, fill up unfamiliar pockets of the same borough.

The human world, again, is itself far from homogeneous. The family of man breaks down into a great diversity of types—into people black, white, brown, yellow, and red, dividing still further, according to their fortunes and faculties, into the long-lived and the short-lived, the healthy and the sickly, the successful and the failures, the gifted and the deprived. Some people are intelligent, others are dull-witted, some are noble, others ignoble, some are spiritually evolved, others spiritually destitute. Human beings range all the way from mental retards who can manage their bodily needs only with great difficulty, to sages and saints who can comprehend the deepest secrets of the universe and lift the moral outlook of their less acute brothers and sisters to heights undreamed of in the common stream of thought.

To the thinker who would dig below the surface presentations and discover the reasons for the manifest phenomena, the question naturally arises why life exhibits itself in such variegated apparel. Reflection upon this question has given birth to a multitude of schools of thought, religious and philosophical, each offering its own speculations as the key to unravel the riddle of nature's kaleidoscopic design. In the intellectual history of humanity, the two dominant positions around which these schools cluster are theism and materialism. Pitted against one another by their antithetical tenets, the two have come down in different guises from ancient times even to the present. Theism refers the diversity of sentient life, including the disparities of fortune evident in the human world, to the will of God. It is God, the theist holds, the omnipotent, omniscient author of the universe, who creates through the fiat of his will the variety of natural forms, allots to beings their respective shares of happiness and suffering, and divides people into the high and the low, the fortunate and the miserable.

Materialism, in contradistinction, rules out any recourse to an extraterrestrial agency to account for the differentiation in the faculties and capacities found amongst living beings, and attempts to provide in its place a system of explanation which works exclusively with naturalistic principles, pertaining to the material order. The entire gamut of living forms together with all life's modes of expression, the materialist claims, can be effectively reduced in the end to the adventures of matter governed by physical, chemical and biological laws. Even consciousness represents, for the materialist, only a secondary superstructure built upon a material base devoid of any larger significance in itself.

It is not our present purpose here to examine at length these two rival doctrines. Let it suffice to note that both, in different ways, throw into jeopardy the postulate of a progressive spiritual evolution of beings by withholding, implicitly or explicitly, the necessary condition for such a course of evolution—namely, an inwardly autonomous will which finds in the diversity of the sentient order the field for the working out of its own potentialities for growth and transformation, in accordance with laws governing freely chosen possibilities of action.

Theism withholds this condition by its basic postulate of an omnipotent deity directing the entire field of nature from above. If all of nature runs its course in obedience to divine command, then the individual will, which belongs to the natural order, must be subject to the same divine supervision as the rest of animate nature. The autonomy of the individual will and its direct impact on the sentient sphere are excluded, and with them also goes the thesis of a genuine long-term spiritual growth, to which they are essential.

Materialism likewise shuts out the notion of a progressive spiritual evolution of beings, but more simply and directly, by explicitly denying the basic presupposition of such a notion. The will's claim to freedom is here rejected, its autonomy usurped by the irresistible pressure of the determinative influences at its base. Consciousness becomes a mere by-product of material processes; the individual life-stream leaves no impact on any continuous current of experience enduring beyond the grave. Both conscious action and evolution in the biotic sphere proceed in the grip of the same play of cosmic forces—blind, brute, and insentient in their fundamental mode of operation.

Buddhism also offers an explanation for the diversity of the sentient order, an explanation which bridges the gap between volition and the diversity and thus opens up the prospect for long-term spiritual development. According to Buddhism, the explanation for the variegation of sentient beings—in their kinds, faculties, and fortunes—lies in their kamma, that is, their volitional action. Beings are, in the words of the Buddha, "heirs of their action." They spring forth from their store of accumulated action as a matrix out of which they are fashioned, inheriting the results proper to their deeds even across the gulf of lifetimes. Through the succession of life-terms, kamma holds sway over the individual evolutionary current. Acts of will, once completed, recede into the forward moving mental stream out of which they emerged, and remaining in the form of psychic potencies, pilot the future course of evolution to be taken by that particular current of experience called an "individual being." Just as the kamma rises up out of the stream of consciousness, so does the stream of consciousness again flow forth from the germinative kamma, which thus serves to link into a single chain the series of separated lives. The kammic force drives the current of consciousness onward into new modes of existence conformable to its nature; it determines the specific form of life in which the individual will take remanifestation, the set of faculties with which the new being will be endowed, and a substantial portion of the happiness and suffering that being will meet during the course of its life.

It is, therefore, not God or chance in the Buddhist picture, but the differentiation in volitional action, functioning across the succession of lives, that accounts for the differentiation in the animate order, and the differentiation in action again that divides beings into the high and low, the happy and the miserable, the gifted and the deprived. As the Buddha declares: "Beings are the owners of their actions, heirs of their actions. Their action is the source from which they spring, their kinsman and their refuge. Action divides beings into the inferior and the superior."

Since the effective determinant of destiny is kamma, and kamma is essentially volition, this means that the operative factor in the formation of future becoming is lodged in the individual will. The will, from the Buddhist perspective, is no accidental offshoot of the machinery of nature, compelled to its course by the conspiracy of cosmic forces; it is, rather, in the deepest sense the artisan behind the entire process of animate evolution. Here will is primary and the material factors secondary, the plastic substance with which the will works and by which it gives tangible expression to its store of dispositional tendencies. The varied landscape of sentient existence, for Buddhism, represents but an outward register of the inward transactions of the will, and the hierarchy of living forms—the "great chain of being"—but a congelation of its functional modalities in the world of spatio-temporal extension.

Differentiation in the biological sphere is thus preceded and paralleled by a set of transformations in the mental sphere, which finds in animate nature the channel for actualizing its own potentialities throughout the series of successive becomings comprising the individual continuum. Through the exercise of our will, therefore, we build for ourselves our own world independent of coercion by extrinsic forces and mould the destiny that awaits us in time to come, whether for happiness or misery, for bondage or liberation.

For the spiritual aspirant, however, it is not sufficient merely to understand the theoretical ground for the differentiation of living beings. For us it is of the utmost importance to know what we can do to further our own progress along the scale of spiritual evolution—to advance to higher levels of attainment during the course of our earthly life, to secure a rebirth conducive to spiritual growth in the life to come, and ultimately to transcend this repetitive cycle of birth and death and attain Nibbāna, the supreme and irreversible deliverance.

The answer to this problem begins with the fact that kamma divides itself, according to its moral quality, into two types—the unwholesome (*akusala*) and the wholesome (*kusala*). Unwholesome kamma is action—physical, verbal, or mental—that springs from the three unwholesome roots of action: greed (*lobha*), hatred (*dosa*), and delusion (*moha*). Any action grounded in these roots is spiritually detrimental and morally defective. It destroys the higher faculties, entails suffering as its consequence, and causes a plunge into lower states of existence; in short, it brings decline along the scale of spiritual evolution and deeper immersion in the mire of phenomenal existence. Wholesome kamma, on the other hand, is action springing from the three contrary wholesome roots—non-greed (*alobha*), non-hatred (*adosa*), and non-delusion (*amoha*), finding positive expression in the qualities of charity, loving-kindness, and wisdom, respectively. Wholesome action functions in a way diametrically opposite to its dark counterpart. It is spiritually beneficial and morally commendable, stimulates the unfolding of the higher faculties, and entails happiness both in the present and in time to come. Consistently practised, it promotes progress along the evolutionary scale, leading to higher states of existence in successive life-spans, and finally to the realization of deliverance.

On ultimate analysis, life is a self-regenerating sequence of occasions of experience, comprising occasions of action and occasions of reception. Action is volition, and volition inevitably involves decision or choice—a selection from the welter of possibilities open to the will of that alternative most conformable to the individual's purpose, a selection even, at a higher level, of the purposes themselves. Every moment of morally significant action, therefore, confronts us with the call for a decision, with the necessity for choice. Choice must work within the gamut of options open to the will, and these options, despite their great differences of qualitative character, necessarily fall into one of two classes according to their ethical nature—into the wholesome or the unwholesome. The one leads to progress, the other to decline.

Thence progress or decline depends entirely upon our choice, and not upon any external agency whether conceived in spiritualistic or materialistic garb. Through our fleeting, momentary decisions, accumulated over long periods, we model our fortune and chisel out of the unshaped block of futurity the destiny that will befall us in the span of time to come. Each call for a decision may be depicted as a ladder, one end leading upward to unknown heights, and the other extending downward into forbidding depths, while our successive decisions may be taken as the steps that lead us up or down the ladder's graded rungs. Or again, each moment of action may be compared to a crossroad at which we stand, a forked road one side of which leads to a city of bliss and the other to a swampland of misery and despair. The two roads stand, fixed and silent, awaiting our choice, and only our decision determines whether we shall reach the one destination or the other.

In sum, then, it is our kamma that precipitates our destiny, for it is kamma that brings about manifestation of all the destinations (*gati*) or realms of sentient existence, and kamma ultimately that fashions the entire variegated landscape of sentient existence itself, according to the ethical tone of its associated moral roots. As the Exalted One explains, speaking not through speculation but through his own direct penetration of the paths leading to all destinations:

It is not celestial beings (*deva*), or humans, or any other creatures belonging to happy forms of existence, that appear through action (*kamma*) born of greed, born of hate, born of delusion; it is rather beings of the hells, of the animal kingdom, of the ghostly realm, or any others of miserable form of existence that make their appearance through action born of greed, hate, and delusion...

It is not creatures of the hells, of the animal kingdom, of the ghostly realm, or any others of a miserable form of existence, that appear through action born of non-greed, born of non-hate, born of non-delusion; it is rather celestial beings, humans, or any other creatures belonging to a happy form of existence that make their appearance through action born of non-greed, non-hate, and non-delusion.

Aṅguttara Nikāya, 6:39

Merit and Spiritual Growth

The performance of deeds of merit forms one of the most essential elements of Buddhist practice. Its various modes provide in their totality a compendium of applied Buddhism, showing Buddhism not as a system of ideas but as a complete way of life. Buddhist popular belief has often emphasized merit as a productive source of worldly blessings—of health, wealth, long life, beauty, and friends. As a result of this emphasis, meritorious activity has come to be conceived rather in terms of a financial investment, as a religious business venture yielding returns to the satisfaction of the agent's mundane desires. While such a conception no doubt contains an element of truth, its popularization has tended to eclipse the more important function merit plays in the context of Buddhist practice. Seen in correct perspective, merit is an essential ingredient in the harmony and completeness of the spiritual life, a means of self-cultivation, and an indispensable stepping-stone to spiritual progress.

The accumulation of a "stock of merit" is a primary requisite for acquiring all the fruits of the Buddhist religious life, from a pleasant abiding here and now to a favourable rebirth in the life to come, from the initial stages of meditative progress to the realization of the states of sanctity that come as the fruits of entering upon the noble path. The highest fruition of merit is identical with the culmination of the Buddhist holy life itself—that is, emancipation from the shackles of *saṃsāric* existence and the realization of Nibbāna, the unconditioned state beyond the insubstantial phenomena of the world. The mere piling up of merit, to be sure, is not in itself sufficient to guarantee the attainment of this goal. Merit is only one requisite, and it must be balanced by its counterpart to secure the breakthrough from bondage to final freedom. The counterpart of merit is knowledge (*ñāṇa*), the direct confrontation with the basic truths of existence through the eye of intuitive wisdom.

Merit and knowledge together constitute the two sets of equipment the spiritual aspirant requires in the quest for deliverance, the equipment of merit (*puññasambhāra*) and the equipment of knowledge (*ñāṇasambhāra*), respectively. Each set of equipment has its own contribution to make to the fulfilment of the spiritual life.

The equipment of merit facilitates progress in the course of *saṃsāric* wandering: it brings a favourable rebirth, the encounter with good friends to guide one's footsteps along the path, the meeting with opportunities for spiritual growth, the flowering of the lofty qualities of character, and the maturation of the spiritual faculties required for the higher attainments. The equipment of knowledge brings the factor directly necessary for cutting the bonds of *saṃsāric* existence: the penetration of truth, enlightenment, the undistorted comprehension of the nature of actuality.

Either set of equipment, functioning in isolation, is insufficient to the attainment of the goal; either pursued alone leads to a deviant, one-sided development that departs from the straight path to deliverance taught by the Buddha. Merit without knowledge produces pleasant fruit and a blissful rebirth, but cannot issue in the transcendence of the mundane order and entrance upon the supramundane path. And knowledge without the factors of merit deteriorates into dry intellectualism, mere erudition or scholasticism, impotent when confronted with the task of grasping a truth outside the pale of intellection. But when they function together in unison in the life of the aspirant, the two sets of equipment acquire a potency capable of propelling him to the heights of realization. When each set of equipment complements the other, polishes the other, and perfects the other, then they undergo a graduated course of mutual purification culminating at the crest in the twin endowments of the Emancipated One—in that clear knowledge (*vijjā*) and flawless conduct (*caraṇa*) which make him, in the words of the Buddha, "supreme among gods and humans."

But while merit and knowledge thus occupy coordinate positions, it is merit that claims priority from the standpoint of spiritual dynamics. The reason is that works of merit come first in the process of inner growth. If knowledge be the flower that gives birth to the fruit of liberation, and faith (*saddhā*) the seed out of which the flower unfolds, then merit is the soil, water, and fertilizer all in one—the indispensable nutriment for every stage of growth. Merit paves the way for knowledge, and finds in knowledge the sanction for its own claim to a place in the system of Buddhist training.

The reason for this particular sequential structure is closely linked to the Buddhist conception of noetic realization. From the Buddhist standpoint the comprehension of spiritual truth is not a matter of mere intellectual cogitation but of existential actualization. That is, it is a matter of grasping with our whole being the truth towards which we aspire, and of inwardly appropriating that truth in a manner so total and complete that our being becomes transformed into a very reflex and effusion of the truth upon which we stand. The understanding of truth in the context of the spiritual life, in other words, is no affair of accumulating bits and pieces of information publicly accessible and subjectively indifferent; it is, rather, a process of uncovering the deepest truths about ourselves and about the world, and of working the understanding that emerges into the entire complex of the inner life. Hence the use of the words "actualization" and "realization," which bring into the open the ontological backdrop underlying the noetic process.

In order to grasp truth in this totalistic manner at any particular stage of spiritual development, the tenor of our inner being must be raised to a pitch where it is fit for the reception of some new disclosure of the truth. Wisdom and character, though not identical, are at any rate parallel terms, which in most cases mature in a delicately balanced ratio. We can grasp only what we are fit to grasp, and our fitness is largely a function of our character. The existential comprehension of truth thus becomes a matter of inward worth, of deservingness, or of merit. The way to effect this inward worthiness is by the performance of works of merit, not merely outwardly, but backed by the proper attitudes and disposition of mind. For the capacity to comprehend truths pertaining to the spiritual order is always proportional to the store and quality of accumulated merit. The greater and finer the merit, the larger and deeper the capacity for understanding. This principle holds at each level of maturation in the ascent towards full realization, and applies with special force to the comprehension of ultimate truth.

Ultimate truth, in the Buddha's Teaching, is Nibbāna, the unconditioned element (*asaṅkhata dhātu*), and realization of ultimate truth is the realization of Nibbāna. Nibbāna is the perfection of purity: the destruction of all passions, the eradication of clinging, the abolition of every impulse towards self-affirmation. The final thrust to the realization of Nibbāna is the special province of wisdom, since wisdom alone is adequate to the task of comprehending all conditioned phenomena in their essential nature as impermanent, suffering, and not-self, and of turning away from them to penetrate the unconditioned, where alone permanent freedom from suffering is to be found. But that this penetration may take place, our interior must be made commensurate in purity with the truth it would grasp, and this requires in the first instance that it be purged of all those elements obstructive to the florescence of a higher light and knowledge. The apprehension of Nibbāna, this perfect purity secluded from the dust of passion, is only possible when a corresponding purity has been set up within ourselves. For only a pure mind can discern, through the dark mist of ignorance and defilement, the spotless purity of Nibbāna, abiding in absolute solitude beyond the turmoil of the phenomenal procession.

The achievement of such a purification of our inward being is the work of merit. Merit scours the mind of the coarser defilements, attenuates the grip of the unwholesome roots, and fortifies the productive power of the wholesome, beneficial states. Through its cumulative force it provides the foundation for wisdom's final breakthrough to the unconditioned. It is the fuel, so to speak, for the ascent of wisdom from the mundane to the supramundane. Just as the initial stages of a lunar rocket work up the momentum that enables the uppermost stage to break the gravitational pull of the earth and reach the moon, so does merit give to the spiritual life that forward thrust that will propel the wisdom-faculty past the gravitational pull of the mundane order and permit it to penetrate the transcendental truth.

The classical Buddhist commentators underscore this preparatory purgative function of merit when they define merit (*puñña*) etymologically as "that which purges and purifies the mental continuum" (*santānaṃ punāti visodheti*). Merit performs its purgative function in the context of a complex process involving an agent and object of purification, and a mode of operation by which the purification takes place. The agent of purification is the mind itself, in its creative, formative role as the source and matrix of action. Deeds of merit are, as we have already seen, instances of wholesome kamma, and kamma ultimately reduces to volition. Therefore, at the fundamental level of analysis, a deed of merit consists in a volition, a determinative act of will belonging to the righteous order (*puññābhisaṅkhāra*). Since volition is a mode of mental activity, this means that merit turns out, under scrutiny, to be a mode of mental activity. It is, at the core of the behaviour-pattern which serves as its vehicle, a particular application of thought by which the mind marshals its components for the achievement of a chosen end.

This discovery cautions us against misconstruing the Buddhist stress on the practice of merit as a call for blind subjection to rules and rites. The primary instrument behind any act of merit, from the Buddhist point of view, is the mind. The deed itself in its physical or vocal dimension serves mainly as an expression of a corresponding state of consciousness, and without a keen awareness of the nature and significance of the meritorious deed, the bare outward act is devoid of purgative value. Even when rules of conduct are observed, or rituals and worship performed with a view to the acquisition of merit, the spiritual potency of these structures derives not from any intrinsic sanctity they might possess in themselves, but from their effectiveness in channelling the current of mental activity in a spiritual beneficial direction. They function, in effect, as skilful means or expedient devices for inducing wholesome states of consciousness.

Mechanical conformity to moral rules, or the performance of religious duties through unquestioning obedience to established forms, far from serving as a means to salvation, in the Buddhist outlook actually constitute obstacles. They are instances of "clinging to rules and rituals" (*sīlabbataparāmāsa*), the third of the fetters (*saṃyojana*) binding beings to the wheel of becoming, which must be abandoned in order to enter upon the path to final deliverance. Even in such relatively external forms of merit-making as the undertaking of moral precepts and ceremonial worship, mindfulness and clear comprehension are essential; much more, then, are they necessary to the predominantly internal modes of meritorious activity, such as meditation or the study of the Dhamma.

The object of the purifying process of merit is again the mind, only here considered not from the standpoint of its immediacy, as a creative source of action, but from the standpoint of its duration, as a continuum (*cittasantāna*). For, looked at from the temporal point of view, the mind is no stable entity enduring self-identical through its changing activities; it is, rather, a serial continuity composed of discrete acts of mentation bound to one another by exact laws of causal interconnection. Each thought-unit flashes into being, persists for an extremely brief moment, and then perishes, passing on to its immediate successor its storage of recorded impressions. Each individual member of the series inherits, preserves, and transmits, along with its own novel modifications, the entire content of the series as a whole, which thus underlies every one of its components. Thence the series maintains, despite its discontinuous composition, an element of uniformity that gives to the flow of separate thought-moments the character of a continuum.

This sequential current of mentation has been going on, according to Buddhism, without discernible beginning. Driven forward from life to life by ignorance and craving, it appears now in one mode of manifestation, now in another. Embedded in the mental continuum throughout its beginningless journey is a host of particularly afflictive and disruptive mental forces known as *kilesas,* "defilements." Foremost among them are the three unwholesome roots—greed, hatred, and delusion; from this triad spring the remaining members of the set, such as pride, opinion, selfishness, envy, sloth, and restlessness. During moments of passivity the defilements lie dormant at the base of the mental continuum, as *anusaya* or latent tendencies. But when, either through the impact of outer sensory stimuli or their own subliminal process of growth, they acquire sufficient force, they surge to the surface of consciousness in the form of obsessions (*pariyuṭṭhāna*). The obsessions pollute the mind with their toxic flow and rebound upon the deeper levels of consciousness, reinforcing their roots at the base of the continuum. If they should gather still additional charge, the defilements may reach the even more dangerous stage of transgression (*vītikkama*), when they erupt as bodily or verbal actions that violate the fundamental laws of morality and lead to pain and suffering as their retributive consequence.

When merit is said to "purge and purify the mental continuum," it is so described in reference to its capacity to arrest the surging tide of the defilements which threatens to sweep the mind towards the perilous deep of transgressional action. Only wisdom—the supramundane wisdom of the noble paths—can eradicate the defilements at the level of latency, which is necessary if the bonds of existence are to be broken and deliverance attained. But the practice of merit can contribute much towards attenuating their obsessive force and establishing a foothold for wisdom to exercise its liberating function. Wisdom can operate only upon the base of a purified mind; the accumulation of merit purifies the mind; hence merit provides the supporting condition for wisdom.

When the mind is allowed to flow according to its own momentum, without restraint or control, like a turbulent river it casts up to the surface—i.e., to the level of active consciousness—the store of pollutants it harbours at its base: lust, hatred, delusion, and their derivative defilements. If the defilements are then given further scope to grow by indulging them, they will wither the potential for good, darken the beam of awareness, and strangle the faculty of wisdom until it is reduced to a mere vestige. The performance of meritorious deeds serves as a means of resisting the upsurge of defiling states, of replacing them with their wholesome opposites, and of thereby purifying the mental continuum to an extent sufficient to supply wisdom with the storage of strength it requires in the work of abolishing the defilements.

The effectiveness of merit in purifying the mental continuum stems from the concordance of a number of psychological laws. These laws, which can only be indicated briefly here, together function as the silent groundwork for the efficacy of the entire corpus of Buddhist spiritual practice.

The first is the law that only one state of consciousness can occur at a time; though seemingly trivial, this law leads to important consequences when taken in conjunction with the rest. The second holds that states of consciousness with mutually opposed ethical qualities cannot coexist. The third stipulates that all the factors of consciousness—feeling, perception, volition, and the remaining states included in the "aggregate of mental formations"—must partake of the same ethical quality as the consciousness itself.

A kammically active state of consciousness is either entirely wholesome, or entirely unwholesome; it cannot (by the second law) be both. Therefore, if a wholesome state is occurring, no unwholesome state can simultaneously occur. A wholesome, spiritually beneficial state of consciousness necessarily shuts out every unwholesome, detrimental state, as well as (by the third law) all unwholesome concomitant factors of consciousness. So at the moment one is performing an act of merit, the consciousness and volition behind that meritorious deed will automatically preclude an unwholesome consciousness, volition, and the associated defilements. At that moment, at least, the consciousness will be pure. And the frequent performance of meritorious acts will, on every occasion, bar the opportunity for the defilements to arise at the time of their performance.

Thus the performance of deeds of merit always induces a momentary purification, while the frequent performance of such deeds induces many occasions of momentary purification. But that some more durable result might be achieved an additional principle is necessary. This principle is supplied by the fourth law.

The fourth law holds that repetition confers strength. Just as the exercise of a particular muscle can transform that muscle from a frail, ineffectual strip of flesh into a dynamo of power and strength, so the repeated exercise of individual mental qualities can remodel them from sleeping soldiers into invincible warriors in the spiritual quest.

Repetition is the key to the entire process of self-transformation which constitutes the essence of the spiritual life. It is the very grounding that makes self-transformation possible. By force of repetition the fragile, tender shoots of the pure and wholesome qualities—faith, energy, mindfulness, concentration, and wisdom—can blossom into sovereign faculties (*indriya*) in the struggle for enlightenment, or into indomitable powers (*bala*) in the battle against the defilements. By repeated resistance to the upsurge of evil and repeated application to the cultivation of the good, the demon can become a god and the criminal a saint.

If repetition provides the key to self-transformation, then volition provides the instrument through which repetition works. Volition acts as a vector force upon the mental continuum out of which it emerges, reorienting the continuum according to its own moral tone. Each act of will recedes with its passing into the onward rushing current of mentation and drives the current in its own direction. Wholesome volitions direct the continuum towards the good—towards purity, wisdom, and ultimate liberation; unwholesome volitions drive it towards the evil—towards defilement, ignorance, and inevitable bondage.

Every occasion of volition modifies the mental life in some way and to some degree, however slight, so that the overall character of an individual at any one time stands as a reflex and revelation of the volitions accumulated in the continuum.

Since the will propels the entire current of mental life in its own direction, it is the will which must be strengthened by force of repetition. The restructuring of mental life can only take place through the reformation of the will by leading it into wholesome channels. The effective channel for re-orientation of the will is the practice of merit.

When the will is directed towards the cultivation of merit, it will spontaneously hamper the stream of defilements and bolster the company of noble qualities in the storage of the continuum. Under its gentle tutelage the factors of purity will awaken from their dormant condition and take their place as regular propensities in the personality. A will devoted to the practice of charity will generate kindness and compassion; a will devoted to the observance of the precepts will generate harmlessness, honesty, restraint, truthfulness, and sobriety; a will devoted to mental culture will generate calm and insight. Faith, reverence, humility, sympathy, courage, and equanimity will come to growth. Consciousness will gain in tranquillity, buoyancy, pliancy, agility, and proficiency. And a consciousness made pure by these factors will advance without hindrance through the higher attainments in meditation and wisdom to the realization of Nibbāna, the consummation of spiritual endeavour.

The Path of Understanding

Prince Siddhattha renounced the life of the palace and entered the forest as a hermit seeking a solution to the problem of suffering. Six years after entering he came out a Buddha, ready to show others the path he had found so that they too could work out their deliverance. It was the experience of being bound to the perishable and unsatisfying that gave the impetus to the Buddha's original quest, and it was the certainty of having found the unperishing and perfectly complete that inspired the execution of his mission. Thence the Buddha could sum up his Teaching in the single phrase: "I teach only suffering and the cessation of suffering." But though the Buddha's Teaching might be simple in its statement, the meaning behind the verbal formulation is profound and precise.

The Buddha envisages suffering in its full range and essence rather than in its mere manifest forms. It is not just physical or mental pain that he means by suffering, but the recurrent revolution of the wheel of becoming, with its spokes of birth, ageing, and death. Taking our immersion in a condition intrinsically inadequate as the starting point of his doctrine, he devotes the remainder to showing the way out of this condition. The solution the Buddha offers to the problem of suffering draws its cogency from the strict logic of causality. Suffering is neither an accident nor an imposition from without, but a contingent phenomenon arising through the force of conditions. It hangs upon a specific set of supports, and is therefore susceptible to treatment by tackling the genetic structure which maintains it in being. By removing the conditions out of which it arises, it is possible to bring the whole phenomenon of suffering to an end.

In order to reach the state of emancipation, it is of the first importance that the causal chain which originates suffering be snapped in the right place. Any proposed solution which does not remedy the problem of suffering at its source will eventually prove to be only a palliative, not a final cure. That the chain be broken in the right place requires an accurate determination of the interconnection of its links. The chain must be traced back to its most fundamental factor and cut off at that very point. Then suffering will no longer be able to arise.

According to the Buddha's Teaching, the primary link in the sequence of conditions generating suffering is ignorance (*avijjā*). Ignorance is a primordial blindness to the true nature of phenomena; it is a lack of understanding of things as they really are. It functions as a mental obscuration cloaking our normal process of cognition and permeating our thought patterns with distortion and error.

Among the various misconceptions produced by ignorance, the most basic is the apprehension of phenomena through the category of substantial existence. Phenomena are not isolated units locked up in themselves, but participants in an interconnected field of events. Their being derives from the entire system of relata to which they belong, not from some immutable core of identity intrinsic to themselves. Thence they are devoid of an abiding essence; their mode of being is insubstantial, relational, and interdependent. However, under the influence of ignorance, this essenceless nature of phenomena is not understood. It is blotted out by the basic unawareness, and as a consequence, phenomena present themselves to cognition in a mode different from their actual mode of being. They appear substantial, self-subsistent, and exclusivistic.

The sphere where this illusion is most immediately felt is the sphere where it is most accessible to us—namely, our own experience. The experiential domain is reflectively divisible into two sectors—a cognizing or subjective sector made up of consciousness and its adjuncts, and a cognized or objective sector made up of the cognitive data. Though the two sectors are interlocking and mutually dependent, through the operation of ignorance they are conceptually bifurcated and reduced to an adventitious subject-object confrontation. On the one side the cognizing sector is split off from the experiential complex and conceived as a subject distinct from the cognitive act itself; the objective sector in turn congeals into a world of external things pointing to the subject as its field of action and concern. Consciousness awakens to itself as a persisting ego standing up against the world as an "other" perpetually estranged from itself. Thence it commences its long career of conquest, control, and domination in order to justify its own suspect claim to a self-subsistent mode of being.

This cognitive error with its consequent solidification of the ego is the source of the afflictions (*kilesa*) which hold us in subjection to suffering. The lurking suspicion that the mode of being we credit to ourselves may be unfounded arouses an inner disquietude, a chronic anxiety compelling a drive to fortify the sense of egoity and give it solid ground on which to stand. We need to establish our existence to ourselves, to give inner confirmation to our conception of personal substantiality, and this need occasions the ordering of the psychic life around the focal point of ego.

The bid for self-confirmation makes its impact felt on both the emotional and intellectual fronts. The dominion of the ego in the emotional sphere appears most conspicuously in the weight of the unwholesome roots—greed, hatred, and delusion—as determinants of conduct. Because the ego is essentially a vacuum, the illusion of egohood generates a nagging sense of insufficiency. We feel oppressed by an aching incompleteness, an inner lack requiring constantly to be filled. The result is greed, a relentless drive to reach out and devour whatever we can—of pleasure, wealth, power, and fame—in a never successful attempt to bring the discomfort fully to an end. When our drive to satisfaction meets with frustration we react with hatred, the urge to destroy the obstacle between our desire and its satisfaction. If the obstructions to our satisfaction prove too powerful for the tactics of aggression, a third strategy will be used: dullness or delusion, an attitude of deliberate unawareness adopted as a shell to hide our vulnerability to pain.

On the intellectual front the ego-illusion engenders a move by reason to establish on logical grounds the existence of a substantial self. The idea "I am" is a spontaneous notion born of ignorance, the basic unawareness of the egoless nature of phenomena. By accepting this idea at its face value as pointing to a real "I," and by attempting to fill in the reference, we develop a "view of self," a belief confirming the existence of a self and giving it an identity in the framework of our psycho-physical constitution.

The theories which emerge invariably fall into one or another of the two metaphysical extremes—either eternalism, when we assume the self to enjoy eternal existence after death, or annihilationism, when we assume the self to be extinguished at death. Neither doctrine can be established on absolutely compelling grounds, for both are founded on a common error: the assumption of a self as an enduring, substantial entity.

Because the pivot of our cognitive adherences and their emotional ramifications is the notion of an ego, a powerful current of psychic energy comes to be invested in our interpretive schemes. And because the notion of an ego is in actuality groundless, the product of a fundamental misconception, this investment of energy brings only disappointment in the end. We cling to things in the hope that they will be permanent, satisfying, and substantial, and they turn out to be impermanent, unsatisfying and insubstantial. We seek to impose our will upon the order of events, and we find that events obey a law of their own, insubordinate to our urge towards control.

The result of our clinging is eventual suffering. Yet this suffering which arises from the breakdown of our egocentric attempts at dominance and manipulation is not entirely negative in value. It contains a tremendous positive value, a vast potential, for by shattering our presumptions it serves to awaken our basic intelligence and set us on the quest for liberation. It forces us to discover the ultimate futility of our drive to structure the world from the standpoint of the ego, and makes us recognize the need to acquire a new perspective free from the compulsive patterns which keep us tied to suffering.

Since the most fundamental factor in the bondage of the ego is ignorance, to reach this new perspective ignorance must be eliminated. To eliminate ignorance it is not sufficient merely to observe rules of conduct, to generate faith, devotion, and virtue, or even to develop a calm and concentrated mind. All these are requisites to be sure, essential and powerful aids along the path, but even in unison they are not enough. Something more is required, some other element that alone can ensure the complete severing of the conditional nexus sustaining the round of *saṃsāric* suffering. That something more is *understanding.*

The path to liberation is essentially a path of understanding. Its core is the knowledge and vision of things as they really are: "It is for one who knows and sees that the destruction of the defilements takes place, not for one who does not know and does not see." The objective domain where understanding is to be aroused is our own experience. Since our distorted interpretations of our experience provide the food which nourishes the process of ego, it is here, in experience, that the ego-illusion must be dispelled. Our own experience is, of all things, that which is "closest to ourselves," for it is through this that everything else is registered and known. And yet, though so close, our own experience is at the same time shrouded in darkness, its true characteristics hidden from our awareness by the screen of ignorance. The Buddha's Teaching is the key which helps us to correct our understanding, enabling us to see things as they are. It is the light which dispels the darkness of ignorance, so that we can understand our own understanding of things "just as a man with eyes might see forms illuminated by a lamp."

The correct understanding of experience takes place in the context of meditation. It requires the development of insight (*vipassanā*) based on a foundation of meditative calm (*samatha*).

No amount of merely intellectual knowledge can replace the need for personal realization. Because our tendency to misconceive phenomena persists through a blindness to their true nature, only the elimination of this blindness through direct vision can rectify our erroneous patterns of cognition. The practice of Buddhist meditation is not a way of dissolving our sense of individual identity in some undifferentiated absolute or of withdrawing into the bliss of a self-contained interiority. It is, rather, a way of understanding the nature of things through the portal where that nature is most accessible to ourselves, namely, our own processes of body and of mind. The practice of meditation has profound effects upon our sense of identity; the alterations it produces, however, do not come about by subordinating the intelligence to some uncritically accepted generalization, but through a detached, sober, and exhaustive scrutiny of the experiential field that provides the locus for our sense of identity.

The focal method of the practice of meditation is reflective awareness, a bending back of the beam of awareness upon itself in order to illuminate the true characteristics of existence implicated in each occasion of cognition. The path of understanding unfolds in three successive stages called "the three full understandings." In the first stage, the "full understanding of the known" (*ñātapariññā*), the domain of experience is broken down by meditative analysis into its constituting factors, which are then carefully defined in terms of their salient qualities and functions. The categories employed in this operation are the key terms in the Buddhist analysis of personality—the aggregates (*khandha*), sense bases (*āyatana*), and elements (*dhātu*). The purpose of this dissection is to dispel the illusion of substantiality that hovers over our gross perception of our experience. By revealing that what common sense takes to be a solid monolithic whole is in reality a conglomeration of discrete factors, the contemplation deprives the sense of self-identification of its chief support, the notion of the ego as a simple unity. The factors which emerge from this analytical investigation are then correlated with their causes and conditions, disclosing their contingency and lack of independence.

The second stage of understanding is the "full understanding of scrutinization" (*tīraṇapariññā*). At this stage the experiential field is examined, not as before in terms of its individuating features, but by way of its universal marks. These universal marks are three: impermanence (*anicca*), suffering (*dukkha*), and non-self (*anattā*). Under the limitations of ordinary cognition, phenomena are apprehended as permanent, pleasurable, and self. In the contemplative situation these assumptions must be corrected, replaced by the perception of phenomena as impermanent, unpleasurable, and non-self. The task of the meditative process, at this level, is to ascribe these qualities to the material and mental processes, and to attempt to view all phenomena in their light.

When the second stage is fully mature, it gives way gradually to the third type of comprehension, the "full understanding of abandonment" (*pahānapariññā*). Here the momentary insights achieved at the previous level blossom into full penetrations. Impermanence, suffering, and selflessness are no longer merely understood as qualities of phenomena, but are seen with complete clarity as the nature of phenomena themselves. These realizations bring about the final abandonment of the deluded perceptions as well as the destruction of the ego-tainted emotions which cluster around them.

To walk the path of understanding is to begin to see through the deceptions which have held our imaginations captive through the long stretch of beginningless time. It is to outgrow our passions and prejudices, and to cast off the mask of false identities we are accustomed to assume, the vast array of identities that constitute our wandering in *saṃsāric* existence. The path is not an easy one, but calls for great effort and personal integrity. Its reward lies in the happiness of growing freedom which accompanies each courageous step, and the ultimate emancipation which lies at the end.

Buddhism and Death

by

M. O'C. Walshe

WHEEL PUBLICATION NO. 261

The Great Unmentionable

(*Note*: It is still often thought today that any form of belief in an afterlife is "unscientific." To disarm any criticisms on that score, readers are referred to the Appendix in which the question is briefly treated.)

It is sometimes said that Death today has replaced Sex as "The Great Unmentionable," and certainly it is, for most people, an uncomfortable subject which they do not care to think about overmuch. Yet if there is one thing that is certain in life it is that we shall all die, sooner or later. There was once a creed which declared: "Millions Now Living Will Never Die," and it had great appeal—but all those who first heard it proclaimed are now dead. So we all have to face death, whether we like it or not. And we all know it, however we may try to forget the fact. Let us, then, at least for a while, *stop* trying to forget it and look death straight in the face. It is, of course, perfectly true that we can be *too* preoccupied with death. There are those who are eaten up with fear of death so that they hardly have any energy or zest for living, and there are some for whom mortality and all its accompaniments and trappings have a peculiar fascination. Facing death realistically does not mean being obsessed by it. Here, as in other respects, Buddhism teaches a Middle Way. For those who have an unhealthy preoccupation with the subject, it can teach a saner and more balanced concern; for those who seek at all costs to avoid thinking about it, it can likewise show a reasonable approach. Fear of death is an unwholesome state of mind, and for this, as for other unwholesome states of mind, Buddhism can show a remedy. In the West today, there are many different attitudes to death and a large number of people are probably quite bewildered by it, not knowing what to believe. But two main ones predominate: the Traditional Christian view and the Modern Secular view. The Traditional Christian view (which has many variations of detail) asserts the reality of an afterlife, which the Modern Secular view denies or at the very least calls strongly into question.

The Traditional Christian View

This asserts that man has an immortal soul, created by God. After death a man will, in some shape or form, receive the reward or punishment for his deeds on earth. In short, the good will go to heaven and the wicked to hell. Heaven and hell are everlasting. Of course, many Christians—even fairly "traditional" ones—are more or less uneasy about this, especially about the eternity of hell, but this doctrine is still taught by many Churches in some form, with whatever loopholes or reservations. It should also be noted that on this view only man has an "immortal soul," and that (non-human) "animals" simply perish at death. A few Christians, especially in England, dislike this and hope to be reunited with their pets in another world. Inquiry would probably show that this is a genuine stumbling-block for more people than might have been supposed.

The Modern Secular View

According to this view, which usually claims to be "scientific," man is just another animal and, like the animals in the Christian view, simply perishes totally at physical death. This could actually be in part an unrecognized heritage from Christian thinking. The Christian says: "Animals have no souls." The Secularist caps this by saying: "Man is an animal, *therefore* he has no soul." Modern biology, medical science, psychology and so on tend markedly (whether quite explicitly or not) to take this view for granted. As has been stated and will be shown, the "scientific" basis for this attitude is at the very least, highly questionable. But its exponents are often people enjoying considerable prestige and are widely listened to by those who do not feel able to form an independent opinion on this subject.

The Buddhist Attitude

The Buddhist attitude to both of these types of view is that they are *extremes*, neither of which is in fact true. The first type of view is called in Buddhism "the heresy of eternalism" (*sassatavāda*), while the second is called "the heresy of annihilationism" (*ucchedavāda*). They both in fact miss the point.

What actually happens according to Buddhism can only be clearly understood if we have some acquaintance with the Buddhist view of the general nature of man. But before considering this (as far as it is relevant to our subject), it may be as well to observe how the Buddhist view can be misinterpreted. If we say, for instance, that in the Buddhist view man is not distinguished from animals by the possession of an "immortal soul," then this looks very like the Modern Secular position. If, on the other hand, it is pointed out that according to Buddhism we reap the rewards and penalties, after death, for our actions in this life, then this looks rather like the Traditional Christian view. If both propositions are stated to be correct, the result looks like a contradiction, though in fact it is not. These misapprehensions about Buddhism result from failure to realize the kind of "optical illusion" which occurs when a middle position is viewed from one of the extremes. If an island is exactly in the middle of a river, then from either bank it looks closer to the opposite bank than to the observer. Only an observer on the island can see that it is equidistant. Viewed from the extreme left, any middle position looks much further to the right than it is, and vice versa. The same phenomenon is commonly observable in politics and other walks of life.

In this case, the true Buddhist view is that the impersonal stream of consciousness flows on—impelled by ignorance and craving—from life to life. Though the process is impersonal, the illusion of personality continues as it does in this life.

In terms of absolute truth, there is no "immortal soul" that manifests in a succession of bodies, but in terms of the relative truth by which we are normally guided, there is a "being" that is reborn. In order to gain Enlightenment, it is necessary to come to a realization of the situation as it is according to absolute truth; in order to face and begin to understand the problem of death we can, in the first instance, view it in terms of that "relative truth" which normally rules our lives and which has its validity in its own sphere. We need merely, for the present, to remind ourselves that this is but a "provisional" view of things. In this connection, too, we have to observe that we are dealing only with the question of death as it affects the ordinary person, not one who has attained Enlightenment.

We may therefore say that Buddhism, rejecting Annihilationism outright, partly agrees with the Eternalists, to the extent of accepting a form of survival, without, for the moment, considering the differences further.

Implications of "Survivalism" and "Annihilationism"

It makes a considerable difference to our outlook on life, whether we believe in *any* form of survival or not. Those who entirely reject the idea of survival inevitably concentrate all their ambitions and hopes, for themselves and others, on this single life on earth. This life, they feel, is all they have and for them the only reasonable goal can be the achievement of *some* kind of mundane satisfaction or contentment in this world—all else being meaningless. The precise implications of such an attitude will depend greatly on a person's character. The idealist may devote himself to all kinds of plans for bettering the human condition. It is claimed, and not without some justice, that this view of things has led to a great many social improvements. Nevertheless, if we look at the whole picture, it may be doubted whether *all* the social consequences of a purely "this-worldly" view have been beneficial. And even the idealist must admit that his hopes are strictly limited, not only for himself but for the race itself which will inevitably die out one day, possibly hastened to its end by man's own wicked folly or even his incompetent attempts to "control nature." Furthermore, those who are less idealistically inclined may tend to regard this "one-life-only" theory as an excuse for enjoying themselves as selfishly as they like while they have the chance, with no fear of any post-mortem retribution.

In addition, there are very many people who are more or less (in some cases greatly) tormented by the fear of utter extinction at death. To point out that this is illogical is useless. For many such, fear of cancer or other fatal diseases, or war and other disasters, is not made any easier to bear because they see no future for themselves beyond the grave. Those who preach the "we have only one life" gospel too enthusiastically may forget in their zeal for good causes the serious psychological harm such talk can do.

Fear of death is not, of course, confined to those who do not believe in an afterlife. It is in fact universal. "In that sleep of death what dreams may come" is a thought that has given pause to many besides Hamlet, and in the past many have gone terrified of hell-fire—and some still do. Probably, however, most believers or would-be believers in survival today settle in fact for something vaguely comforting, a trifle wishful, and with few clearly envisaged details.

It should be noted that lack of belief in survival is not entirely incompatible with a religious attitude, though probably most sincere believers in all religions have some such faith, however vague. The Jewish religion, for instance, has little to say on an afterlife (though this is not denied), and probably many orthodox Jews have little or no faith in one. This is partly due to the reticence of most of the Hebrew Bible (known to Christians as the Old Testament) on the subject, and in this connection the well-known concern of Jews with their race and its continuance is significant—as in the case of the secularists noted above. The relation, of course, is an inverse one: the Jew, concerned with racial survival, thinks little about personal survival. The secularist, rejecting personal survival, pins his hopes on that of the race. The concern of many Christian churchmen with social problems today often goes together with a marked reticence on the subject of survival, and occasionally even with a degree of open skepticism. In some cases this looks like a scarcely-veiled capitulation to the dominant materialistic outlook of the present age.

Of course there are many who believe—rightly or wrongly—that they can get in touch with the departed. Mediums who claim to be able to do this are numerous, and while some (it is impossible to say how many) are fraudulent, and some others are self-deluded, it would be unwise in the extreme to suppose that this is always the case. Genuine clairvoyants, spiritual healers and other such specially gifted people unquestionably exist, as anyone who is prepared to undertake an impartial investigation can readily discover. But in the public mind such people tend still (though perhaps rather less than formerly) to be dismissed *en masse* as fraudulent or at best cranky. Those who consult them often do so surreptitiously, guarding the fact from their friends as a guilty secret they would be ashamed to divulge. While excessive concern with such matters is not necessarily a good thing, the loudly voiced scornful skepticism of many materialistic-minded people is simply an inadequate response to something of which they are woefully—sometimes even culpably—ignorant.

Repression

Since in fact a fear of death is deep-rooted in everybody, the propagation of an attitude of total skepticism can do much harm. Even a great psychologist like the late Dr. Ernest Jones, the biographer of Freud, considered it necessary to declare that it was important to eliminate from one's mind all belief in an afterlife. Now if, in fact, it could somehow be finally proved (which it cannot) that there is no such thing, and if further it were *possible* through psychoanalysis or some such methods to get rid of all fear of extinction, this might be a good thing. But since these premises cannot be substantiated, the claim falls to the ground. The fact is that orthodox psychoanalysis was able to find out a great deal about the problem of sex, with which it was largely (though not entirely) able to cope. But it had not and has not the equipment to adequately deal with the problem of death. What Dr. Jones (Freudian though he was) failed to see is that the only result of such an attempt can be repression! Repression may be briefly defined as "the active process of keeping out and ejecting, banishing from consciousness, the ideas and impulses that are unacceptable to it."[1] We can call it successful self-deception. Its deleterious effects on the psyche are well-known, thanks above all to the work of Sigmund Freud and his followers. In this case it means that we deceive ourselves into believing that we are not afraid of death—and in fact very many people do this. Buddhism is actually an even better and more radical method of dealing with one's repressions than psychoanalysis, and it is often a hard task to convince people that they have in fact not "transcended," but merely *repressed* their fear of death! The reader is earnestly advised at this point to consider seriously the possibility that he or she has done just this, bearing in mind that in the nature of things an immediate negative reaction

1. Hinsie and Shatzky, *Psychiatric Dictionary*, Oxford University Press, 1940.

proves nothing! If in fact there is any instinctive tendency to shy away from the whole subject, the answer is actually obvious, though it may be hard to accept. This is due not only to the fear itself but to conceit—the belief that one is "advanced."

Consequences

The consequences of a definite denial of the possibility of survival (so highly praised by Dr. Jones) are the persistence of the fear of death, in either an overt or repressed form. Either way there is a distortion of the psyche with resultant suffering, whatever the exact form it may take. Since such an attitude of denial is very widespread in many parts of the world today (and even officially prescribed in some places), these deleterious effects, on a very wide scale, are quite inevitable. In passing, it may be presumed that if in fact there were no survival, we would not have this built-in fear of death.

In present circumstances, the man who thinks, or wants to think, otherwise is in something of a dilemma. Assuming that he is not a psychic or drawn to spiritualism or the like, nor on the other hand an orthodox believer in one of the traditional faiths, he is probably plagued by doubts and has at best only a hazy notion of what it is he "believes." He may indulge in many fanciful speculations. It is not at all clear to him on what basis he can judge of the possible validity of these ideas. Under the impact of his surroundings, his belief, vague though it may be but perhaps based on some genuine intuition, is liable to be weak and fail him in times of crisis. In such a case, a resolute dismissal of all such ideas as "wishful thinking" may for the time being even bring a sense of relief (especially where his thoughts of the hereafter tend to arouse exaggerated fears of some awful retribution). All this must be admitted, and it is presumably for just such reasons that thinkers like Dr. Jones advocate the course they do. In fact, of course, it does not solve the real problem.

The social and personal drawbacks of the "Jonesian solution" do not end there. This negative attitude is the outcome of a materialistic view of the world which—though it is still held by many scientists—is in fact outmoded. Being in essence materialistic, it tends also to reduce our respect for human life. The traditional

Christian view that "animals have no souls" is in fact semi-materialistic in this sense. Those who think that man is a special case tend all too easily to take the view (for which, unfortunately, there is Biblical support) that animals are totally subservient to him and can be treated as of no account—hence factory-farming and many other such horrors. The true materialist goes a step further and regards man himself as an "animal" in this sense. The extreme consequences of a radical application of this idea can be witnessed in many places at this day, and are often utterly appalling. But even when tempered with "liberal humanism" they can be pretty bad. Power over life and death is given to the medical profession and others to a degree which is sometimes quite irresponsible. Transplant surgery, to take an example, is based on a view of death which is entirely unethical by traditional standards, apart altogether from any "religious" considerations, and similar objections apply to demands for virtually indiscriminate abortion.

Death and the Buddhist

What, then, should be a truly Buddhist attitude towards death? Let us first note that in traditional Christianity, as for instance in the Roman Catholic Church (which has more wisdom—despite all reservations that may be made—than it is often given credit for!), great attention is paid to the dying. Special rites are performed, and every effort is made to help the dying person to pass on in what is considered to be a right frame of mind. To those with no belief in a hereafter, all such things are meaningless. To Buddhists and other non-Catholic "survivalists," they may be open to certain criticisms, but the *principle* is wholly admirable. In Tibetan Buddhism especially, there are observances of a very similar nature, while in Theravada countries it is part of the duties of a *vipassanā* bhikkhu to assist the dying. Of course, the frame of mind in which a Buddhist should die is not quite the same as that expected of an adherent of a theistic religion. But at least it is better to try to give the dying such understanding as one can, than to drug them into unconsciousness as an almost routine measure. That way they will pass on to another existence in much the same state of blindness and confusion with which they have gone through this life. Let us note once again that such considerations can only be rejected as quite valueless if we are *perfectly certain* that there is no form of afterlife—and even on that basis it might be very cruel to deprive many of the dying people of such comfort. Therefore the suggestion made in the humanist circles that hospital chaplains should be abolished can only be characterized as downright wicked. Some such chaplains may be pretty useless, but the majority can give the sick and dying at least *some* comfort. Ideally, of course, they should all be highly-trained bhikkhus!

However, when one is actually dying it is a bit late to *begin* thinking seriously about death. We should familiarize ourselves with the thought long before we hope it will happen! And besides, even for the young and strong, it can still come with unexpected suddenness. *Mors certa—hora incerta*, "Death is certain—the hour is uncertain." To bear this in mind is for the Buddhist an important aspect of Right Understanding. And therefore the Buddhist practice of Meditation on Death—not very popular in the West—should be encouraged. Death for the Buddhist is not indeed the absolute end—but it does mean the breaking of all ties that bind us to our present existence, and therefore, the more detached we are from this world and its enticements, the more ready we shall be to die, and, incidentally, the further we shall get along the path that leads to the Deathless—for this is one of the names of Nibbāna: *amataṃ*, "the Deathless State." Meanwhile, for those who have not got so far along the Path, death is inseverable from birth. Existence in the phenomenal world (*saṃsāra*) is continual birth-and-death. The one cannot be understood without the other, and cannot exist without the other.

We all fear death, but actually we should also fear the rebirth that follows. In practice, this does not always happen. Fear of rebirth is less strong than death. This is part of our usual short-sighted view (for those who do actually believe in rebirth), and the fact must be faced. Full Enlightenment will only be achieved when there is the will to transcend *all* forms of "rebirth"—even the pleasantest. Though as a first step, then, acceptance of the fact of rebirth may help to overcome the fear of death, the attachment to rebirth itself must then also be gradually overcome.

Death-Wish

Though there is a strong fear of death, there is, strangely enough, also a desire for it. Psycho-analysis has a good deal to say about this, though it is perhaps not very illuminating. But the fact remains that many people show suicidal tendencies, or even actually commit suicide, whatever be the explanation. The Buddha in fact included this "death-wish" as the third of three kinds of craving: besides desire for sense-pleasures we find in the formula of the Second Noble Truth the desire for becoming (*bhavataṇhā*) and the desire for cessation (*vibhavataṇhā*). Since life is by its very nature frustrating, we can never get it *on our own terms*, and therefore there is an urge to be quit of the whole thing. The fallacy, of course, lies in the fact that one cannot just "step out" so easily, since death by suicide, like any other death, is followed immediately by rebirth in some plane or other—quite possibly worse than that which one had left. The traditional Christian view indeed is that suicide is a mortal sin—with the implication that it would be a case of "out of the frying-pan and into the fire." Some psychoanalysts speak—ignorantly—of the Nirvana-principle" in connection with the death-wish. But what we are here dealing with is not in fact the urge to true liberation, but merely an escape-reaction. Only if, by insight more profound than that of the Freudians, this revulsion is followed by complete equanimity can it be turned towards the Supramundane, which alone is the goal of Buddhism. This will not happen spontaneously. It should be noted that the "death-wish" here referred to is associated in Buddhism with the "heresy of annihilationism" already mentioned. In a somewhat aggressive form it can even serve to mask repressed death-fear. This would seem to explain the vehemence with which people like Dr. Ernest Jones assert the desirability of their anti-survivalist views. By way of curiosity, it may be mentioned that a distinguished biologist has gone on record as declaring that whether or not we believe in survival is entirely determined by our genes. This would seem to be pushing determinism pretty far!

Psychology of Survivalism and Anti-Survivalism

It is, of course, easy to suggest that those who believe in some form of survival are victims of wishful thinking, fantasy and the like. And in many cases there is a good deal of truth in the allegation. But what is less often realized is the fact that the opposite situation also exists. As has been indicated, quite a number of cases can be found of a curiously fanatical and intolerant belief in "death as the end." That this attitude masks a repressed death-fear has been suggested above. It also betrays a measure of conceit: by adopting it one appears "scientific," "realistic," "tough" and so on. It may even to some extent be an assertion of one's masculinity (disbelief in "old wives' tales," etc.). The fact that more women than men are churchgoers may be partly due to the fact that women in general feel less urge than men to put on this particular "act" (they have others!).

Apart from these factors, this attitude also, curiously enough, gives a certain sense of "security." One has made up one's mind on that particular question and can now dismiss it, and turn to other things. This enables the scientist—and the politician—to make "realistic" decisions without reference to traditional objections. Also, by excluding one whole branch of phenomena from the need for investigation, it helps to make our scientific knowledge more "neat and tidy." Unfortunately for this type of view, however, there is a whole field of knowledge which runs directly counter to any smug mechanistic-materialistic view of the world. A wide variety of paranormal phenomena—some with direct relevance to the question of survival—is so well attested that to brush them aside is a trifle difficult. Some scientists contrive to ignore the whole lot and just go on behaving as if there were nothing "there." A few—but a growing minority—investigate, and as a result are convinced that there is at least *something* "there," however you may explain it. Others can do neither of these things, that is, they can neither ignore the whole lot nor investigate with genuine objectivity. They therefore set themselves up as "debunkers." They set out to "expose" or "disprove" whatever they disapprove of.

The assumption is in effect that since, admittedly and obviously, there are some fraudulent mediums and so on, therefore *all* such people are fraudulent or at any rate deluded. Quite a number of books and articles have appeared in recent years, assiduously "debunking" various classical cases of paranormal phenomena. But genuinely impartial investigation frequently shows that, whatever may have been the weaknesses in the reporting of these cases, the debunkers have in fact gone widely beyond all reasonable criticism and have sometimes themselves been—unconsciously no doubt—quite unscrupulous. The well-known case of "Bridey Murphey" a few years ago illustrates this. Some very confident "debunking" of this story turned out on further investigation to be quite wide of the mark. One book on hypnotism, too, pours scorn on attempts to recall past lives by this method. The author calls these "a hunk of junk" (note the emotive language), and clearly implies deliberate fraudulent suggestion by the hypnotist—a suggestion which is not only ridiculous but libelous. And the present writer once heard a very intelligent lady psychologist say: "I'd rather believe *anything* than accept precognition: it would upset my entire scientific conception of the universe!" Perhaps one can even sympathize a little with this lady; nevertheless since precognition, however mysterious, is a well-attested fact, it is up to her to revise her conception of the universe. She did, however, neatly phrase the dilemma in which a lot of scientifically trained people find themselves today.

In view of all this, it is important to be aware of the psychological motives which may underlie different attitudes to this whole problem—not only in others but in oneself. While excessive credulity and uncritical dabbling in the occult is to be deplored (and has its own serious dangers), the opposite extreme of total rejection should also be treated with more suspicion and reserve than it often gets.

Spiritualism and the Occult

While Buddhism certainly does not encourage too much preoccupation with these matters, it does not of course deny the existence of various classes of "discarnate" beings. They dwell in various realms and on various planes, some higher and happier than this world, others, such as the so-called "hungry ghosts" (*petas*), more miserable. They are relatively real—i.e., no less "real" than we ourselves in this world. They all, without exception, belong to the realm of *saṃsāra* or "birth-and-death," and their stay in any of the realms they inhabit is therefore temporary, though in some cases it may be fantastically long-lasting by human standards. There is no contradiction here with the idea of rebirth on earth, since the realm one is born in depends on one's *kamma*, the human condition being only one of the various possibilities (though a specifically important one, since Enlightenment from any other realm is held to be virtually impossible). Therefore, human rebirth is considered to be as desirable as it is rare—a precious opportunity which it is a folly to waste. It is also stated in the scriptures that man has a "mind-made body, complete in all its parts," which would seem to correspond to the "astral" or "etheric" body referred to by occultists.

Responsible occultists—of whom there are many—are themselves, of course, thoroughly well aware of the dangers of incautious involvement with these matters, which they often stress. The inhabitants of the various realms are *not* enlightened beings, and while some are undoubtedly much wiser and more advanced than the average human, others are not, and can even exert a definitely malevolent power.

It is not in the province of Buddhist monks to practice any of the occult arts—it is in fact forbidden them in terms—although it is not infrequently done in the East. Western Buddhists should actually also not concern themselves with such matters. If they nevertheless do so (as many will, whatever is said to the contrary), they should at least be extremely careful to consult only responsible and conscientious practitioners, with a high moral standard. Such people are not hard to find, and are often very fine characters. But it should always be borne in mind that even quite genuine messages from the departed can be misleading, since they are still, in varying degrees, ignorant. For this reason, too, the well-known triviality of so many "spirit" messages proves nothing about their genuineness.

The beings of higher worlds are known in Buddhism as *devas*, and it seems certain that many of them are truly concerned to help mankind as far as lies in their power. It might even be suggested that there is perhaps no essential difference between the higher devas and the *bodhisattvas* of the Mahāyāna tradition.

Some people are naturally psychic, and some even develop psychic powers as a result, or by-product, of meditation. Such powers are perfectly real, but should not be sought after or clung to, if attained. If they are gained without sufficient insight or moral purification, they can be disastrous. It is another of the many illusions of the modern liberal humanist that such things as "witchcraft" do not exist. Righteous indignation at the cruel treatment of real or alleged witches in the past should not lead us to imagine that the whole thing was completely mythical. So we should be very wary of seeking contact with the psychic planes, not because they do not exist (if that were the case, comparatively little harm would be done), but because they *do*.

What Is Death?

We now come to the Buddhist definition of death. According to the Ven. Nyanatiloka,[2] it is ordinarily called "the disappearance of the vital faculty confined to a single lifetime, and therewith of the psycho-physical life-process conventionally called 'man,' 'animal,' 'personality,' 'ego,' etc. Strictly speaking, however, death is the continually repeated dissolution and vanishing of each momentary physical-mental combination, and thus it takes place every moment."

This definition is very important. Each moment (i.e., millions of times a second) "I" die and "I" am reborn, in other words, a new "I" takes over from the old which has vanished forever. At the end of "my" physical life there is at the same time a severing of the link between this mental process and the body, which quickly decays in consequence. But rebirth in exactly the same way is instantaneous in some sphere, whether as conception in a fresh womb or elsewhere.

Death, then, except in the case of the *arahant* (to which we shall briefly refer), is in the Buddhist view inseparable from rebirth. But two kinds of rebirth are distinguished: rebirth from life to life, and rebirth from moment to moment, as indicated in the above definition. Some people today maintain that the Buddha taught only the latter. This is nonsense. There are many hundreds

2. Buddhist Dictionary, Colombo, 1950.

of references to rebirth throughout the Buddhist scriptures of all schools, and they cannot be simply explained away as either "symbolic" (whatever that means) or as "concessions to popular beliefs" (it is not true, incidentally, that in the Buddha's day "everybody believed in rebirth"). Nor is there any need for such explanations, since there is plenty of convincing evidence for the reality of the process (see Appendix).

What Is Rebirth?

Though "rebirth from moment to moment" is very important to understand and should not be overlooked, what we are really concerned with here is "rebirth from life to life." In this connection, two general, somewhat minor points should be made. The term "birth" (*jāti*) here is not confined to extrusion from a womb; it includes other processes such as the spontaneous appearance of beings in certain states. Birth of the human type is thus simply a particular case. There is also the question of "intermediate states" between births. Some Buddhists, and others, speak of such states. This is really just a question of semantics: in the Theravada view, at least, any such so-called intermediate state between existences of a certain type is itself a "rebirth."

The reason why rebirth, of whatever kind, takes place is because of the unexpended force of *taṇhā* or craving, conditioned by ignorance. This force of ignorance and craving is comparable to a powerful electric current. To suppose that it just ceases at physical death is actually quite unreasonable, and contradicts the law of conservation of energy. As to the question of the identity of the being that is reborn with the one that died, the best answer is that given by the Venerable Nāgasena to King Milinda: "It is neither the same nor different" (*na ca so na c'añño*). The whole process is really quite impersonal, but seemingly a being exists and is reborn. We can thus make a clear distinction between the terms "Reincarnation" and "Rebirth."

"Reincarnation" is the term used by those who hold that a real entity (a "soul") exists and passes on from life to life, occupying successive bodies. Literally, this should only apply to manifestation in "fleshy" bodies, though it is commonly applied to discarnate states as well. "Rebirth" denotes the Buddhist view that while this is indeed what seems to happen, the true process is entirely impersonal. What, therefore, in terms of relative truth appears (and can be experienced by some) as Reincarnation, is in terms of absolute truth Rebirth. The formulation of Dependent Origination (*paṭicca-samuppāda*) describes the process as follows: ignorance conditions *sankhāras* (the karmic of personality patterns), the *saṅkhāras* condition consciousness, consciousness conditions mind-and-body, and so on. This means that the pattern or "shape" of a person's character is based on ignorance; this pattern is impressed, like a seal on wax, on the new consciousness arising in the womb (or otherwise), on which the development of a new being (mind-and-body) depends.

The Western assumption that character and mental traits are genetically inherited is not accepted in Buddhism; true, there may be some genetic element, apart from the purely physical side, but essential inheritance here is karmic. The apparent inheritance of mental traits can be explained in many other ways. In part, it is mere assumption. If a child turns out to be musical, people will recall that his uncle George used to play the clarinet, a fact which would have been forgotten had the child been tone-deaf. Parental and other environmental influences can undoubtedly account for much, especially when we allow for unconscious (telepathic) influence. Sir Alister Hardy has even suggested that genes may be capable of being influenced telepathically. Further, the "choice" of one's parents is bound to be influenced by some affinity, and even by karmic links from the past. By the same token, suggestions that it would be possible to breed a race of "clones" with identical reactions belongs, no doubt very fortunately, strictly to the realm of science fiction. Such people even if bred would *not* be karmically identical, any more than identical twins are. Life is not as mechanical as all that.

Death and the Arahant

For one who has attained full Enlightenment in this life, the death of the body brings with it the end of all individual existence: this at least is the Theravada teaching. This is called *anupādisesa-nibbāna*, "Ṅibbāna without the groups remaining." While the final attainment of Nibbāna should not be understood as mere annihilation in the materialistic sense (though some scholars seem to interpret it in this way), nothing positive can be predicated of it. It is not the extinction of self, for that self never was real in the first place, nor is it "entering into Nibbāna," for there is no being who enters. It is the final cessation, however, of the five aggregates which were the product of greed, hatred and delusion. We may think of it as a state of utter peace, and perhaps we can leave it at that. It is the Deathless State.

Meditation and Death

In his elaborate survey of Buddhist meditation methods, the Ven. Dr. Vajirañāṇa says this of the meditation on mindfulness of death: "It virtually belongs to the Vipassanā meditation, for the disciple should develop it while holding the perception of *anicca*, *dukkha*, and *anattā*."[3]

When the Ven. Somdet Phra Vanarata, the then Vice-Patriarch of Thailand, visited Wat Dhammapadīpa, Hampstead, London, on 23rd October 1968, he spoke on the subject of death. He said that we are fortunate to be born in the human condition, in full possession of all our faculties, as this gives us the possibility of hearing the Dhamma and practicing it. This is an advantage we should not neglect, because birth in the human state is a rare thing. If people are born blind or deaf, or without other faculties, this is the result of *kamma*. They may have to wait for another opportunity. We should always remember the inevitability of death. The awareness of this should make us cease from clinging too much to worldly things. If we constantly keep the thought of death before our minds, this will be an instigation to work hard on ourselves and make good progress.

The standard Meditation on Death is given by Buddhaghosa in Chapter VIII of the *Visuddhimagga* (*Path of Purification*). It may be summarized as follows: Buddhaghosa begins by stating the kinds of death he is not considering: the final passing of the Arahant; "momentary death" (i.e., the moment-to-moment dissolution of formations); or metaphorical uses of the term "death." He refers to *timely death*, which comes with exhaustion of merit, or the

3. *Buddhist Meditation*, Colombo, 1962, p. 209.

life-span, or both, and to *untimely death* produced by *kamma* that interrupts other (life-producing) *kamma*. One should go into solitary retreat and exercise attention wisely thus: "Death will take place, the life faculty will be interrupted," or "Death, death." Unwise attention may arise in the form of sorrow (at the death of a loved one), joy (at the death of an enemy), indifference (as with a cremator), or fear (at the thought of one's own death). There should always be mindfulness, a sense of urgency and knowledge. Then "access-concentration" may be gained—and this is the basis for the arising of Insight.

"But," says Buddhaghosa, "one who finds that it does not get so far should do his recollecting of death in eight ways, that is to say: (1) as having the appearance of a murderer, (2) as the ruin of success, (3) by comparison, (4) as to sharing the body with many, (5) as to the frailty of life, (6) as signless, (7) as to the limitedness of the extent, (8) as to the shortness of the moment." Some of these terms are not quite self-explanatory: thus (3) means by comparing oneself with others—even the great and famous, even Buddhas, have to die; (4) means that the body is inhabited by all sorts of strange beings, "the eighty families of worms." They live in dependence on, and feed on, the outer skin, the inner skin, the flesh, the sinews, the bones, the marrow, "and there they are born, grow old and die, evacuate, and make water, and the body is their maternity home, their hospital, their charnel ground, their privy and their urinal." (6) means that death is unpredictable, (7) refers to the shortness of the human life-span.

Buddhaghosa concludes: "A bhikkhu devoted to mindfulness of death is constantly diligent. He acquires perception of disenchantment with all kinds of becoming (existence). He conquers attachment to life. He condemns evil. He avoids much storing. He has not stain of avarice about requisites. Perception of impermanence grows in him, following upon which there appear the perceptions of pain and not-self. But while beings who have not developed mindfulness of death fall victims to fear, horror and confusion at the time of death as though suddenly seized by wild beasts, spirits, snakes, robbers, or murderers, he dies undeluded and fearless without falling into any such state. And if he does not attain the deathless here and now, he is at least headed for a happy destiny on the break up of the body.

"Now when a man is truly wise, his constant task will surely be this recollection about death blessed with such mighty potency."[4]

Appendix: Science and Survival

There are still those who suppose that it is somehow "unscientific" to believe in any form of survival. There is actually no justification for this view, and certainly today not all scientists would endorse it.

As has been pointed out earlier, there are psychological reasons why some scientists almost willfully shut their eyes to all evidence for the paranormal; this enables them to continue operating on the assumption that all manifestations of "mind" are simply by-products of the body, determined by it and perishing with it. In this way, mental activities are reduced to "mere" functions of the brain, and so on. In fact, however, it should be stressed that the brain *does not think*.

The human brain is a very remarkable organ, which has still been only very superficially explored, owing to obvious practical difficulties in addition to its own quite extraordinary complexity. But quite certainly not all mental activities can be related to it. The various forms of ESP (extra-sensory-perception) phenomena are facts, and nothing in the physical brain has been found to account for them, even by officially materialist Soviet-bloc scientists who have a vested interest in establishing such a connection. Telepathy, for instance, is not (except metaphorically) a form of "mental radio": as the late G.N.M. Tyrrell, who was both a distinguished psychic researcher and a radio expert, long ago pointed out, it does not obey the law governing all forms of physical radiation, the inverse square law connecting intensity with distance.

4. The full text of this passage is to be found in *The Path of Purification* (*Visuddhimagga*) by Bhadantācariya Buddhaghosa, translated from the Pali by Bhikkhu Ñāṇamoli, Kandy, 1975 (BPS), pp. 247–259. A lucid, learned and witty commentary is provided by Edward Conze in *Thirty Years of Buddhist Studies*, Oxford, 1967, pp. 87–104. The reader may also consult with profit V. F. Gunaratna, *Buddhist Reflections on Death* (Wheel Publications 102/103), Kandy, 1966.

Now while the existence of telepathy does not in itself prove survival or rebirth—indeed it is often rather freely invoked to "explain" evidence pointing to survival—it does prove that something mental can "jump" through space (and even time!) with no physical link. And this is of the very essence of rebirth in the Buddhist view. And since telepathy is certainly a fact, and widely accepted as such, all arguments against the possibility of rebirth fall to the ground on this point alone. The shrinking band of hardened skeptics who still doubt the fact of telepathy have quite clearly not faced up to the overwhelming evidence for it; indeed they have not even observed it in themselves, though it probably occurs to some extent with everybody, even if unrecognized as such.

There is, of course, a wealth of positive evidence for survival in general and for rebirth in particular. The material collected by the Society for Psychical Research over nearly a century is highly impressive, and every single item in these records has been subjected before acceptance to the most stringent tests—far more stringent in fact than for many modern scientific "discoveries." On rebirth in particular, reference can now be made to *Rebirth as Doctrine and Experience: Essays and Case Studies* by Francis Story (Buddhist Publication Society, Kandy, 1975), which incorporates the same writer's Wheel publication, *The Case for Rebirth*. Dr. Ian Stevenson, Carlson Professor of Psychiatry and Director of the Division of Parapsychology in the University of Virginia School of Medicine, who collaborated with Francis Story, is the author of a number of important works on the subject, including *Twenty Cases Suggestive of Reincarnation* (2nd edition, University of Virginia, 1974), and three volumes of *Cases of the Reincarnation Type* (University of Virginia 1975–6). A Penguin book probably still obtainable which gives an admirable survey of the general field of psychic phenomena is G.N.M. Tyrrell's *The Personality of Man*; some further fascinating material can also be found in *The Cathars and Reincarnation* by a distinguished English psychiatrist, Dr. Arthur Guirdham (Neville Spearman, London, 1970). The extraordinary career of Edgar Cayce (1877–1945), who has now become something of a cult-figure in the U.S.A., is well worth studying; one of the best books on him is *Many Mansions* by Dr. Gina Cerminara, first published in 1950 and often reprinted.

Faith in the Buddha's Teaching and Refuge in the Triple Gem

by

Soma Thera

Saddhā: Buddhist Devotion

by

Sister Dhammadinnā

WHEEL PUBLICATION NO. 262

Faith in the Buddha's Teaching

by Soma Thera

> "Bhikkhus, in the doctrine so rightly made known by me, which is plain, open, explicit, and speckless, all who have but faith in and affection for me have heaven as their lot."
>
> (M I 142)

"*Who have but faith in and affection for me.*" By this phrase those persons who develop insight, but have in them no noble mental state beside mere faith in and affection for the Perfect One are referred to. In these persons arise, after their insight practice, a singular faith in and singular affection for Him who is endowed with the ten powers, the Buddha. With that faith and affection they are as it were taken by the hand and placed in heaven. It is said that they are possessed of an assured destiny. Ancient elders speak of such a bhikkhu as a lesser Stream-entrant.

There is no doubt that faith is a cardinal virtue in the Dhamma: it is the means of entry into the dispensation. Everyone who (after listening to the Buddha) went for refuge to him, the teaching, and the community of bhikkhus was impelled by faith. Often those who went for refuge to the Buddha after receiving instruction from him spoke thus:

> "Marvellous, venerable sir! As if, venerable sir, a person were to turn face upwards what is upside down, or to uncover the concealed, or to point the way to one who is lost, or to carry a lamp in the darkness believing, 'Those who have eyes will see forms,' so has the Dhamma been set forth in many ways by the Blessed One. I, venerable sir, go to the Blessed One for refuge, to the Dhamma for refuge, and to the community of bhikkhus for refuge. Venerable sir, may the Blessed One regard me as a follower who has gone for refuge for life from today" (D I 85).

This form of going for refuge to the three jewels, the noblest objects for the Buddhist, appears as one of the ways of declaring the disciple's faith in the presence of the Buddha.

Criticism in the sense of careful judgment belongs to the fundamentals of the doctrine and is necessary for reaching right understanding (*sammādiṭṭhi*). A teaching should not be accepted by a reasonable person without investigation, particularly if he wants to live in conformity with it. The Buddha says:

> "Bhikkhus, a person who causes another's establishment in a wrongly-explained doctrine-and-discipline, the one he establishes in it, and the established one who practises to realise what he has been taught, all these produce much demerit. Why is that? Because of the wrong explanation of the doctrine. ... Bhikkhus, a person who is energetic in a wrongly-explained-doctrine dwells unhappily. Why is that? Because of the wrong explanation of doctrine" (D I 34).

Study of a teaching through inquiring into it is unfavourable to credulity; but such study may produce faith in the teaching if it is true and intelligible. There are some people who, without examining the Dhamma properly, speak of it as a kind of rationalism, and of the Buddha "as an early rationalist introducing the blessings of common sense into a world which knew nothing better than the mysticism of the Upanishads."[1] By such talk they cause a good deal of misunderstanding. There is no doubt that the Buddha was rational and that his teaching accords with reason. But it is incorrect to call him a rationalist. He was one of robust faith. His faith was connected with knowledge and founded on it. It is because the Bodhisatta had faith in truth and his ability to find it that he went forth from home to homelessness. It was because of his faith that he was able to renounce his princely state. He underwent all the great troubles, vexations and sufferings of his six years of search for light only because he believed that there was a way out of the miseries of existence to freedom. He was of an analytical turn of mind from the very start of his quest. He would not accept anything without scrutiny. But for applying what he found out by analysis to life he required faith, and he saw that it was indispensable in his experiments with aspects of the truth he reached as a seeker. It was his faith that carried him from partial understanding ever onward.

1. A. E. Keith, *Buddhist Philosophy*, pp. 13f.

The Bodhisatta's reasonableness is seen nowhere more than in his wisdom in venturing forth beyond what he learned from his teachers, especially from Ālāra Kālāma and Uddaka Rāmaputta. This is the aspect of faith that won for him his goal. It is owing to the strength of the venturesome or aspiring characteristic (*sampakkhandana lakkhaṇa*) of the Bodhisatta's faith that his striving for enlightenment was unremitting till he reached the supreme goal. But it is wrong to think that he ceased to have faith after that. It was his faith in human nature, in the supremacy of the truth, and its ability to conquer the hearts of men, that made him toil for forty-five years in the service of the world till he passed away at the ripe old age of eighty (having founded a dispensation that for its virility is as remarkable today as it was when the Blessed One set in motion the Wheel of his incomparable doctrine at the Deer Park in Benares, twenty-five centuries ago). Therefore it is said of this indefatigable worker for the welfare of all living beings:

> Marvellous is the tireless Victor ever
> Striving for all beings' weal and bliss.[2]
>
> (Cariyāpiṭaka)

The Buddha did not teach rationalism. His teaching is beyond all *isms* in its essential portion. *Isms* have to do with being (*bhava*). The essence of the Dhamma, the knowledge and vision of uttermost freedom, belongs to the sphere of the transcending of being. The Buddha was not contemptuous of common sense, but the core of his doctrine is uncommon. Common sense cannot grasp it. What can grasp it is a mental state beyond normal sensitivity. That does not mean that the Dhamma is a mysticism. Since faith that is accordant with facts is necessary to bring that state into being, and not the faith of mysticism, which is based on what does not exist, the Dhamma is different from mysticism in its methods and principles no less than its goal.

What is the faith a disciple of the Buddha needs? Faith in the fruit of action (*kammaphala-saddhā*) and faith in the three jewels (*ratanattāya-saddhā*). Because of faith in these real things, things that are, the Dhamma is not founded on vague abstractions or unrealities. And since the Dhamma is inseparably bound to

---

2. *Sabbadā sabbasattānaṃ hitāya ca sukhāya ca.*

faith, and has faith for its great motivating power, the Dhamma cannot be a rationalism. Without faith (and without faith founded on what exists and not on empty concepts as in mysticism), no one can expect to obtain what he expects to get from a religion or follow a truly religious life. Faith deriving its authority from facts is the chief sign of genuine religion and also the important principle that affects it from its foundations upwards. According to what has been stated above, the Dhamma is a religion in the sense of a way of life founded on faith that is reasonable. Such faith is always ready to examine things and it encourages open-mindedness, an indispensable ingredient of a truth-seeker's mind, together with the quality of responsiveness or amenability to the influence of truth.

As faith increases in a disciple of the Buddha it becomes a faculty (*indriya*) and a power (*bala*). In the form of believing in the virtues of the Buddha, the Dhamma, and the community of the ennobled disciples of the Master, faith comes to be, or is what believes in or relies on, the jewels beginning with the Buddha. Trust is what plunges us into the ocean of the Buddha, the Dhamma and the community of ennobled disciples, and enters their virtues, having as it were broken into them. Strong confidence is that by which living beings become very confident in the virtues of the Buddha, the Dhamma and the community, or it is that by which they become very confident themselves. Faith is a faculty (*indriya*) in the sense of predominance through its vanquishing disbelief, or because it exercises mastery through its typical quality of conviction. What does not waver with disbelief is the power of faith.

Faith has the characteristic of confidence and of venturing or aspiring. In the form of confidence faith suppresses the hindrances, makes the defilements come to a halt and causes the mind to become bright and not turbid. This feature of faith has been compared to the water-purifying crystal of a universal monarch (*cakkavatti raja*). With a mind that is clear owing to confidence, a man devoted to religious activities gives freely, undertakes the observance of the precepts, performs the practices of the fast-day and sets about his mental development for enlightenment. Confidence is born when there is esteem, admiration and affection for the jewels. Hindrances to faith are doubts about the fruit of action (*kammaphala*) and the meaning and value of the jewels. Faith arises only when doubts are shed through carefully investigating details of evidence and facts concerning the credibility of these objects of faith. So long as a man has doubts about them he cannot be pleased or satisfied with the Buddha's teaching. But when the doubts disappear the mind becomes as clear as a blue sky freed from clouds. That freeing takes place when a person avoids unbelievers, resorts to those who are endowed with faith, associates and keeps close contact with them and reflects on confidence-producing suttas.

The other characteristic of faith (venturing mentioned with the faith of the Bodhisatta earlier) is to go beyond what is actually known with hope or expectation of success in a useful enterprise, or to take the risk of trusting or confiding in a person for some good purpose, or to have the courage to undertake the doing of noble actions (having decided to take what comes). The faith-characteristic of venturing has been compared to the action of a stout warrior, a great soldier, who leads safely to and fro from bank to bank those too timid to cross a swollen river infested with crocodiles and other dangerous creatures, repelling them as they come towards him with his mighty sword. The faith-characteristic of venturing like that of strong confidence precedes acts of liberality, precept-observance, performance of fast-day practices and the beginning of inner development for liberation.

Again, faith is considered according to characteristics, function, intelligibility and the condition closest to its arising. Believing or trusting is its characteristic. Its function is producing the serenity and placidity of confidence through dispelling the sludge, slush and mud of doubt and uncertainty like the water-purifying crystal of a universal monarch (*cakkavatti rāja*), or the spirit of venturing comparable to the seasoned warrior's crossing of a swollen river infested with dangerous creatures. Faith is understood, or becomes intelligible, when either there is freedom from impurity of doubt or when there is conviction or certitude. The condition closest to the arising of faith is an object that inspires faith or the factors of stream-entrance. These factors are following good men (the Buddhas and those who approximate them), listening to the Dhamma, systematic right attention and practice that conforms to the Dhamma (S V 347).

It has also been said that faith should be seen as a hand, as wealth and as a seed. That means that faith is like a hand for grasping meritorious, wholesome states, like wealth in obtaining all kinds of happiness and like seed harvesting immortal fruit.

From what has been so far set forth it can be seen that faith gives subjective certainty of the Buddha's teaching on reasonable grounds. Common credulity is a form of blind trust. When blindness falls away from common credulity owing to the arising of authentic and relevant knowledge about an object of faith, a man is established in faith provided the object is worthy of belief. Blind faith is not compatible with the reasonable doctrine of the Buddha and is repugnant to the intelligent. Both common credulity and meaningless scepticism have to be shunned. Without confidence in a teaching no progress can be made in it. If a person cannot engender belief in Nibbāna, conditioned arising (*paṭiccasamuppāda*) and the fruit of action here and hereafter (*kammaphala*), then for him there will never come into being the energy to set himself to work for liberation from ill, in the doctrine of the Buddha. Firm trust and the spirit of venturing, it may be said, is the core of faith, and it is difficult to conceive how one could ignore these aspects of faith in any effort for liberation from ill in the Dhamma, even if one would. It is because of the very great place that faith has in the dispensation of the Blessed One and in all undertakings to increase the welfare of mankind that the Buddha taught thus:

> "Ānanda, in these three places you should establish, fix and make firm friends, companions and kith and kin, who think they ought to hear the doctrine. In what three places? In confidence founded on knowledge concerning the Buddha you should establish them, fix them and make them firm, thus: 'So is the Blessed One consummate, fully enlightened, endowed with knowledge and practice, sublime, knower of the worlds, peerless, guide of tameable men, teacher of divine and human beings, enlightened, blessed.'
>
> "In confidence founded on knowledge concerning the Dhamma, you should establish them, fix them and make them firm, thus: 'The Dhamma of the Blessed One is revealed well, realisable now, immediate, open for seeing, leading onwards and knowable by the intelligent by themselves.'
>
> "In confidence founded on knowledge concerning the community of bhikkhus, you should establish them, fix them and make them firm, thus: 'The community of the disciples

of the Blessed One has practised well, the community of the disciples of the Blessed One has practised uprightly, the community of the disciples of the Blessed One has practised in the right path, the community of the disciples of the Blessed One has practised what befits it. The community of the disciples of the Blessed One, that is to say, the four pairs of persons and the eight kinds of individuals, is worthy of offerings, worthy of hospitality, worthy of gifts, worthy of reverential salutations and is the world's unsurpassable field of merit.'

"Ānanda, there may be change in the four great elements, earth, water, fire and air, but the noble disciple who is endowed with confidence founded on knowledge concerning the Buddha, with confidence founded on knowledge concerning the Dhamma, with confidence founded on knowledge concerning the community of bhikkhus, cannot change. That is to say, it is impossible for him to be reborn in hell, or as an animal, or where unhappy spirits dwell.

"Ānanda, in these three places of confidence founded on knowledge you should establish, fix and make firm, friends, companions and kith and kin, who think they ought to listen to the doctrine" (A I 222).

Thus it becomes clear how important it is to have faith, confidence or trust in objects worthy of belief, in objects connected with the realisation of Nibbāna (the peace that arises with the final destruction of craving in all forms). The faith mentioned in the sutta cited above belongs to the *sotāpanna*, the Stream-entrant,[3] who has reached the supramundane path (*lokuttara magga*). But it is not possible to come to have that faith of the noble disciple (*ariya sāvaka*) without cultivating, before entry into the supramundane path, all the qualities that reach perfection in that path. The faith of those who have not reached the noble path is feeble in regard

3. This is the first fruit-attainer (*paṭhama-phala-lābhi*); he is the first noble one who attains intelligent faith (*aveccappasāda*) in the Buddha, Dhamma and the Sangha. The first path-attainer (*paṭhama-magga-lābhi*) has yet to attain perfection in it; he has only the faculty of faith (*saddhindriya*) in its initial stage along with the other four faculties of energy, mindfulness, concentration and wisdom.

to certitude and consistency. Yet the faith of the man intent on the realisation of the first holy path (*paṭhama-ariya-magga*), from the time he goes for refuge to the three jewels, is superior to the faith of those with no such high aim, that is, of those who have not made the supramundane the basis for their spiritual growth. In the dispensation of the Buddha, however, even the going for refuge to the jewels, the very first act of faith has the thought of reaching the supramundane as basis, if the going for refuge is properly done.

Failure in development of mind (*cittabhāvanā*) and of wisdom (*paññābhāvanā*) particularly is due to lack of faith in the genuine teaching of the Buddha and to resorting to deviations of it, which are often contravenes of the original teaching of the Buddha in the Pali canon. Faith in the Buddha, the Dhamma and the Sangha, respect for the precepts, and application to the teaching of concentration taught by the Blessed One, ensure the continuation of the Buddha's dispensation. But all that makes for the swift disappearance of the doctrine and the discipline of the Blessed One stems from lack of faith, disregard for the precepts, the neglect of the way of concentration taught by the Master, which is in the Pali canon. Of these destructive things the worst is the waning of faith. Therefore it is said: "The bhikkhu who is wanting in faith (*assaddho bhikkhu*) falls away from good qualities (*guṇehi cavati*) and is not able to establish himself in the good law, in the true doctrine of the dispensation" (*sāsana-saddhamme patiṭṭhātuṃ na sakkoti*) (A III 6-7).

Faith is indispensable for mundane as well as supramundane progress. In the instruction to Āḷavakā (S I 214), the Master said, "Faith is man's best wealth here," affirming the words of his predecessor in the lineage of the noble ones, the Buddha Kassapa, and setting forth the mundane and the supramundane aspects of faith.

It is said in our books that as jewels and gold bring about worldly enjoyment, do away with hunger and thirst, end poverty, become the cause of getting various other valuable things and produce worldly honour, so do mundane and supramundane faith bring into being the bliss of the world and of what is beyond it. Supramundane faith destroys birth and old age, and producing the gems of the enlightenment factors, gives bliss here and now, and deathlessness hereafter. Both kinds of faith bring the praise and appreciation of the good at all times. The riches of faith never depart from one, always accompany one and are one's own unfailing treasure. Mundane faith is the cause of all gains in the world, even that of silver and gold; the man endowed with faith, having given freely and acquired merit, becomes a possessor of material wealth. The one who lacks faith, however, comes to harm and hurt even with the material wealth he possesses now. So it is said, "Faith is man's best wealth in the world."

The aspirant to spiritual perfection acknowledges on trust the truth of his yet-unrealised goal. Without faith in the truth and realisability of his aim the impulse to achieve it becomes very weak (if it does not entirely disappear) through misgivings and doubts. Faith gives the impetus and makes him take not merely the first step but every step in his long pilgrimage to uttermost purity. That is because faith is one of the powerful good (*sobhana*) mental properties universal to all wholesome conscious states connected with inner development, and every effort that tends goalward belongs to such a conscious state of merit.

Faith is the trunk, the hand, of the great bull elephant, the powerful tusker, the Buddha said (Th 694). It is with faith that the highest is reached by the Enlightened One. It is thus the means of gaining supreme bliss.

Faith gathers the provisions for the journey (S I 44), that is to say, the journey from *saṃsāra* to Nibbāna along a happy road of good rebirths, as it causes the doing of meritorious deeds. Faith is the first of the seven treasures of the noble (*ariyadhana*). It has been shown above that faith is a faculty (*indriya*) and a power (*bala*). Around faith cluster the forces of effort, conscientiousness, fear of reckless action censured by the wise, mindfulness, concentration and wisdom.

Material treasures are subject to destruction by the moth and rust of change and decay. Worldly possessions are in danger of being taken away by rulers and robbers, destroyed by fire and flood and run through by one's own heirs. But faith and other treasures of the mind last. So the man with faith and other virtues can never be a pauper, empty, or helpless by himself.

Faith is the first of the five factors necessary for noble exertion (*pañca padhāniyaṅgāni*). The others are health, candour through absence of hypocrisy and deceit, energy and the wisdom of renunciation. Faith is also the forerunner of all things of value, beginning with giving freely, in the Buddha's dispensation.

Four kinds of faith are recognised in the Dhamma: faith of the *sammā bodhisatta* beginning with his first resolve to become a Supreme Buddha (*āgamana-saddhā*); the faith of the hearers of the Buddha who realise the paths and the fruits of sanctitude (*adhigama-saddhā*); the firm trust in the three jewels after considering their qualities (*okappanā-saddhā*); and the trusting in what is wholesome, meritorious and generally good (*pasada-saddhā*). Thus every kind of faith, concerning things leading to well-being from the attainment of short-lived belief (*khaṇika pasāda*), through a momentary dispelling of doubt, to faith of the *ariyas*, can be found in the Dhamma.

Faith exists in the form of a predominant condition (*adhipac-caya-bhāvana*) of the function of believing (*saddhādhana kiriyāya*) of conscious mental properties. When there is this functionally conditioning predominance of believing belonging to mental properties in a conscious state, it is said, "A person believes."

Faith is like a boat to ferry one across the flood of wrong views to safety, a strong branch to lift a man on to the giant tree of virtue when pursued by the wild oxen of the passions and is the door that shuts out the serpent of unbelief. Like a strong cable that holds a ship to its anchor in stormy weather, faith keeps a man attached to the Triple Gem during the destructive storms of scepticism that trouble him while he is still far from the noble path.

As a pillar of the king's fort firmly fixed on the ground and unable to be shaken (for the protection of those in the fort and for repulsing enemies), so is faith for keeping off all enervating influences in the course of a man's struggle for virtue, concentration and wisdom, as well as for his protection. There is no possibility of a disciple falling into demeritorious states, says the Blessed One, as long as the disciple places faith on wholesome things; but when faith goes, the disciple becomes possessed of unbelief and gets himself involved in evil actions.

Until a disciple of his is not impelled by faith and other good impulses, the Buddha says that he watches him, but once faith and other qualities connected with faith begin to operate in him, the Master, knowing that his disciple is guarded and incapable of slackening, no longer keeps his eye on him.

About the saying of the Buddha that faith is the seed, the ancients have written thus: Just as a grain-growing farmer cannot cultivate his field without seed, so the farmer of the spirit cannot produce anything of real value without faith in the rightness, desirability and practicability of the Buddha's teaching for the extinction of ill. The farmer's seed does two things: it establishes itself in the earth by its roots, and sends upward shoots and sprouts. In like manner, the seed of faith establishes itself in the field of the human heart with the roots of virtue and sends upward the shoots of serenity and insight (*samatha-vipassanā*). As the material seed (after drawing up the essences of earth and water by its stem) grows for the purpose of making its fruit reach maturity, so the faith of the yogi grows for the purpose of bringing the fruit of *ariyan* wisdom to ripening after drawing up the essence of serenity (*samatha*) and of insight (*vipassanā*) through the stem of the *ariyan* path. The material seed, having established itself in the soil, having grown, increased and become great, by developing roots, shoots, leaves, and stem, produces milky juice, and brings into being ears of corn heavy with a multitude of grain. Likewise, the seed of faith planted in the mind, having grown, increased, and become great on account of the purification of virtue (*sīla-visuddhi*), the purification of mind (*citta-visuddhi*), the purification of view (*diṭṭhi-visuddhi*), the purification of transcending doubt (*kaṅkhāvitaraṇa-visuddhi*), the purification of knowledge and vision of what is and is not the path (*maggāmagga-ñāṇadassana-visuddhi*), and the purification of knowledge and vision of practice (*paṭipadā-ñāṇadassana-visuddhi*), produces the milk of the purification of knowledge and vision (*ñāṇadassana-visuddhi*) and brings into being the crop of consummate saintship, heavy with manifold analytical and supernormal knowledge. So the Blessed One said, "Faith is the seed" (Sn 77). Though faith arises with many other wholesome mental states, it is (on account of its function) called the seed. As consciousness performs the function of knowing, so faith performs the function of a seed and is the source of all wholesome things. Accordingly it is said:

> "One who is endowed with faith in the Buddha's teaching resorts to a preceptor or a teacher and performs the duties of a pupil. Through association with the teacher he gets instruction; bearing the instruction in mind he ponders on

it, gets at the general meaning of the doctrine and is pleased with the understanding of it. The pleasure of understanding it produces zest for the practice of it; and imbued with zest, he endeavours to grasp the deep aspects of the Dhamma, while practising for reaching the supramundane. When his practice becomes perfect, he realises the highest truth and becomes one with it."

Refuge in the Triple Gem

by Soma Thera

Taking refuge in the Buddha is really taking refuge in what one understands as the qualities of the Buddha. Whatever the qualities of the Buddha may be, one cannot understand those which one's mind is incapable of apprehending, those which one's imagination is not virile enough to seize.

Just as it requires a great artist to take in the wonder and charm of a grand landscape and transfer it on to a canvas, so it needs a man of cultivated mind even to know, abstractly, the might and majesty, the fascination and purity, the compassion and love, and the other great traits of the Master in a worthy way.

No true idea of the Buddha, however, can be got by merely studying the books or by mere logical thinking and the working up of religious emotion. To gain a fairly clear idea of the Buddha and to take effective refuge in him we must produce in our own selves some small fraction at least of the qualities which constitute the Buddha.

We can understand a thing rightly and fully only by making it a part of ourselves mentally, and where possible, translating what we see in thought into action as the artist translates his impressions on to a canvas. If we want to understand the renunciation of the Buddha, we must ourselves give up things; we must renounce, as he renounced, things that we hold dear in this crumbling, dissolving world. To understand his compassion our hearts must melt in mercy for our suffering fellow beings. To understand his uprightness we ourselves must be straight. And if by such practice we approximate to the Master in pitch of actual achievement in spirituality we shall feel that we have taken refuge in him for very good reasons. We shall then feel in some way a new light dawning on us and shall rise to a clearer view than we had ever before of life and its possibilities. Then we shall be taking refuge in the Buddha not through words but through deeds, and also because we have found him an efficient guide to happiness by following his instructions and proving the truth of his word.

Through experience of the truth of the Buddha at first hand one comes to see that in the Buddha is reached the full extinction of sorrow through the extinction of all the possible causes of sorrow, namely, lust, hatred and ignorance; that other teachers are not invulnerable to sorrow as he; that they are not all-compassionate as he; and that they are not detached from all things as he. One finds them holding on to some form or another of life and as no life is unchanging they are all subject to the pain which change brings directly or indirectly. Further, as what changes cannot be the true self, they are all under some form of delusion as regards an abiding soul, or both an eternal soul and God.

Sentient life is consciousness, and every other goal of religion (except Nibbāna), be it in the form of the Vedantic absorption in the *paramātman* or of the Christian communion with Father in Heaven or of the emancipated soul of the Jainas, is based on something fleeting. For in all these non-Buddhist goals there is some kind of consciousness, and consciousness will not keep to just one form (unchanging) if it is consciousness. It is only in the Buddhadhamma that we find uttermost release from sorrow through the uttermost release from every vestige of consciousness. And when Buddhists take refuge in the Dhamma they take refuge in just this uttermost release, knowing from their own experience that to be conscious is to be sick as the Buddha unambiguously teaches us. Here too, taking refuge in the Dhamma is taking refuge in the conception of the Teaching in us.

This uttermost release, Nibbāna, the *summum bonum*, the highest in the sense of the most excellent of all things, is what the Buddha discovered and revealed to us. And we who follow him resemble him in that we too are seekers of Nibbāna (*nibbāna-pariyesaka*). For though he revealed to the world the existence of Nibbāna and pointed out the direction in which it lies, each one has to tread the way leading to the goal, see it for oneself and thus rediscover it personally.

There is in the Buddhadhamma no quest for a hare's horn, for something that does not exist, but for something borne witness to by the Buddha and his disciples and which we ourselves can test and see. There is nothing mystical or occult in it; it is accessible to anyone who has the courage and wisdom to tread the path to perfection through unceasing endeavour.

Says a scripture: "Well-expounded is the Dhamma by the Master, realisable here and now, timeless, inviting, leading truthwards, to be known by the wise, individually, namely, the crushing of the libidinous, the subjugating of life's thirst, the uprooting of desire, the breaking of the circle of becoming, the void, the hard-to-get-at dissolution of craving, detachment, cessation, Nibbāna."

Of this same Teaching the Buddha says: "Seeking Nibbāna I realised the birthless, peerless, perfectly secure blowing out; the unageing, the unailing, the undying, the sorrowless, the speckless ... Difficult to see, to understand, tranquil, excellent, is what I reached."

To reach that goal, far-off at the moment to many of us, we can set forward just now by becoming mindful of our actions, words and thoughts, so that we do not lust or hate or get deluded with the delusion of permanence, beauty, pleasure, or immortal soul in regard to anything. By such practice we move Nibbāna-wards and when we see that by such mindfulness of the real nature of things we are freed from sorrow temporarily, we can infer that if we increase such mindfulness and make it a settled feature of our thought we shall be finally freed of all ill. Thus it will become clear that taking refuge in the Teaching of the Buddha is no act of blind belief but a practical method ever provable as an efficient one, if we are serious about abolishing suffering in ourselves.

In the same way on sure ground, inferred from our well-founded belief in the Buddha and the Norm, is taking refuge in the Order of Pure Persons (the Ariya Sangha) established. Through even a little practice of the Teaching we know that it is realisable. And, when we read the records of the pure persons from the Buddha downwards, we feel that they are the perfect patterns of the good life in its highest meaning, and that what they have done we too could do. This confidence which they inspire causes to arouse in us all that is lofty and pure when we dwell upon their virtues. They become for us fields of the highest yield, for in them we sow the seed of our faith in human nature at its best and reap the fruit of the very noblest endeavour: the final ceasing from all ill.

This is the statement in brief of the great triple theme of refuge, the basis of the Buddhist outlook. Without this refuge progress in good is not settled and steady. With it, work on the path becomes easy to a great extent because of clarification of purpose and of the emergence of a sense of proper values.

Saddhā: Buddhist Devotion

by Sister Dhammadinnā

The object of Buddhist devotion is what is known as the Triple Gem or the Threefold Refuge, comprising the Buddha, Dhamma and Sangha, viz., the fully Enlightened One, His Doctrine, and the Order of His Noble Disciples.

And the practice of devotion consists in meditating on the qualities of these Three Refuges.

These qualities are embodied in the most simple yet profound formula familiar to all Buddhists from the time they learn how to speak, and which they recite on most occasions.

Buddha comes first in the Triple Gem, worshipped and followed as the Great Teacher and Spiritual Master. The word Buddha implies the attainment of Supreme Enlightenment (*sammā sambodhi*). In other words, Buddha implies a state of perfection and not a person.

Hence Buddha is not a personality, a God, an Avatar, nor an incarnation of some God. Prayers to Him, rituals, blind faith in Him, have no meaning whatsoever.

Dhamma or Nirvana (in this context the transcendental truth) is also the supermundane Path (*magga*) leading to the perfect Truth, which has been discovered by the Buddha.

Reflection on the Dhamma means reflection on the nature of its transcendental attributes; in other words reflection on the state of perfect deliverance, being freed from all *saṃsāric* turmoils, and a blissful condition of peace which has once and for all done with death and rebirth.

The Sangha is the Order of the Noble Disciples who have achieved the Goal or have entered the Path which leads to the Goal, thus forming the living example for those still striving. In brief, the Buddha is the way-finder, the Teacher, the Guide; the Dhamma is the Way, the Teaching; and the Sangha refers to those teaching the way, or treading the way, the real followers of the Teaching.

In the course of the actual practice of devotion, however, these three embody, and culminate in, one idea: the Truth.

Hence devotion is directed towards an ever-present reality and not towards a dead teacher or empty abstractions. Devotional acts call into play many forces and faculties of the mind. The most important of these is *saddhā*, or confidence in the Triple Gem (the Refuges) which is associated with other factors such as gratitude, love, joy, and deep reverence and worship, forming a whole that we call the devotional aspect.

It must be clearly understood that this *saddhā* (confidence), born of knowledge, is essentially different from the Hindu "*bhakti*" or Christian "faith" since there is no element of a purely emotional affection or any personal relationship or blind credulity.

Saddhā has the background of understanding with regard to the nature of *saṃsāra*, and also with regard to the significance of the Refuges. At the last it must be accompanied by a conviction in the operation of the Law of Karma as a factor that sustains and perpetuates this endless course of life and death. Since *saddhā* is an indispensable factor governing all spiritual growth, it is called the seed from which is born the tree that bears the fruit of deliverance.

Among the five factors of spiritual powers and spiritual faculties, *saddhā* (faith or confidence), *viriya* (energy), *sati* (mindfulness), *samādhi* (concentration), *paññā* (intuitive wisdom), the primary factor is *saddhā*, which, if properly cultivated, conditions the development of the rest. In its highest supermundane sense, *saddhā* is unshakable faith in the Triple Gem (the Refuges), achievable through the attainment of the Noble Path. Only in this sense is it true "self-surrender" which is the culmination of devotion.

Self-surrender, in the Buddhist sense, is not becoming one with any "universal spirit," etc., but it is the entire abandonment, down to the last vestige, of all self-notion and personality-belief which, if accomplished, brings to pass the overcoming of two other mental fetters: "doubt and wavering" and "clinging to rites and rituals."

Lastly, *saddhā* arouses concomitant factors such as assurance, joy and gratitude. As one realises the tremendous significance of the Refuges, as the True Refuge from the toils and tumults of *saṃsāra*, a deliberate and conscious cultivation of this one factor means the development of the entire devotional aspect, which forms the fount and source of all mental energy.

Mahā-Moggallāna

by

Hellmuth Hecker

WHEEL PUBLICATION NO. 263/264

Life of Mahā-Moggallāna

> Homage to him, to that bhikkhu who, Brahmā-like, can see in a moment's flash the thousandfold universe before his eyes; who, master of magic powers, can also see in the flow of time the gods' arising and their death
>
> Theragāthā (Verses of the Elders), verse 1181

His Youth[1]

Near the capital of the kingdom of Magadha (today in the Indian State of Bihar) there were several townships. In one of them, Kolita Moggallāna was born in a Brahmanic family which claimed descent from Mudgala, one of the ancient seers. Thus this clan was named "the Moggāllans." The small town was inhabited entirely by Brahmins and was "ultra-conservative." Kolita's father was born of the most prominent family from which usually the town's mayor was appointed. Being a member of such a high caste and of the town's most respected family, his father was almost like a petty king. Thus Kolita grew up in an environment of wealth and honour, knowing of no sorrows. He was educated entirely in the Brahmanic tradition, which was based on the law of the seeds and ripening of actions. As a matter of course, that education included the belief in a life beyond, making it part and parcel of everyday life and its rituals.

Kolita's family lived on very friendly terms with another Brahmanic family from a neighbouring village. On the very day of Kolita's birth, also to the other family a son was born whom they named Upatissa. When the children grew up they became friends and soon they were inseparable. Whatever they did, they did together, whether it was play or study, pleasure or work. Always they were seen together, and their undisturbed friendship was to last for life, for more than eighty years. They never quarrelled nor bore a grudge against each other. Always they lived amicably

1. Sources for chapters 1 and 2 are the ancient records in the Commentaries to the Aṅguttara Nikāya and Dhammapada.

and stuck together in whatever difficulties. Yet in their character dispositions they were quite different. Upatissa was more of a pioneer type, daring and enterprising, while Kolita's way was to preserve, to cultivate and to enrich what he had gained. Also their place within their families was different. Kolita was the only child, but Upatissa had three brothers and three sisters. To both, their friendship meant so much and filled their daily life to such an extent that as young men, they had little interest in the other sex, though they were not quite free from the light-heartedness and indulgences of their youthful age. Each of them was the leader of a group of friends with whom they undertook many kinds of play and sport in high spirits. When they went to the river, Kolita's companions came on horseback and those of Upatissa were carried in palanquins. It was similar with Francis of Assisi: he, too, had been the leader of a group of playboys, and like him, both friends, too, had been enamoured by the intoxications of youth, health and life.

In Rājagaha, Magadha's capital, there was annually a great public celebration with popular shows and amusements, which was called "the hill festival." Of course, both friends, too, went to enjoy it. They had places reserved for them from where they could easily watch the entertainments. When there was something to laugh, at they too joined in the laughter, and when there was something fascinating they too got excited. They enjoyed these entertainments so much that they went there also for a second day and continued to watch keenly the performances, which were a mixture of folksy comedies and old legends. But the heightening of their joyful mood which they had expected failed to come. Still they had their places reserved for the third day too, as a new program of entertainments had been announced in glowing terms. They slept badly that night as the impressions of the previous day still haunted their minds. While thus kept awake, Kolita thought: "What's the use of all that for us? Is there really anything worthwhile to be seen? What benefit does it give? After a few years, these glamorous actors will be old and feeble; they will leave the stage of life and continue their migrations through existence, driven by their cravings. The same it is with us. These actors cannot help themselves to solve the problem of existence. How, then, can they help us? We just waste here our time instead of thinking of our liberation!"

Upatissa, too, had spent a restless night, and quite similar thoughts had come to him. He reflected how these ancient myths and legends dramatised in those performances, actually concerned the reality of rebirth; but the jokes and frolics overlaying those ideas in the plays pretended that there was only this present life one need be concerned with. Was this not an artificial suppression and repression of truth by vain illusions?

When, on the morning of the third day, they went to their places at the festival, Kolita said to his friend: "What is the matter with you? You are not as merry as you have been. What depresses you?" His friend replied: "Tell me, what is the use to us of all these pleasures of eye and ear? It is absolutely useless and worthless! What I would rather do is seek a way of release from that devastating law of impermanence, a way to liberation from the fleeting illusions of life which alluringly haunt us and yet leave us empty. That is what went through my head and made me think. But you, too, dear Kolita, look anything else but cheerful!" Kolita replied: "I have felt the same as you did. Why should we stay any longer here, in this unholy vanity show? We should seek the way to the Holy!" When Upatissa heard that his friend had the very same wish, he happily exclaimed: "That is a good thought that came to us independent from each other! We have wasted our life and our time long enough with all those unprofitable things. But if one earnestly seeks a teaching of deliverance, one has to give up home and possessions and go forth as a homeless pilgrim, free of worldly and sensual bonds, rising above them like a feathered bird."

So the two friends decided to take to the life of ascetics who then, as they still do now, wandered in large numbers along the roads of India in search of a spiritual teacher, a Guru, who could guide them. When they told their followers about their decision, these young men were so deeply impressed that most of them joined in that spiritual quest. So all of them gave up home life, took off the sacred Brahmanic thread, cut hair and beard and put on the pale earth-coloured garments of religious wanderers. Discarding all distinguishing marks and privileges of their caste, they entered the classless society of ascetics.

The Years of Wandering and Spiritual Search

It was about the same time when Prince Siddhattha married (and thus, for the time-being at least, made another step into worldly life) that Kolita and Upatissa left behind their worldly homes and started upon their quest for inner peace and salvation. Together with their friends, they began a period of training under a spiritual teacher, just as the Bodhisattva did later.

At that time, there were many teachers with many different views. Some of them even taught amoralism, others taught fatalism and again others taught materialism. Both friends realised the hollowness of such teachings early enough and thus did not take them too seriously. In Rājagaha, however, there was one teacher who appealed to them. His name was Sañjaya, who, according to tradition, was identical with Sañjaya Belaṭṭhaputta, mentioned in the Pali Canon as one of six non-Buddhist teachers. Under him the group of friends was ordained, which added considerably to Sañjaya's reputation. What did he teach them? The texts do not provide an answer to this question in a way we are used to, but only some key ideas are briefly indicated, which, for the Indian of those days, was sufficient for making them understand the substance of these teachings.

Contrary to other ascetic teachers who made definite dogmatic statements about specific topics, Sañjaya posed what may be called "the deepest existential problems" in a more comprehensive way. Firstly: Is there another world beyond our empirical surface experience? Secondly: After the death of this material body, does one appear in that other world by way of a purely mental birth process as a spontaneously arisen being? Thirdly: Whatever action one has committed in this carnal existence, be it good or bad, will it take effect in the next life, be it of a spiritual or human type, by way of reward or punishment, thus constituting our destiny? Fourthly: What, finally, is the destiny of a Perfected One after death? In which way is it possible to conceive and describe his state or condition? Whenever such questions were raised by ancient Indian thinkers, four alternative types of answers were thought to be possible: affirmation; negation; partial affirmation and partial negation; neither affirmation nor negation. Sañjaya, however, taught that, with regard to the questions mentioned, none of those four positions was acceptable as a solution; they all contained unresolvable contradictions (antinomies), and therefore one should refrain from any judgment about these problems. Here it may be noted that, from the four sets of antinomies which often occur in the Pali scriptures (e.g., MN 63), only the fourth set is identical with Sañjaya's problems, namely, the one concerning the after-death state of a Perfected One.

While other ascetic teachers as a solution to their problems always advocated one of the four logical alternatives—yes, no, yes and no, neither-nor—Sañjaya did not commit himself to any of them. Especially, he did not commit himself dogmatically to the unprovable assertion (made, for instance, by popular natural science) that there is no world beyond, no mind-made (astral) body, no Law of Karma and no survival after death. In that attitude, he clearly differed from the materialists of his time. He rather taught that, in view of the unresolvable nature of these problems, one should keep to a stance of detachment and impartiality, not tolerating the slightest bias towards approval or disapproval of any of these theories and their consequences. From that we can see that he was a confirmed agnostic and sceptic of a peculiar brand who tried to convert the purely negative "*ignorabimus*" ("we cannot know") into a definite philosophical attitude. In some ways, he was what we nowadays would call an existentialist. He taught, so to speak, a kind of dialectical existentialism, instead of dialectical materialism.

An Indian king Ajātasattu reported to the Buddha the following talk he had with the ascetic Sañjaya:

"One day I went to Sañjaya of the Belaṭṭha clan and I asked him: 'Can you, sir, declare to me an immediate fruit, visible in this very world, of the life of a recluse?' Being thus asked, Sañjaya said: 'If you asked me whether there is another world—well, if I thought there were, I would say so. But I don't say so. And I don't think it is thus or thus. And I don't think it is otherwise. And I don't deny it. And I don't say there neither is nor is not another world. And if you asked me about the beings produced spontaneously; or whether there is any fruit, any result, of good or bad actions; or whether a Tathāgata continues or not after death—to each or any of these questions do I give the same reply.'

"Thus, Lord, did Sañjaya of the Belaṭṭha clan, when asked what was the immediate fruit and advantage in the life of a recluse, show his manner of prevarication."

—DN 2; adapted from the translation by T.W. Rhys Davids

But Kolita and Upatissa, who, at that time, had not found any better teacher, were attracted by Sañjaya as they must have felt that his philosophical stance was something more than mere evasion. Yet, after a short time, they realised that Sañjaya did not know what they were searching for: a cure for the illness of universal suffering. Besides, they intuitively felt sure that there actually was another world, that there were mind-born beings (as, e.g., deities) and that there was a moral recompense of actions. In so far, their understanding went beyond that of their sceptical teacher. Furthermore, Sañjaya, in total contradiction to his dogmatic scepticism, had once declared that his best disciples had been reborn at such and such a place (SN 44:9). Hence, one day, the two friends approached Sañjaya and asked him whether he had still other teachings to convey than those they had learned from him. To this he replied: "That is all. You know my entire teaching." Hearing this, they decided to leave and to continue their search. They felt that it was for finding liberation that they had left their families, and not for the sake of endless and futile agnostic arguments.

Thus, for a second time, they took up the life of wanderers in search of truth. Again, they walked across India for many years, from North to South, from East to West. They endured the dust of the road and the tormenting heat, the rain and the wind, being spurred on by thoughts that moved the mind of many Indians:

> "I am a victim of birth, ageing and death, of sorrow, lamentations, pains, griefs and despairs. I am a victim of suffering, a prey of suffering. Surely, an end of this whole mass of suffering is discovered!"

—MN 28; trans. Ñāṇamoli

In their travels they met many ascetics and brahmins who had the reputation to be exceptionally wise. With them they had religious talks on God and world, heaven and hell and on the meaning of life and the way of salvation. But with their keen and critical minds trained by Sañjaya's scepticism, they very soon realised the emptiness of all those assertions and the learned ignorance of these philosophers. None of these teachers could answer their probing questions, while the two friends themselves were quite able to reply when questioned.

There is no record that tells us to which other teachers they had gone. But it would be surprising if the two truth-seekers had not met such mystics and sages as for instance the seer Bāvari of great meditative power or the two teachers of Formless Infinity whose disciple the Bodhisattva was for some time. But from their life story we can conclude that the two attained as little to the world-transcending experience of liberation as the Bodhisattva did. What may have been the cause of that lack of attainment?

There are two possibilities for spiritual seekers: either to gain inner peace and serenity by deep meditation (*samādhi*) or to seek for a clear teaching about the meaning of existence in its entirety, which encompasses the meaning of that inner peace. Those who had achieved such inner peace through meditation, mostly gave up any further search as they had found an overwhelming bliss which they believed to be the goal. But at its best, this bliss would last a few aeons in one of the celestial worlds, and then its kammic force would be spent, leaving the meditators in the same *saṃsāric* imprisonment as before. In former lives, this must have happened often to the Bodhisattva as well as to Kolita and Upatissa. Though the two friends had no recollection of such previous experiences, they obviously had an intuitive feeling that meditative bliss and its rewards were not the final goal, but only a temporary relief within the continuing cycle of suffering. Hence their foremost quest was for clarity about the concatenation of existence, how things hang together in this complex *saṃsāra*. But such clarity cannot be found without the help of a Buddha. Hence they had to continue their search until it had led them to the Buddha.

In ages void of a Buddha's appearance, their search would have been as futile as the recurring attainment, enjoyment and again losing of *samādhi*. It may have been an undefinable inner urge within them, which did not allow them to rest until they had found the Buddha, who, like them, had gone forth in search of liberation, during the last years of their own quest. If even the

Bodhisattva, the future Buddha, only in the pressing situation of a great spiritual crisis remembered the meditative experience of his young years and only then could see it and use it as a gate to liberation, it was not to be expected that the two friends would find out by themselves that meditative absorption (*jhāna*) was to be used as a gate of access to higher stages of the mind's emancipation. They had neither the meditative experience nor the wide and independent mental range of a Buddha. This is one of the aspects of existential misery, of prison-like ignorance: either one settles down at the gate, regarding it, as the mystics do, as one's true home of peace and bliss; or one by-passes it quickly. In retrospect, the friends' wanderings in search of truth were just a going in circles, in expectation of a Buddha's message of the liberating Path.

Finding the Teaching[2]

Without knowing anything of the Buddha, they gave up their life as wanderers and, after about twenty years, returned to their home country Magadha. This happened not long after the Buddha had set in motion the Wheel of the Dhamma at Benares.

But the two friends still had not given up hope and they decided now to do their search separately, for doubling their chances. They agreed between themselves that he who had first learned about a convincing path to the Deathless should quickly inform the other.

At that time, when both were about forty years old, the Buddha had sent out the first batch of his disciples, sixty-one in number and all of them saints, so that they may proclaim the Teaching for the well-being and happiness of men. The Buddha himself had gone to Rājagaha, where the Mahāraja of Magadha soon became his follower and donated to him the Bamboo Grove Monastery (Jetavana). At that monastery he lived when Kolita and Upatissa returned to Rājagaha, staying at Sañjaya's place. One day Upatissa had gone to the town while Kolita had stayed back at their dwelling. Kolita saw his friend returning but never had he seen him like that: his entire being seemed to be transformed, his appearance was buoyant and radiant. Eagerly Kolita asked him:

2. Source: Vinaya Mahā-Vagga I, 23–24.

"Your features are so serene, dear friend, and your complexion is so bright and clear. Should it have happened that you have found the road to the Deathless?"

Upatissa then replied: "It is so, dear friend, the Deathless has been found." He then reported how it happened. In town, he had seen a monk whose behaviour impressed him so deeply that he addressed him and asked who his teacher was. The monk, whose name was Assaji, was one of the first five disciples of the Buddha and one of the sixty-one saints (Arahants). Assaji replied that he was a disciple of the ascetic of the Sakya clan. When Upatissa begged him to explain his teacher's doctrine, Assaji said that he could not do so as he had been ordained only a few months ago. He could only tell him in brief the quintessence of the Teaching. When Upatissa said that he would be satisfied knowing just the gist of the teaching in short, Assaji replied by way of that short stanza which was to become famous wherever the Buddha's Teaching spread in the centuries and millennia that followed. This is the original Pali text and its translation:

Ye dhammā hetuppabhavā
tesaṃ hetuṃ Tathāgatāha
tesaṃ ca yo nirodho
evaṃvādi mahāsamaṇo.

The Perfect One has told the cause
of causally arisen things
And what brings their cessation, too:
Such is the doctrine taught by the Great Monk.

In literal translation:

Of things conditionally arisen
the Thus-gone the condition told
and what is their cessation,
thus the Great Ascetic proclaimed.

When Upatissa heard this stanza, the vision of truth (the "Dhamma-eye") arose in him on the spot, and the very same happened to Kolita when he listened to the stanza retold by his friend. He, too, realised: Whatever arises is bound to vanish. The realisation that was evoked by this stanza may be called a truly mystical event. For us, these four lines do not contain an explanation explicit enough for a full understanding. The deeper and wider meaning of the stanza reveals itself only to those who have trained themselves for long in wisdom and renunciation and have reflected long upon the impermanent and the Deathless, the conditioned and the Unconditioned. This stanza will have such a revolutionary impact only on those who are so single-minded that they have become accustomed to investigate things only in those terms of the conditioned and Unconditioned. As the two friends were inwardly prepared, Assaji's stanza had the power to lead them to the attainment of stream-entry (*sotāpatti*), which bestows the first vision of the Deathless (Nibbāna) beyond the transience of phenomenal existence where death ever reigns. In a flash of awakening they had seen the Uncreated.

Here it is of interest to note that the three monks who were closest to the Buddha, Ānanda and the two chief disciples, did not attain to stream-entry by the Buddha's own instruction, but through the guidance of others: Ānanda through his Sangha-teacher, the Arahant Puṇṇa Mantāṇiputta, Upatissa through the Arahant Assaji, and Kolita even through one who was not an Arahant, but only a stream-enterer. For making such an attainment possible, Kolita needed to possess strong confidence in his friend as well as in truth; and Kolita did have this confidence.

After Kolita had listened to that powerful stanza, he asked at once where the Great Ascetic, the Perfected One was staying. Hearing that he was staying not far away at the Bamboo Grove Monastery, he wished to go there immediately. But Upatissa asked him to wait, saying, "Let us first go to Sañjaya and tell him that we have found the Deathless. If he can understand, he is sure to make progress towards the truth. But if he cannot comprehend at once, he may perhaps have confidence enough to join us when we go to see the Master. Then, on listening to the Awakened One, himself, he will certainly understand."

Thus the friends went to their former Master and said, "Listen, O Teacher, listen! A fully Awakened One has appeared in the world. Well proclaimed is his Teaching and his monks live the fully purified life of ascetics. Come with us to see him!" But Sañjaya could not bring himself to join them, but, on the contrary, offered them to take over the leadership of his following, along with him, as his equals. If they accepted this, they would gain a great reputation, because spiritual teachers enjoyed, at that time, the highest respect. But the two replied that they would not mind remaining pupils for life, whether under him or under the Buddha. But they would ask him to make up his mind now, as their own decision was final. Sañjaya, however, torn by indecision, lamented: "I cannot, no I cannot! For so many years I have been a teacher and had a large following of disciples. Should I now become a pupil again, it would be as if a mighty lake were to change into a miserable puddle!"—Thus he was moved by conflicting sentiments: his longing for truth and the desire to keep to his superior position contended within him. Yet, the urge to preserve his status was stronger, and he yielded to it.

At that time, Sañjaya had about five hundred disciples. When they learned that the two friends had decided to follow the Buddha, spontaneously all of them wanted to join. But when they noticed that Sañjaya remained behind, half of them wavered and returned to their accustomed habitat. Sañjaya, seeing that he had lost so many of his disciples, was stricken by grief and despair so much that, as the texts tell, "hot blood spurted from his mouth."

The Struggle for the Realisation of the Teaching[3]

Now the two friends, at the head of the two hundred and fifty fellow ascetics, approached the Bamboo Grove. There the Buddha was just teaching Dhamma to his monks, and when he saw the two friends approaching, the Awakened One said: "Here, monks, they are coming, the two friends Kolita and Upatissa. They will be my Chief Disciples, a blessed pair!" Having arrived, all respectfully saluted the Buddha, raising their folded palms to the forehead and bowing at the feet of the Master. Then the two friends spoke: "May we be permitted, O Lord, to obtain under the Blessed One the Going-Forth and the Full Admission?" Then the Blessed One responded: "Come, monks, well proclaimed is the Teaching. Live now the Life of Purity, for making an end of suffering!" These brief words served to bestow ordination on the two friends and their following.

3. Sources: AN 4:167; 7:58. SN 21:1; 40:1–9. Mv I.24. Th 1172.

From now, Upatissa was called Sāriputta, that means "the son of Sari," which was the name of his mother. Kolita was called Mahā-Moggallāna, "the Great One of the Moggallāna clan," to distinguish him from other monks of that clan, such as Gaṇaka-Moggallāna and Gopaka-Moggallāna.

After all of them had obtained ordination, the Buddha addressed the two hundred and fifty disciples and explained to them the Teaching in such a way that before long they attained to the first stage of emancipation, stream-entry, and in due course became Arahants. Sāriputta and Moggallāna, however, went into solitude, but this time separate from each other.

Sāriputta remained in the vicinity of Rājagaha and went to meditate in a cave called "Bear's Den." From there he walked to the city for his alms, which afforded him the opportunity to listen often to the Buddha's discourses. What he had heard from the Master, he independently worked over in his own thoughts and he methodically penetrated to clear understanding of the mind and its laws. He needed fourteen days for reaching Sainthood (*arahatta*), the utter destruction of all Taints (*āsavakkhaya*).

Moggallāna, however, for reasons not known to us, chose as his abode the forests near the village of Kallavalaputta in Magadha. With great zeal, he meditated there while sitting or walking up and down. But in these efforts, he was often overcome by sleepiness. Though he did not wish to fall asleep, he was unable to keep his body erect and his head upright. There were times when he had to keep his eyes open even by force of will. If one thinks of the tropical heat, the strain of his long years of a wandering life and the inner tensions he had gone through, one can well understand that now, at the end of his quest, his body reacted by fatigue.

But the Awakened One, with a great teacher's solicitude for his disciples, did not lose sight of him. With his supernormal vision he perceived the difficulties of the new monk, and by magic power he appeared before him. When Moggallāna saw the Master standing before him, a good part of his fatigue had already vanished. Now the Awakened One asked him:

"Are you nodding, Moggallāna, are you nodding?"—"Yes, Lord." —

1. "Well, then, Moggallāna, at whatever thought drowsiness befalls you, to that thought you should not give attention and not dwell on that thought. Then, by doing so, it is possible that your drowsiness will vanish.
2. "But if, by doing so, drowsiness does not vanish, then you should reflect upon the Teaching as you have heard and learned it, you should ponder over it and examine it closely in your mind. Then, by doing so, it is possible that your drowsiness will vanish.
3. "But if, by doing so, drowsiness does not vanish, then you should repeat in full detail the Teaching as you have heard and learned it. Then, by doing so, it is possible that your drowsiness will vanish.
4. "But if, by doing so, drowsiness does not vanish, then you should pull both ear-lobes and rub your limbs with your hand. Then, by doing so, it is possible that drowsiness will vanish.
5. "But if, by doing so, drowsiness does not vanish, you should get up from your seat and, after washing your eyes with water, you should look around in all directions and upwards to the stars and constellations. Then, by doing so, it is possible that your drowsiness will vanish.
6. "But if, by doing so, drowsiness does not vanish, you should give attention to the perception of light, to the perception of day(-light): as by day so by night, as by night so by day. Thus, with your mind clear and unclouded, you should cultivate a mind that is full of brightness. Then, by doing so, it is possible that your drowsiness will vanish.
7. "But if, by doing so, drowsiness does not vanish, then, with your senses turned inward and your mind not straying outward, you should take to walking up and down, being aware of going to and fro. Then, by doing so, it is possible that your drowsiness will vanish.
8. "But if, by doing so, drowsiness does not vanish, you may, mindfully and clearly aware, lie down, lion-like, on your right side, placing foot on foot, keeping in mind the thought of rising; and on awakening, you should quickly get up, thinking 'I must not indulge in the comfort of resting and reclining, in the pleasure of sleeping.'

"Thus, Moggallāna, should you train yourself."

—AN 7:58

Here the Buddha gives Moggallāna a graded sequence of advice how to overcome drowsiness. The first and best device is not to pay attention to the thought causing or preceding the state of drowsiness. This is, however, the most difficult method. If one does not succeed with it, one may summon some energising thoughts or one may reflect upon the excellence of the Teaching, or recite parts of it by heart. If these mental remedies do not help, one should turn to bodily activity as, for instance, pulling one's ears, shaking the body, activating the circulation by rubbing one's limbs, refreshing one's eyes with cold water and, at night, looking at the grandeur of the starry sky, which may make one forget one's petty drowsiness, as it happened to the monk of old who spoke the following verse:

"Nay, not for this that you may slumber long,
Comes the night, in starry garlands wreathed.
For vigils by the wise this night is here."

—Theragāthā 193, trans. by C.A.F. Rhys Davids

If all that, too, does not help, then he may recall the inner light of which many mystics speak and which arises in the meditations of a purified mind that has turned away from the world. Then, in his practice, he will be unconcerned about day or night, because an inner light is shining within him. Then, with his self-radiant mind, he will be able to leave behind, like a Brahmā-deity, the whole realm of days and nights as perceived by the senses. This indicates that Moggallāna had experienced such states before, so that the Buddha could refer to them as something known to Moggallāna. This "Perception of (inner) Light" (*āloka-saññā*) is mentioned in the 33rd Discourse of the Dīgha Nikāya, as one of four ways of developing *samādhi* and as leading to "Knowledge and Vision" (*ñāṇadassana*).

If this method, too, does not help, he should walk up and down mindfully and thus, by resorting to bodily movement, try to get rid of fatigue. If, however, none of these seven devices proves helpful, he may just lie down and rest for a short while. But as soon as he feels refreshed, he should quickly get up, without allowing drowsiness to return.

The Buddha's instruction on that occasion did, however, not stop here, but continued as follows:

"Further, Moggallāna, should you train yourself in this way. You should think, 'When calling at families (on the alms-round), I shall not be given to pride.' Thus should you train yourself. For in families it may happen that people are busy with work and may not notice that a monk has come. Then a monk (if given to pride) may think, 'Who, I wonder, has estranged me from this family? These people seem to be displeased with me.' Thus, by not receiving an offering from them, he is perturbed; being perturbed he becomes excited; being excited he loses self-control; and if uncontrolled, his mind will be far from finding concentration.

"Further, Moggallāna, should you train yourself in this way: 'I shall not speak contentious talk.' Thus should you train yourself. If there is contentious talk, there is sure to be much wordiness; with much wordiness, there will be excitement; he who is excited will lose self-control; and if uncontrolled, his mind will be far from finding concentration."

Here the Awakened One points out two ways of behaviour which lead to excitement and restlessness, and both of them arise from too close a social contact of the monk with the laity. In one case, there is the desire for recognition on the part of a monk who is proud of his status and expects respect from the laity. But if lay people pay more attention to their own business than to him, he soon becomes unsure of himself, is perturbed and upset. In the other case, there is the intellectual delight in discussions, in the conceit of one who "knows better," or in the pleasure of defeating others in debate. By all this, one's mental energy is diverted into unprofitable channels and wasted in futile excitement. One is slack and careless in practising the Way if one cannot keep the senses under control, or allows one's mind to get excited or easily diverted. Such a condition is far from the unification of mind and inner peace obtained in meditation.

After the Awakened One had instructed him on the overcoming of sleepiness and the avoidance of excitement, Moggallāna asked the following question:

"In what way, O Lord, can it be briefly explained how a monk becomes liberated by the elimination of craving; how he becomes one who has reached the final end, the final security from bondage, the final Holy Life, the final consummation, and is foremost among gods and men?"

"Herein, Moggallāna, a monk has learnt this: 'No thing is fit to be clung to!' When a monk has learnt that no thing is fit to be clung to, he fully knows everything; by fully knowing everything, he fully comprehends everything; when fully comprehending everything, whatever feeling he experiences, be it pleasant, painful or indifferent, he, with regard to these feelings, abides contemplating impermanence, contemplating dispassion, contemplating cessation, contemplating relinquishment. When thus abiding, he is not attached to anything in the world; without attachment he does not hanker; and without hankering he reaches within himself complete extinction (of craving): 'Ceased has rebirth, lived is the holy life, done is the task, there is no more of this or that state,' thus he knows."

After Moggallāna had received all these personal instructions of the Master (as recorded in AN 7:58), he devoted himself again to his training with great ardour. With still greater vigour he fought against the five inner hindrances. During his many years of ascetic life he already had, to a great extent, suppressed sensual desire and ill-will, which are the first and the second of these hindrances. Now with the help given by the Buddha, he conquered sloth and torpor, the third hindrance; then he overcame the fourth hindrance, restlessness and worry, by avoiding unprofitable social contacts. Finally he gave up doubt, the fifth hindrance, by following the concluding instruction of the Buddha, contemplating on the transiency of all phenomena and thus severing emotional attachment.

By overcoming the five hindrances, he was able to gain the experience of meditative states transcending the world of materiality; and by his penetrative knowledge of existential reality, he approached the gate to Nibbāna.

He first attained and enjoyed the overwhelming bliss of the first meditation (*jhāna*), that state of mystical absorption of mind. Yet, gradually, some worldly ideas intruded again, claiming his attention. When thus he fell back to the level of the mental hindrances, the Buddha came to his help again. This time, however, not with a detailed instruction as before, but with a brief indication that helped him to get over the impasse. The

Exalted One warned him he should not light-heartedly believe himself to be secure in the attainment of the first *jhāna*, but to gain more firmness in it, so that his mind becomes fully immersed in it and unified. When Moggallāna followed that advice his state of concentration in the first *jhāna* was no longer disturbed by mundane thoughts.

Having thus found a firm footing on the first *jhāna*, he gained the second absorption, which he called "the noble silence" (SN 20:1), because all thoughts are silenced in it. Thus he advanced up to the fourth absorption (SN 40:2f). As he later told, he had practised the absorptions in a twofold way, first by cultivating the "Ways of Power" (*iddhi-pada*, SN 51:31),[4] and then by the "Liberations" (*vimokkha*, Th 1172). On his path towards the final Deliverance by Wisdom (*pañña-vimutti*), the absorptions (*jhāna*) served as stages to the "Ways of Powers," which led to various kinds of super-normal faculties and also opened up many gateways to wisdom. This twofold approach was his strong point when he became an Arahant, a Saint. For attaining to the "Liberation of Mind" (*ceto-vimutti*) the absorptions led him to the eight Liberations (*vimokkha*), culminating in the four formless (immaterial) absorptions (*arūpajjhāna*). On his way to become one "Liberated in Both Ways" (that is, through both concentration and insight),[5] he used the fourth absorption as basis for both. In doing so, he gained the "Signless Concentration of Mind,"[6] which is free from all that marks (or signifies) conditioned existence and which affords a glimpse of the "Signless Element," Nibbāna (SN 40:9). But this attainment, too, was not final as yet. For even here he lapsed into a subtle enjoyment of it. Such refined

4. Or "Four Bases of Success"; see *Requisites of Enlightenment*, Ledi Sayādaw, Wheel 171/174, p. 64ff.

5. *Ubhato-bhaga-vimutta*; see *Buddhist Dictionary*, by Nyanatiloka.

6. "Signless Concentration of Mind" (*animitta-ceto-samādhi*). The Comy explains it as a high level of insight-concentration (*vipassanā-samādhi*) that keeps the mind free from the delusive "signs" of permanency, etc. and of greed, etc. This explanation appears plausible in view of the fact that Mahā-Moggallāna was "liberated in both ways," through concentration and insight. On the related term "Signless Deliverance of Mind" (*animitta-cetovimutti*) see MN 43 (Editor, "The Wheel").

attachment is still a delusive "sign" or "mark" superimposed on a high spiritual attainment of greatest purity. But aided by the Master's instructions, he could free himself from these last fetters and attain to perfect "Deliverance of Mind" and "Deliverance by Wisdom," in all their fullness and depth. Thus the venerable Mahā-Moggallāna had become one of the Saints. He admitted that he could well say about himself that "Supported by the Master a disciple may obtain the great state of the super-knowledges."[7]

This entire development took place within one single week. These were, indeed, seven days of a tremendous impact, with a significance far beyond that of its individual relevance. One must try to imagine the intensity and depth of Moggallāna's determination during this short period, because for a person with such a wide range of great natural gifts it was an especially heroic effort to undertake within his own active mind that hard struggle to cut through all those fetters binding him to this world of vast potentialities. It has been reported that the Buddha, in the four hours of the first watch of the night of his Enlightenment, remembered ninety-one world periods. The appearance of time-space may have dissolved by way of contraction, or something similar must have happened to Moggallāna when an immensity of inner experience was condensed into one short week. Here notions of measurable duration of time fail entirely. Immured in the prison of the senses, one week is no more than seven days for an ordinary person who is unaware of the infinities that burst through the limits of the common time concepts.

Moggallāna, as he later said, attained sainthood by quick penetration (*khippābhiññā*), that is, in one week, but his progress was difficult (*dukkha-paṭipadā*), requiring the helpful prompting (*sasaṅkhāra*) of the Master. Sāriputta, too, attained sainthood by quick penetration (in two weeks), but his progress was smooth (*sukha-paṭipadā*); see AN 4:167–168. Moggallāna had advanced to sainthood more speedily than Sāriputta because the Buddha

7. *Mahā-abhiññāta.* This refers to the six Supernormal Knowledges (*abhiññā*) of which the first five are magical and mystical powers and are mundane (*lokiya*), while the sixth consists of the attainment of sainthood by the elimination of the Cankers (*āsavakkhaya*) and is supramundane (*lokuttara*) (Editor, "The Wheel").

directed and inspired him personally and intensively; but Sāriputta was superior to him in regard to the independence of his progress.

The Most Excellent Pair of Disciples

In the 14th text of the "Longer Discourses" (Dīgha Nikāya: *Mahāpadāna Sutta*), the Awakened One speaks of six Buddhas of the past and says that each of them had two chief disciples and one attendant; and elsewhere (SN 47:14) he says that all the Buddhas of the past and future had or will have one preeminent pair of disciples. When a Perfectly Awakened One is going to appear these three are as necessary to him just as the ministers of war, of the interior, and of finance are necessary to a king. The Buddha himself uses this comparison with a state's administration. He spoke of Ānanda, who could remember all discourses of the Buddha, as the Treasurer of the Teaching (minister of finance), of Sāriputta as its general in command, and of Moggallāna as child's nurse (minister of the interior). Of these four (including the Buddha), two groups of two had certain things in common: the Buddha and Ānanda belonged to the warrior caste (*khattiya*) and were born on the same day; Sāriputta and Moggallāna, however, were Brahmins, and likewise born on the same day. This affinity showed itself also in their lives. Ānanda was always with the Buddha; since the time when he started to be his attendant, he followed him like a shadow; whereas Moggallāna was almost inseparable from Sāriputta and nearly always together with him. Whenever the Buddha, in advancing years, felt physically tired, these three men were the only ones whom he asked to expound the Teaching on his behalf. This happened, for instance, at Kapilavatthu when Moggallāna gave a long discourse on sense-control as remedy against being submerged in the flood of the six sense impressions (SN 35:202).

After Sāriputta and Mahā-Moggallāna had attained Sainthood, the Buddha announced to the Order that they were his chief disciples. Some of the monks were surprised and began to grumble why the Master did not treat with such distinction those ordained first, the "men of the first hour," as for instance the Group of Five, or Yasa or the three Kassapas. Why did he overlook them and give prominence to those who had entered the Order last and were young in seniority? To this the Awakened One replied that each reaps according to his merit. For aeons Sāriputta and Moggallāna had been progressing towards this state, by gradually cultivating the necessary faculties. Others, however, had developed on different lines. Although both chief disciples were of another caste and from another region than the Buddha's, their special position within the community of saints was an outcome of the Law of Karma.

In many ways the Buddha had spoken in praise of this noble pair of disciples:

> "Outstanding they are among my disciples, exceptional they are among my disciples. They truly acted upon the Master's instructions and followed his advice. How dear and amiable are they to the fourfold assembly,[8] worthy of their respect and reverence!"
>
> —SN 47:14

> "If a devout lay woman should admonish her only son whom she dearly loves, she would rightly do so by saying: 'My dear son, you should be like Citta the householder or Hatthaka of Āḷavi!'—because these two are model and exemplar for my lay devotees. (And she should further say:) 'But if, my dear, you should go forth from home into the homeless life (of a monk), you should be like Sāriputta and Moggallāna!'—because they are model and exemplar for bhikkhu disciples."
>
> —SN 17:23

> "Seek and cultivate, O monks, (the company of) Sāriputta and Moggallāna! They are wise and are helpful to their fellows in the Holy Life. Sāriputta is like a mother, and Moggallāna is like a nurse. Sāriputta trains (the monks) for the Fruit of stream-entry, and Moggallāna for the supreme goal."
>
> —MN 141

The characterisation of the two in the last text may be interpreted as follows. Sāriputta urges his pupils to cut through the first and basic fetters and thus helps them to attain stream-entry. In this way he "converts" men by vigorously diverting them from the

8. That is, bhikkhus and bhikkhunīs (nuns), male and female lay followers.

futility of the round of existence, and guides them into the zone of safety. Sāriputta, like a mother, watches and guides the first steps on the path of emancipation; or it may be said, he causes, or at least assists, the birth of final emancipation in the pupil. Moggallāna, however, leads on those who thus far have been saved, guiding them along their way upwards; he supports them in their practice of meditation up to sainthood, in the same way as he himself was helped by the master; he is like a wet nurse, nourishing the strength and sustaining the growth of the pupil.

Both aspects are found perfectly united in a Fully Awakened One; but in Sāriputta and Moggallāna they were separate qualifications. Though both were "liberated in both ways," yet with Sāriputta the major emphasis was on wisdom, and with Moggallāna on the meditative "Liberation of the Mind" (*cetovimutti*).

This fact found perfect expression when these two spiritual sons of the Buddha had to look after Rāhula, the Buddha's own son. As every newly ordained monk, Rāhula had two teachers, one in knowledge and one in conduct. Sāriputta was appointed as his teacher in knowledge, and Moggallāna as his teacher in conduct and spiritual practice.

Once Sāriputta said to his friend that, compared with Moggallāna's great supernormal powers, he was like a small splinter of rock set against the mighty Himalayas. Moggallāna, however, replied that, compared with Sāriputta's power of wisdom, he was like a tiny grain of salt set against a big salt barrel (SN 21:3).

About the differing range of wisdom, the Buddha once said that there are questions which only he could conceive and answer, but not Sāriputta; there are other questions which only Sāriputta could clarify, but not Moggallāna; and there are those which only Moggallāna could solve, but not the other disciples (J 483). Thus the two chief disciples were like a bridge between the supreme qualities of the Buddha and the capacities of the other disciples.

When Devadatta voiced his claim to lead the Order, the Buddha said that he would not entrust anybody with the leadership of the Sangha, not even his two chief disciples, let alone Devadatta (Cv VII, 3). Between the high point of discipleship, Sāriputta and Moggallāna, on one end of the scale, and at the other Devadatta, the most depraved of the disciples, there is a long and varied line of others with different degrees of accomplishments and virtues.

It is characteristic that the only slander uttered against the chief disciples came from a follower of Devadatta. The monk Kokālika, wishing to malign them, told the Buddha that the two had evil intentions, which, in fact, was the case with Devadatta. The Buddha, however, replied: "Don't say so, Kokālika, don't speak like that! Let your heart have glad confidence in Sāriputta and Moggallāna! They are capable monks" (SN 6:10). But Kokālika, in spite of this emphatic admonition, persisted in his slander. According to the old texts, Devadatta and Kokālika were reborn in a state of utter suffering, in the deepest hellish abode, while Sāriputta and Moggallāna won the highest bliss, Nibbāna.

The Activities of the Chief Disciples in the Order

In the canonical scriptures there are many reports about common activities of the two chief disciples, who were the best assistants of their Master in taking care of the Order. Both did much work for the advancement and benefit of the community of monks. Their activities directed to maintain inner concord, stability and discipline within the Order deserve special mention. At the request of the Buddha they brought about the banishment of an extremely reckless and undisciplined group of monks known as the "group of six" (*chabbaggiya*), on whom the Buddha's admonition had no effect, as reported in Majjhima Nikāya No. 70 (*Kīṭāgiri Sutta*). It was on account of them that a great part of the disciplinary rules of the Order had to be proclaimed. Finally, they behaved in such a frenzied way that, on the Buddha's bidding, Sāriputta and Moggallāna, at the head of the virtuous monks, had to banish those six from the place of their mischief, which was near Kīṭāgiri. Thereafter most of them left the Order (CV I.13–16).

Above all, the two great disciples were able to convince those newly ordained monks who had fallen away, having been instigated by Devadatta, to return to the Buddha's fold and to the right conduct of monk life. When at that time, Sāriputta gave his exhortation to those misguided monks, he showed his power of thought-reading, while Moggallāna used his magic powers (CV VII.4). Also the following incident led to a strengthening of concord in the Order: Once when Sāriputta was treated with hostility by a certain monk and was wrongly accused by him, Moggallāna and Ānanda called together all the monks, so that, for their instruction and edification, they could hear Sāriputta's dignified answer to those accusations (AN 9:11).[9]

Once when Moggallāna was ill, the Buddha went to see him and gladdened him by a discourse on the Seven Factors of Enlightenment. Inspired by it, Moggallāna regained mastery over his body and recovered (SN 46:15).

The two chief disciples often lived together in one cell of the monastery, and they held many dialogues in the presence and for the benefit of their fellow monks, as shown in the Discourse on Stainlessness (MN 5), and frequently they gave discourses to the monks. Some of those given by Moggallāna are, for instance, those in Majjhima Nikāya No. 15, AN 10:84 and SN 35:202. They also spent much of their time in giving seminar-like instructions to their disciples (see SN 14:15). Besides, they had conversations with Anuruddha about the meaning of the Four Foundations of Mindfulness (SN 47:26–27) and the difference between a Noble Learner (*sekha*) and a person who has "finished his learning" (*asekha*) (SN 52:4–6).

Both chief disciples were highly praised by the Awakened One for their beneficial work, which, however, left them unmoved by pride as they were Saints. Such a situation occurred when they were seated near the Buddha and were both immersed in deep concentration focused on the Recollection of the Body. Then the Buddha spoke one of the following two verses to each of them, first to Sāriputta and then to Moggallāna:

> "Just as a rocky peak cannot be shaken, being firmly grounded,
> So will not waver anymore a monk when he delusion has destroyed.
> "With mindfulness directed on the body
> and well restrained in sixfold sense contact,
> his mind remaining always well collected,
> such monk will come to know his own Nibbāna."
>
> —Ud III.4–5

9. See *Aṅguttara Nikāya: An Anthology Part III* (The Wheel 238/240), p. 19f.

It happened only once that the Buddha preferred Moggallāna's attitude in a certain matter to that of Sāriputta. The Master, after having dismissed from his presence some noisy and unmannered monks, later asked his two chief disciples what they had thought when he sent away those monks. Sāriputta said, he thought that the Master wanted to enjoy a blissful abiding in the present (through *jhāna*) and that they, the chief disciples, were to do the same. But the Buddha reproached him, saying that he should not have such thoughts again. Then the Buddha turned to Moggallāna, with the same question. Moggallāna replied that he, too, had thought the Master wanted to enjoy the bliss of *jhāna*; but if so, then it would have been Sāriputta's and his task to take care of the community of monks and to look after them. The Buddha praised him and said that if both his chief disciples took care of the community, it would be as good as if he himself looked after the monks (MN 67).

Moggallāna's Magical Powers

In the discourse about the disciples who excelled in special capacities and qualities (AN 1:13), the Buddha said that Moggallāna was foremost among the bhikkhus who possessed magical faculties. One day when Moggallāna with some of his disciples walked up and down, the Buddha told his monks that Moggallāna possessed great supernormal powers, and so did his pupils; thus beings congregate according to their nature and dispositions (SN 14:15). There were, of course, also other prominent disciples highly skilled in one or the other of the various magical powers. But they mastered only some of them: the monk Anuruddha and the nun Sakulā, for instance, possessed the supernormal vision of the Divine Eye; the monk Sobhita and the nun Bhaddakāpilānī could recollect far into the past; the monk Sāgalo had masterly control of the fire element; Cūḷa Panthaka was skilled in "astral travel"; and Piliṇḍa excelled in communication with heavenly beings. Mahā Moggallāna, however, was perfect master of the magical faculties in a very comprehensive way. He mastered the various kinds of supernormal powers altogether, surpassing in them the other disciples. He also excelled by far the nun Uppalavaṇṇā, who was foremost among the nuns in regard to magical faculties.

For appreciating the old reports on Moggallāna's magical (parapsychological) faculties, one ought to know how such things can be possible at all. The world of so-called matter as perceived through our five senses—which today's physicists conceive as a manifestation of energy—is only a small section of that much wider reality which consists of other vibrational forms of energy. Inklings of it, under terms like "anti-matter," "Psi-power," the "Astral," or "Prana," have penetrated into our range of experience. As we perceive only the narrow sector of our human world, we are inclined to regard its limited laws as absolutes. But the universe as experienced by the wise, is much larger, and the laws in force in it have also an impact upon our own world. It is that impact of different laws which is called a miracle. But whenever a higher or wider world manifests itself, the true miracle is that people can be so imprisoned within their narrow outlook that they just ignore all that is beyond their limited faculties, in spite of the fact that the effects of those other forces and laws are undeniably present. But whosoever, as the Buddha and Moggallāna, has highly developed his capacity to experience that wider reality with his higher sense faculties refined by cultivating the Four Ways of Power (*iddhipada*) will realise a sheer infinite widening of experience in space and time. His horizon and experiential knowledge will grow universal and immeasurable, transcending all boundaries and limitations.

When Sāriputta asked (in MN 32) to which type of monk would those assembled give the highest praise, Moggallāna replied that from his point of view such a monk would be truly brilliant who can engage best in dialogues and discussions on the Teaching. Later the Buddha confirmed that Moggallāna was indeed a very capable speaker on Dhamma. In fact, talks on Dhamma gain in range and depth when they issue from an experience that transcends the realm of the senses. The more one has widened one's consciousness by such experiences, the more one has to say. One who has personal experience of those many avenues of liberating wisdom will best be able to conduct talks on Dhamma and make them lively and stimulating. Examples of such discourses given by Mahā-Moggallāna are MN 15 and 37, AN 10:84, SN 35:202, SN 44:7–8.

We shall now turn to what the Buddhist canonical texts relate about Moggallāna's supernormal faculties, presenting the material grouped according to the types of faculties concerned.

1. Penetration of others' minds and thought-reading (telepathy)

Once on an Uposatha day, the Buddha sat silently throughout the whole night in front of the assembly of monks. When the morning dawned, he only said: "This assembly is impure." Thereupon Moggallāna surveyed with his mind the entire assembly from monk to monk and saw that one monk was entirely corrupted. He went towards him and asked him to leave. When that monk did not move though asked thrice, Moggallāna took him by his arm, led him out of the hall and bolted the door. Then he begged the Exalted One to recite the Rules of Monastic Discipline (Pātimokkha), as the assembly was now pure again (AN 8:20).

Once the Master stayed together with a community of five hundred monks who all were Saints. When Moggallāna joined them, he at once discerned in his heart that all these monks were canker-free Arahants. Then one of these saintly monks who, on his part, cognised Moggallāna's supernormal perception, rose from his seat and praised Moggallāna in the following verses:

> "Him who serenely sits on mountain's slope,
> a sage who has transcended ill entire –
> to him disciples pay their homage,
> themselves of triple knowledge, vanquishers of death.
>
> "He has discerned them by his mental power,
> the master of the supernormal, Moggallāna.
> He probed their minds with his
> and found them free and unattached."

—SN 8:10

A third report says: Once, while the venerable Anuruddha was meditating in solitude, he considered how, by means of the Four Foundations of Mindfulness (*satipaṭṭhāna*), the Noble Path that leads to the extinction of suffering can be perfected. Then Moggallāna, penetrating Anuruddha's mind by his own, appeared before him through supernormal power and requested him to describe in detail this method of practice (SN 52:1–2).

2. *The Divine Ear (clair-audience)*

One evening when Sāriputta went to see Moggallāna, he found that his features had such a strikingly serene expression that Sāriputta felt moved to ask Moggallāna whether he had dwelt in one of the peaceful abodes of mind. Moggallāna replied that he had dwelt only in one of the less refined abodes, but that he had been engaged in a talk on the Teaching. On being asked with whom he had such a talk, he replied that it had been with the Exalted One. Sāriputta remarked that the Master was now dwelling very far away, in Sāvatthī, while they themselves were here in Rājagaha. Did Moggallāna, by way of his supernormal power, go to the Buddha, or did the Buddha come to him? Moggallāna replied that neither had been the case. It was rather the Divine Eye and the Divine Ear, which had been purified and perfected in both of them, that enabled them to have a Dhamma talk on the mental faculty of energy. Then Sāriputta exclaimed that Moggallāna, being endowed with powers so great, might be able to live through an entire aeon (*kalpa*), like a Buddha, if he so wished (SN 21:3).

With the Divine Ear, Moggallāna could also hear the voices of non-human beings, deities, spirits, etc., and receive messages from them. So, for instance, a spirit had warned him against Devadatta, who harboured evil intentions towards the Buddha and planned a plot against him (Culla Vagga VII, 2).

3. *The divine eye (clairvoyance, second sight, visions)*

As mentioned above, Moggallāna, with his Divine Eye, was able to perceive the Buddha over a long distance (SN 21:3).

Once the following happened. While Sāriputta was sitting in quiet meditation, a wanton demon (Yakkha) hit him on the head. Moggallāna saw it and asked his friend whether he had felt much pain. Sāriputta smiled and said that he had just felt a slight touch of a headache. Then Moggallāna praised his strength of concentration, but Sāriputta said that Moggallāna had been able to see that demon while he himself could not (Ud IV.4).

Once Moggallāna saw with the Divine Eye how King Pasenadi had been defeated in battle by the Licchavis, but that afterwards he had gathered his troops again and vanquished the Licchavis. When

Moggallāna told this, some monks accused him of falsely boasting about his supernormal faculties, which is a disciplinary offence making a monk subject to expulsion from the Order. The Buddha, however, explained that Moggallāna had told only what he saw and what had actually happened (Pārājika IV.95; case No. 17).

Above all, he often saw the operation of the law of *kamma* and its fruits. Again and again he saw how human beings, due to their evil actions that harmed fellow-beings, were reborn among unhappy ghosts undergoing much suffering; while others by their charitable deeds rose upwards to lower heavenly worlds that were close to the human plane. He often gave instances of this for exemplifying the law of *kamma*. The reports about this are numerous. In two books of the Pali Canon, dealing with the ghost realm (the *Petavatthu*) and the heavenly abodes (the *Vimānavatthu*), respectively, nine and fifty-one of such reports are given. From this it can be readily understood why Moggallāna was famous as one who knew the worlds beyond as well as the workings of *kamma*. The reports are too numerous for inclusion, but at least one of his visions recorded in the Saṃyutta Nikāya should be mentioned here (SN 19:1–21 = Pārājika IV.9; 15th case).

Once Moggallāna lived on Vulture Peak, near Rājagaha, together with the Bhikkhu Lakkhaṇa, one of the thousand Brahmin ascetics who had been converted together with Uruvela-Kassapa. One morning when they had descended from the peak for going on alms-round in the town, Moggallāna smiled when they reached a certain place on the road. When his companion asked him for the reason, Moggallāna said that now it was not the right time to explain it, he would tell it in the presence of the Master. When they later met the Buddha, Lakkhaṇa repeated his question. Moggallāna now said that at that spot he had seen many miserable ghosts flying through the air, chased around and tormented by various kinds of afflictions and sufferings. The Buddha confirmed this as absolutely true and added that he himself spoke only reluctantly about such appearances because people with superficial minds would not believe it. Then the Buddha, out of his universal knowledge, explained what propensities and behaviour had brought those ghosts seen by Moggallāna to their present pitiable position.

4. *Travel by "mind-made body" ("astral travel")*

"Just as a person may bend his stretched arm or stretch his bent arm," so quickly was Moggallāna able to depart bodily from the human world and reappear in a celestial realm. Repeatedly he made use of this capacity for instructing other beings and looking after the affairs of the Order. Thus he taught the Gods of the Thirty-three the Factors of stream-entry, or tested Sakka, King of Gods, whether he had understood the teaching about the extinction of craving (MN 37). Once when the Buddha was preaching for three months in one of the heavenly worlds, Moggallāna appeared in that heaven and informed the Master of happenings in the Order, asking him for instructions (J 483E). He visited not only the Gods of the Sense-sphere, but also those of the Brahmā world. Thus he appeared before a Brahmā deity who believed that there were no ascetics capable of entering his realm, and through questioning and supernormal feats Moggallāna shook the self-assurance of that deity (SN 6:5). Or he appeared in front of a Brahmā named Tissa—who formerly had been a monk and had died recently—and gave him instructions about stream-entry and the realisation of final deliverance (AN 4:34; 7: 53).

5. *Telekinesis (supernormal locomotion)*

Moggallāna also had mastery over what appears to be solid matter. Once there were monks staying at a monastery who were negligent and of distracted minds, busying themselves too much with material trifles. Learning this, the Buddha asked Moggallāna to shake their excessive faith in materiality by a supernormal feat and to stir them on to renewed and serious effort. In response to the Buddha's request, Moggallāna pushed the building with his big toe, so that the entire monastery, called "The Terrace of Migāra's Mother," shook and trembled as if there was an earthquake. By this experience the monks were so deeply stirred that they became again receptive when the Buddha instructed them, explaining the four roads to power (*iddhipāda*), from which Moggallāna's great supernormal prowess derived (SN 51:14; J 299).

When Moggallāna visited Sakka in his heavenly realm and saw that Sakka was living rather light-heartedly and was captivated by the heavenly sense pleasures of his world, forgetful of the

Teaching, Moggallāna performed a similar magic feat by shaking slightly the celestial palace, called "Banner of Victory," in which Sakka took much pride. This had a "shock effect" on Sakka too, and he now recalled the teaching on the extinction of craving, which the Buddha had briefly taught him not long ago. It was the same teaching by which the Buddha had once helped Moggallāna to attain sainthood (MN 37).

Once there was a famine in the area where the Buddha and his community of monks stayed, and the monks could not obtain sufficient alms food. On that occasion Moggallāna asked the Buddha whether he may overturn the ground, so that the nourishing substance underneath would be accessible and could be eaten. But the Buddha told him not to do so, as this would cause the destruction of a large number of living beings. Then Moggallāna offered to open by his magical power a road to the (mythical) Uttara Kuru country, so that the monks could go there for alms. This, too, was rejected by the Buddha. But all survived the famine unharmed, even without such supernormal devices (Pārājika I.2). This was the only occasion when the Buddha disapproved of Moggallāna's suggestions.

Moggallāna's supernormal power expressed itself also in his ability to bring things from long distances by his magical locomotion. Thus for instance he brought lotus stalks from the Himalayas when Sāriputta was ill and needed them for medicine (Mahāvagga VI.20; Cūlavagga V. 34). He also fetched a shoot of the Bodhi tree for Anāthapiṇḍika to be planted at the Jetavana Monastery (J 78). But when his fellow-monk Piṇḍola asked him to prove the superiority of the Buddha's Sangha over the sectarians by magically bringing down a precious bowl that had been hung up in town so high that nobody could take it down, Moggallāna refused, saying that Piṇḍola himself possessed sufficient powers to do it. But when Piṇḍola actually performed that feat, the Buddha rebuked him: a monk should not display supernormal powers for the sake of impressing the laity (Cūlavagga V.8).

Moggallāna's Previous Lives

About his recollection of his own former existences, Moggallāna spoke only once, in the 50th Discourse of the Middle Length Discourses (Majjhima Nikāya). With that text we shall deal in the following chapter.

In the Jātakas, the stories about the Buddha's former existences, it is reported that the Buddha-to-be and Moggallāna had lived together quite often. In no less than thirty-one lives the Buddha and Moggallāna had met, and in thirty of them Moggallāna and Sāriputta had lived together. So strong was the bond that in previous lives had already connected these three. To be sure, the thirty-one which have been recorded, is a very small number compared with the infinity of lives through which every being in *saṃsāra* has passed. Yet some general conclusions concerning Moggallāna can be drawn from them. It is, of course, not possible to reproduce here these thirty-one Jātakas, with all their details and embellishments. Only some general points can be mentioned here, which are important for understanding Moggallāna's life and personality.

The first thing we find from the Jātakas is his close relationship to the Bodhisattva. Moggallāna and Sāriputta were often his brothers (J 488, 509, 542, 543), his friends (J 326) or his ministers (J 401). Sometimes they were his disciples as ascetics (J 423, 522), or even his teachers (J 539). Sometimes Sāriputta is the son and Moggallāna the general of the royal Bodhisattva (J 525). When the Buddha was Sakka, King of Gods, they were the moon-god and the sun-god respectively (J 450).

The second point worth noting is the relationship of Sāriputta to Moggallāna. When, in the Jātaka stories, both are seen to traverse all the heights and depths of *saṃsāra*, they sometimes play quite inferior parts in relation to the main figures of the respective stories. There appears a certain lawfulness in the stories insofar as in most cases the difference between them (e.g., in status) is larger to the degree in which their level of rebirth is lower and there is less difference when their rebirth is on a higher level. When reborn as animals, they rarely were equals (only as swans, in J 160, 187, 215, 476) and mostly Sāriputta was born in a higher species of animals. Thus they were snake and rat (J 73), bird and tortoise (J 206, 486), lion and tiger (J 212, 361, 438), monkey and elephant (J 37), snake and jackal (J 315), man and jackal (J 490). When born as human beings in worldly careers, Sāriputta was always in a higher position than Moggallāna: as a royal prince and royal minister (J 525), royal minister and son of a slave (J 544), charioteer of the royal Bodhisattva and charioteer of King Ānanda (J 151). Once Moggallāna was the moon-god and Sāriputta the wise ascetic Nārada (J 535). But when both are ascetics or deities, they are mostly of equal status. But once it happened that Sāriputta was only the moon-god and Moggallāna the superior sun-god (J 450); once Sāriputta was the king of the Nāgas (serpent deities) and Moggallāna the king of their foes, the Supannas (mythical birds of deity status) (J 545).

The only time when Moggallāna appears in the Jātakas without Sāriputta is a life in which he holds the office of Sakka, King of Gods. In MN 37, he admonishes one of his successors to that office. At that time, as Sakka, he also appeared on earth to a miser in order to urge on him the virtue of giving and thus to lead him to a better rebirth (J 78). But another time, when Sāriputta and Moggallāna lived on earth, they were stingy merchants who had buried much money. After death, they were reborn close to their buried treasure, but as a snake and a rat (J 73).

There is also a story in which Moggallāna was reborn as a jackal. Seeing a dead elephant, he was so greedy for its flesh that he crept through an intestinal aperture right into the elephant's belly, ate as much as he could, but was then unable to get out again, suffering mortal fear—an impressive symbol of the perils of sensual enjoyment (J 490).

In the famous Jātaka about the Law of the Kuru people (J 216), Moggallāna is a keeper of grain stores and Sāriputta a merchant. Both were very careful in observing the law of not-stealing.

The Last Days of Moggallāna

Half a year before the Final Passing Away of the Awakened One, death separated the two friends for the last time. Sāriputta died on the full-moon day of the month Kattikā (October/November); it was at his birth place, in his parental home, far away from Moggallāna. Just as their attainment of sainthood occurred at different places, they were also separated in death, though they had been so close to each other for a long time.

Soon after the death of Sāriputta, Māra, the embodiment of evil and the Lord of Death, claimed Moggallāna's mortal frame, by entering his bowels. He could not make him possessed by entering his head, because he had access only to the lowest Chakra. Moggallāna, however, told him calmly to get out and away as he had well recognised him. Māra was very surprised that he had been found out so soon, and in his delusion he thought that even the Buddha would not have recognised him so quickly. But Moggallāna read his thoughts and ordered him again to get away. Māra now escaped through Moggallāna's mouth and stood at the hut's door post. Moggallāna told him that he knew him not only from today but was aware of his karmic past and his descent. In that way, Moggallāna manifested here three supernormal faculties: the Divine Eye, telepathy and recollection of past lives. It was only on this occasion, reported in Majjhima Nikāya No. 50, that Moggallāna spoke of his recollection of his own distant past.

The following is the gist of what he said. The first Buddha appearing in our "fortunate aeon" (*bhadda-kappa*) with five Buddhas, was Kakusandha. He lived when the lifespan of man was 40,000 years and when the first darkening of the golden age became evident because of a king's lack of concern and the occurrence of the first theft. Because of that, man's vital energy became reduced to half. At that time, Moggallāna was Māra, chief of demons, lord of the lower worlds, and his name was Māra Dūsī. He had a sister by the name of Kālī, whose son was to become the Māra of our age. Hence Moggallāna's own nephew was now standing in front of him at the door post. While being the Māra of that distant time, Moggallāna had attacked a chief disciple of the previous Buddha by taking possession of a boy and making him throw a potsherd at the holy disciple's head so that blood was flowing. When the Buddha Kakusandha saw this, he said: "Verily, Māra knew no moderation here"—because even in satanic actions there might be moderation. Under the glance of the Perfect One the astral body of Māra Dūsī dissolved on the spot and reappeared in the deepest hell. Just a moment ago he had been the overlord of all the hellish worlds and now he himself was one of hell's victims. A moment ago he had been the greatest torturer and now he himself was undergoing one of those terrible torments. Such is the rapid change in *saṃsāric* situations. For many thousands of years Moggallāna had to suffer in hell as a punishment for his frivolity towards a saint. Ten thousand years he had to spend alone in a hellish pool, having a human body and the head of a fish, just as Pieter Breughel had painted such beings in his pictures of the hells. Whenever two lances of his torturers crossed in his heart, he would know that a thousand years of his torment had passed (MN 50).

After this encounter with Māra, which once more brought to his mind the terrors of *saṃsāra* from which he now was free forever, Moggallāna felt that the time of his last existence was running out. Being a Saint he saw no reason for making use of his ability to extend, by an act of will, his life span up to the end of this aeon, and he calmly allowed impermanence to take its lawful course.

As many great sages of the East and many saints of the Buddha did, he left behind a kind of autobiography in verses in which he summarised how he, as a liberated one, had passed through all the situations of his life, unperturbed and unshaken. Events that completely overwhelmed others left him calm. His verses in the Theragāthā could be summed up by saying that none of *saṃsāra*'s upheavals appeared to him extraordinary, nor could anything disturb the equipoise of his sainthood. The *dukkha* of the world no longer touched him as he lived in a peace that transcended all the pain and restlessness of existence.

The verses begin with events of his life in this world. Wherever others craved for possessions, he, as a forest hermit, was content in an austere life of few wants (Th 1146–1149). Once when a harlot tried to seduce him, he rejected her, just as the Buddha had rejected Māra's daughters (1150–1157). When Sāriputta, his best friend died, he was not agitated by sorrow as was Ānanda who had not yet become an Arahant, but remained unshaken in his serenity (1158–1163). Then the verses turn to events of a supernormal nature as his shaking a monastery building with his toe (1164) and his undisturbed meditation in a mountain cleft, in the midst of thunder and lightning (1167). Living with mind pacified in remote places, he, a true heir of the Buddha, is venerated even by Brahmā (1169). The following verses (1169–1173) are addressed to a superstitious Brahmin of wrong views who, on seeing Mahā-

Kassapa going for alms, had abused him. Moggallāna warns him against the dangers of such conduct and urges him to respect the Saints. He then praises Sāriputta (1176) and it seems that the next verses (1177–1181) are Sāriputta's own praise of Moggallāna. He now reviews his attainments and rejoices in the consummation of the goal of his monk life (1182–1186). The last verses (1187–1208) are identical with those concluding his encounter with Māra recorded in Majjhima Nikāya No. 50 and briefly related above.

The Death of Mahā-Moggallāna

The Awakened One, surrounded by many of his monks, passed away peacefully during a meditative absorption which he entered with perfect mastery. Sāriputta's death in his parental home, likewise with fellow monks in attendance, was similarly serene, though, unlike the Buddha, he had been ill before his end. Ānanda died at the age of 120, before which he entered with meditative skill the fire element so that his body vanished in a blaze, as he did not wish to burden anyone by his funeral. Considering the serene death of the Master and these two disciples, one would have expected that, in the case of Mahā-Moggallāna, too, the final dissolution of the body at death would take place in external circumstances of a similarly peaceful nature. But in Moggallāna's case it was very different, though the gruesome nature of his death did not shake his firm and serene mind.

He passed away a fortnight after his friend Sāriputta, namely, on the new-moon day of the month Kattikā (October/ November), in the autumn. The Great Decease of the Buddha took place in the full-moon night of the month Vesākha (May), that is half a year after the death of his two chief disciples. The Buddha was in his 80th year when he passed away, while both Sāriputta and Mahā-Moggallāna died at 84.

These were the circumstances of Moggallāna's death.

After the death of Nigaṇṭha Nāthaputta, the leader of the ascetic Order of the Jains (*Jinas*),[10] there arose among his followers bitter contentions about his teaching, and consequently there was a loss of devoted adherents and of support. The Jains had also learned

10. In the Pali texts, they are called "Nigaṇṭhas."

what Moggallāna reported from his celestial travels: that virtuous devotees of the Buddha were seen to have a heavenly rebirth while followers of other sects lacking moral conduct had fallen into miserable, subhuman states of existence. This, too, contributed to the decline in the reputation of other sects, including the Jains.

Particularly the very lowest type of Jains in Magadha were so enraged about that loss of public esteem and support that they wanted to get rid of Moggallāna. Without investigating the causes in themselves, they projected blame externally and concentrated their envy and hate on Mahā-Moggallāna. Hesitating to commit a murder themselves, they conceived another plan. Even in those days there were professional criminals ready to do a killing for payment. There are always unscrupulous men willing to do anything for money. So some evil-minded Jains hired such a gang and ordered them to kill Moggallāna.

At that time, Mahā-Moggallāna lived alone in a forest hut at Kālasilā. After his encounter with Māra he knew that the end of his days was near. Having enjoyed the bliss of liberation, he now felt the body to be just an obstruction and burden. Hence he had no desire to make use of his faculties and keep the body alive for the rest of the aeon. Yet, when he saw the brigands approaching, he just absented himself by using his supernormal powers. The gangsters arrived at an empty hut and, though they searched everywhere, could not find him. They left disappointed, but returned on the following day. On six consecutive days Moggallāna escaped from them in the same way. His motivation was not the protection of his own body, but saving the brigands from the fearsome karmic consequences of such a murderous deed, necessarily leading to rebirth in the hells. He wanted to spare them such a fate by giving them time to reconsider and abstain from their crime. But their greed for the promised money was so great that they persisted and returned even on the seventh day. Then their persistence was "rewarded," for on that seventh day Moggallāna suddenly lost the magic control over his body. A heinous deed committed in days long past (by causing the death of his own parents) had not yet been expiated, and the ripening of that old *kamma* confronted him now, just as others are suddenly confronted by a grave illness. Moggallāna realised that he was now unable to escape. The brigands entered, knocked him down, smashed all his limbs and left him lying in his blood. Being keen on quickly getting their reward and also somewhat ill as ease about their dastardly deed, the brigands left at once, without a further look.

But Moggallāna's great physical and mental strength was such that his vital energies had not yet succumbed. He regained consciousness and was able to drag himself to the Buddha. There, in the Master's presence, at the holiest place of the world, at the source of the deepest peace, Moggallāna breathed his last (J 522E). The inner peace in which he dwelt since he attained to sainthood never left him. It did not leave him even in the last seven days of his life, which had been so turbulent. But even the threat of doom was only external. This is the way of those who are finally "healed" and holy and are in control of the mind. Whatever *kamma* of the past had been able to produce a result in his present life, nevertheless, it could affect only his body, but no longer "him," because "he" no longer identified himself with anything impermanent. This last episode of Moggallāna's life, however, showed that the law of moral causality (*kamma*) has even greater power than the supernormal feats of this master of magic. Only a Buddha can control the karmic consequences acting upon his body to such an extent that nothing might cause his premature death.

Sāriputta and Mahā-Moggallāna were such wonderful disciples that the Buddha said the assembly of monks appeared empty to him after their death. It was marvellous, he said, that such an excellent pair of disciples existed. But it was marvellous, too, that, in spite of their excellence, there was no grief, no lamentation on the part of the Master, when the two had passed away.[11]

Therefore, inspired by the greatness of the two chief disciples, may a dedicated follower of the Dhamma strive to be his own island of refuge, have the Dhamma as his island of refuge, not looking for any other refuge, having in it the powerful help of the Four Foundations of Mindfulness (*satipaṭṭhāna*)! Those who are thus filled with keen desire to train themselves in walking on the Noble Eightfold Path, they will certainly pass beyond the realms of darkness which abound in *saṃsāra*. So the Master assures.[12]

---

11. See Ukkacela Sutta (SN 47:24), translated in *The Life of Sāriputta*, (The Wheel 90/92), p. 84.
12. SN 47:23.

ABOUT PARIYATTI

Pariyatti is dedicated to providing affordable access to authentic teachings of the Buddha about the Dhamma theory (*pariyatti*) and practice (*paṭipatti*) of Vipassana meditation. A 501(c)(3) nonprofit charitable organization since 2002, Pariyatti is sustained by contributions from individuals who appreciate and want to share the incalculable value of the Dhamma teachings. We invite you to visit www.pariyatti.org to learn about our programs, services, and ways to support publishing and other undertakings.

Pariyatti Publishing Imprints

Vipassana Research Publications (focus on Vipassana as taught by S.N. Goenka in the tradition of Sayagyi U Ba Khin)

BPS Pariyatti Editions (selected titles from the Buddhist Publication Society, copublished by Pariyatti)

MPA Pariyatti Editions (selected titles from the Myanmar Pitaka Association, copublished by Pariyatti)

Pariyatti Digital Editions (audio and video titles, including discourses)

Pariyatti Press (classic titles returned to print and inspirational writing by contemporary authors)

Pariyatti enriches the world by

- disseminating the words of the Buddha,
- providing sustenance for the seeker's journey,
- illuminating the meditator's path.

www.ingramcontent.com/pod-product-compliance
Lightning Source LLC
Chambersburg PA
CBHW020348170426
43200CB00005B/99
9781681721880